BREAD OF EXILE

Dimitri Obolensky

BREAD OF EXILE

A RUSSIAN FAMILY

Translated from the Russian by
Harry Willetts
with an Introduction by
Hugh Trevor-Roper

HARVILL PRESS
LONDON

First published in 1999 by
The Harvill Press
2 Aztec Row
Berners Road
London N1 0PW

www.harvill.com

1 3 5 7 9 8 6 4 2

A CIP catalogue record for this title is
available from the British Library

ISBN 1 86046 511 0

Designed and typeset in Quadraat at
Libanus Press, Marlborough, Wiltshire

Printed and bound in Great Britain by Butler & Tanner Ltd
at Selwood Printing, Burgess Hill

This book is dedicated to James Howard-Johnston

Tu lascerai ogni cosa diletta
  più caramente; e questo è quello strale
  che l'arco dello essilio pria saetta.
Tu proverai sì come sa di sale
  lo pane altrui, e come è duro calle
  lo scendere e 'l salir per l'altrui scale.

Thou shalt leave everything loved most
dearly, and this is the shaft which the bow
of exile shoots first. Thou shalt prove how
salt is the taste of another man's bread
and how hard is the way up and down
another man's stairs.

Dante, *Divina Commedia* (Paradiso: Canto XVII)
(Translated by John D. Sinclair, The Bodley Head, 1958)

CONTENTS

Preface

The memoirs in this book are of two kinds. Some were written by different members of my family: my father, Dimitri Obolensky; my mother, née Maria Shuvalov, later married to André Tolstoy, with an account by her of our escape from Bolshevik Russia in March 1919; my (maternal) grandmother, Sandra Shuvalov, née Vorontsov-Dashkov; her sister and my great-aunt, Sofka Demidov; and my stepfather, André Tolstoy.

The second type of memoir has been written by me. It covers the principal episodes of my own life, as an infant in the Crimea, as I remember them, from my Russian-bound childhood in Nice, vicissitudes in an English preparatory school, later studies in a Parisian lycée, and experiences as a teacher at Cambridge and Oxford.

Three of the authors are men, and three women. The odd man out is myself: alone of the six I belong to the youngest of the three generations. Two women married Russian public figures of Tsarist times: Sandra, the City Governor of Moscow, Sofka, a diplomat. Professionally the men fared rather less well, except for André Tolstoy, aide-de-camp and secretary to General Wrangel, the outstanding anti-Bolshevik leader in 1920.

Two opposing worlds jostle and succeed each other on these pages: the world of privilege and power of imperial Russia, generally before 1917, close to throne and government, struggling during the next few years to survive Communist persecution and military attack; and, on the other hand, the life of dispossession and exile. My family, whose members lived through those successive phases of their country's history, belonged to the upper layers of the Russian aristocracy. Some were close friends of the Emperors Alexander III and Nicholas II, and of Nicholas' mother, the Empress Maria Feodorovna. Their reminiscences shed light on these royal personages that is intimate, credible, and sometimes startlingly new; and they show how, in their later capacity as political refugees, members of my family responded to life in what was at first a largely alien environment.

They were written, probably without thought of publication, mostly as diaries, to be read and remembered in family circles. The relative absence of literary sophistication has often, however, endowed these texts with a freshness and immediacy which may strike the reader as both moving and informative.

For me this pilgrimage into the past has proved an enriching experience, filled with unexpected discoveries. All the more reason for feeling thankful for the help I received in my twin aims of bringing together these biographies and exploring their relationship and points of contact.

My greatest debt is to Harry Willetts. I was indeed fortunate to have secured the collaboration of so renowned a translator who is also a professional historian. Many of the footnotes were contributed by him.

To others too, who helped me in a variety of ways, I wish to express my thanks. They include Philipp Blom, Ian Pindar, Francis and Larissa Haskell, Richard and Anne Kindersley, Chloe Obolensky, Ihor Sevcenko, Ron Truman, and Ivan and Paul Tolstoy. I am also grateful for the forbearance of my ever-patient publishers.

DIMITRI OBOLENSKY
Oxford, May 1998

Introduction

Sir Dimitri Obolensky has been one of my closest friends for nearly 50 years. He has been a valued colleague in Oxford and a delightful travelling companion in Eastern Europe in its communist days, when a friend with linguistic knowledge and a well-developed sense of humour was much needed. We have enjoyed some difficult and some comical experiences on such occasions. But these are personal memories. In the world of scholarship he is known and admired as a historian of the Byzantine Empire and, in particular, of its political and cultural relations with its Balkan and Slavonic neighbours. But in this book he appears in a new guise: first as the editor (and sometimes the object) and finally as the author and subject, of a series of personal memoirs illustrating the experiences of his own Russian family on the eve and morrow of the Bolshevik Revolution.

I have always known that Dimitri's* family was distinguished in Russian history, but he is too modest, and too sensible, to make any claims for it on that score, except under extreme provocation. I did indeed once hear him so provoked. It was at an embassy dinner in Bucharest. He had been introduced under his (by then discarded) princely title, and his host opened the conversation with the words: "I suppose you are descended from one of the lovers of Catherine the Great?" This was too much for Dimitri and elicited the slightly dry response: "My ancestors ruled Russia in the ninth century" – for

* Sir Dimitri's correct title, until he became a British subject, was Prince Dimitri Obolensky; but as his father had the same name, I distinguish them in this Introduction by referring to the father as Prince Dimitri and the son simply as Dimitri

indeed, as I now know, he is directly descended, in the male line, from Rurik, the Viking founder of the first and longest lasting ruling dynasty in Russian history. Relations between the various branches of that dynasty were not always harmonious, if there is any truth in the story that Ivan the Terrible, the Tsar so admired by Stalin, once caused 40 Obolenskys to be boiled in a single pot. On which one can only comment by echoing the response of G. M. Trevelyan, the Master of Dimitri's Cambridge college: "Some pot!"

By the later nineteenth century, when the history illustrated by these memoirs begins, relations between the Obolenskys and the ruling dynasty of Russia were much improved. Indeed, some of the contributors to this volume take us into the very heart of the Romanov court. They were there thanks to what we may call the Vorontsov connection.

The Vorontsovs were very rich and grand, and by that time, like many great families in Russia, they were Westward-looking, liberal and anglophile. In the reign of King George III, Count Simon Vorontsov had come to London as Russian ambassador, and had kept that position for 22 years (1784–1806). His daughter had married the Earl of Pembroke, and his son "the illustrious Prince Michael Vorontsov", Governor of Bessarabia, had commissioned the English architect Edward Blore to build his new palace at Alupka, close to Yalta, in the Crimea. He had also built another palace in Odessa. Both palaces feature in these memoirs. Later, the Vorontsov family was represented by Count Ilarion Vorontsov-Dashkov, who, though he does not speak for himself in these memoirs, is a constant presence in them, through the accounts of his devoted and admiring daughters, Sandra, Countess Shuvalov, and Sofka, Princess Demidov, the grandmother and great-aunt respectively of Sir Dimitri. Count Ilarion Vorontsov-Dashkov was an important figure under the last three emperors of Russia, his career lasted almost to the outbreak of the Revolution (he ended it as Viceroy of the Caucasus), and after the Revolution he received a rare tribute from the left-wing press, cited here, as a man whose counsels might have prevented it.

The three Romanov reigns correspond with three generations of Dimitri's family, and these memoirs offer, from different personal viewpoints, a picture of court life, and sometimes political events and country life, under the last three Tsars: Alexander II (1855–81), Alexander III (1881–94) and Nicholas II (1894–1917). In those three reigns, the Russian aristocracy and the Russian old regime, though superficially intact, were gradually undermined. Responsible Russian statesmen, looking to the West, recognised the need for change, but the old structures resisted, well-intentioned reforms created new problems, and the would-be reformers were ultimately overtaken by radicals and revolutionaries who also looked to the West for their ideas, albeit very different ones. The fatal process was hastened by that common agent of revolution, defeat in war.

It was in the reign of Alexander II that the first stone of the old edifice was dislodged. In the preceding era, the 30-year reign of Nicholas I, the Russian monarchy, victorious over Napoleon, had been the most formidable model and the most active defender of autocracy in Europe. At home, it had crushed the national revolt of the Poles in 1830; abroad, it had intervened to crush the revolt of the Hungarians in 1849. But in the 1850s, the tide had turned. Alexander II began his reign by conceding defeat in the Crimean War, and five years later he loosened the structure of rural society by emancipating the serfs – a step which would hasten the gradual industrialisation of the country. After several previous attempts on his life, he was assassinated on 1 March 1881 by means of a bomb on the Ekaterinsky Embankment in St Petersburg.

This act of violence, organised by a terrorist group calling itself "The People's Will", began the brief reign of Alexander III. It also pointed forward to an increasing tempo of terrorism which came to a climax under his successor Nicholas II. Defeat by Japan then led to the revolution of 1905 and the brief experiment of the new parliament, the Duma. That same year saw the assassination of the Governor-General of Moscow, the Grand Duke Sergei, and of his deputy, the City Governor, Dimitri's grandfather, Count Paul Shuvalov. In the following years, Nicholas II's energetic minister, Peter Stolypin, sought both to impose and to control reform, but in 1912 he, too, was assassinated. Assassination, by this time, had become a habit. Habits are catching, and soon the aristocracy too had caught it. In 1916, Prince Yusupov and his friends brutally murdered Grigori Rasputin, the fraudulent holy man who had become the fatal *guru* of the Empress, and Yusupov's mother openly boasted of her son's glorious deed. Next year, defeat in another and greater war would lead to a more terrible revolution and the even more brutal massacre of the whole imperial family.

Such was the political background to life in the court into which Dimitri's grandmother and great-aunt, thanks to the position of their father, (for he was Minister of the Court), first entered as children at the end of the reign of Alexander II, and in which they would continue to live until the eve of the Revolution. Both Sandra and Sofka begin their memoirs with the assassination of Alexander II. This was a great shock, of course, but to them the Tsar was a remote figure and the sight of his corpse lying in state in his coffin elicited no emotion, no tears, only curiosity and some distaste – it seemed so strange, unnatural, doll-like, and the face, bluish in colour, was mutilated by fragments of the bomb. Anyway, in the long term, there were compensations. The late emperor, influenced by his second (and morganatic) wife, Princess Yurevskaya, who disliked the Vorontsovs and their friends, had just signed an order to Count Ilarion to go out and govern Siberia – or was it Turkestan? – a dismal prospect indeed for the girls! But now all was changed. Princess Yurevskaya was in eclipse. The new emperor, who could not dispense with the company and advice of Ilarion, cancelled the order, and from now on life at court was assured. The children of the two families would be brought up together. A particular bond would unite Sandra and Sofka with the Tsarevich Nicholas, afterwards emperor, and his sister the Grand Duchess Xenia. There would be romps and games in the royal palaces, parties and picnics together, ice-hockey with the Emperor himself; afterwards, when they had grown up, there would be grand ceremonies and state banquets. When Sandra was married to Count Paul Shuvalov, the Emperor himself gave her away and kissed her hand. "I am proud of that," she wrote long afterwards, "to this day."

Talleyrand once said, towards the end of his long and versatile career, that only those who had lived in France under the *ancien régime*, before the Revolution (he meant, of course, in the top layer of society) could know the true meaning of the words "*douceur de vivre*"; and the same phrase (with the same limitation) could no doubt be applied to pre-revolutionary Russia. The Russian aristocracy, like the French, were a privileged class, enlightened, sophisticated, cosmopolitan, semi-detached from the nation around them. In their fine houses on the English Embankment in St Petersburg, "swarming with menservants", they spoke mainly French among themselves, and French was the language at court! Of Dimitri's great-grandmother we read that "her Russian was shaky". For their children they employed English nannies, governesses, tutors. For recreation they visited each other's estates or went abroad, to Paris or Biarritz, Baden-Baden or Nice. There was a special railway service direct from St Petersburg to Nice, "*le train des grands ducs*". If they visited their own estates, they arrived there in a procession of carriages followed by a train of carts. Prince Dimitri, who loved his estate at Gorodishche in Penza province, south-east of Moscow, has vivid childhood memories of those regular family migrations. And once there, their peasants would come to them on their knees, with their humble petitions on their heads, for legal emancipation has not changed old habits. Twenty-five years after emancipation, the peasants on a distant estate of Count Ilarion would make a long journey to petition him to receive them back into serfdom: exposure to "liberty" had been more than they could bear. Humble petitions went all the way up the social hierarchy and could be a risky business. When Andrei Shuvalov, Sandra's grandfather, as marshal of the nobility in his province, presented a petition to Alexander II suggesting a modification of the terms of emancipation, he was ordered to leave St Petersburg and either go to live on his estate at Perm, on the edge of the Urals, or to leave the country altogether. Predictably, he preferred to go abroad, and was not seen in St Petersburg "for a long time". And Count Ilarion's brother-in-law, Prince Paskevich, for supporting the petition, was similarly exiled from the court.

We are reminded that it was an autocracy, and the function of the nobility is not merely to enjoy it but to make it work as such; which they do, for a time. The court nobility merged with the official nobility and even with the expanding world of commerce and industry. Prince Dimitri had a glass factory on his estate which employed 2,000 workers and had agents in the major Russian cities and even in Persia: he used it to produce elegant *objets d'art* by Fabergé to present to the Tsar. The Vorontsovs, on one of their estates, had a sugar refinery. And, of course, the great noble estates in the Ukraine, "billowing with corn", were the granary of Europe – until they were destroyed by Stalin, and Russia itself became dependent on imported corn. Prince Elim Demidov, the husband of Dimitri's great-aunt Sofka, had inherited highly profitable mines and factories in the Urals, which periodically diverted his attention from his duties as a diplomat. Meanwhile, as state servants – viceroys, governors, ministers of the court, marshals of the nobility in the provinces – such men sought to keep the system going. Sandra and Sofka, those devoted daughters, dwell on their father's attempts to sweeten it in action. Prince Dimitri recounts with relish his responsibilities in his province: his functions as marshal of the nobility, his care of the workers in his factory, their medical services, their education, their entertainment. He interested himself in every process of production, whether of the factory or of the land.

Might the system have been saved – by gradual reform, political skill, French loans? Prince Dimitri thought that it might – if Stolypin had lived to complete his work. But who can answer such a question? Necker could not save the French monarchy, and anyway none of the other great continental empires would survive defeat in the coming war. Could Nicholas II have succeeded where the emperors of Germany, Austria, and Turkey failed? It would be unreasonable to put such questions to those who were enclosed in the court. To them, the fate of the Tsar and his family was a personal tragedy. To Sandra and Sofka, the reign of Alexander III had been a brief, golden age: he was "the soul of honour". How sad that he died so soon! He would have stood up to those Bolsheviks. But Nicholas II, whom they loved – who was so charming, so shy, so affectionate, who had such "purity and nobility of character" – was, alas, too weak, too pliable, too easily ruled by his wife. In her memoir, which she dedicated to his memory, Sofka meditated on this fatal weakness of her martyred childhood friend. It came, she decided, from his Danish mother. The Danish royal family were all like that: handsome, charming, but indecisive. She knew all about them because her husband, Prince Demidov, had been first secretary of the Russian Embassy in Denmark. Indeed, it pleased her to think that it was by her sick-bed in a hotel in Copenhagen, where she was visited, at the same time, by King Edward VII, then on a state visit, and by Izvolsky, the Russian ambassador (soon to be Foreign Minister), that the Anglo-Russian Treaty of 1907, the culmination of the Triple Entente, was conceived. Sofka had known King Edward in England, where her husband had served at the embassy. There had been an unfortunate *malentendu* for a time, but that was now happily cleared up.

The Anglo-Russian Treaty could not save Russia from defeat by Germany and revolutionary violence. By 1919, with Lenin in power in St Petersburg and Moscow, and a reign of terror beginning, the family group prepared to flee the country.

The patriarch Count Ilarion had died in 1916, *felix opportunitate mortis*. His great-grandson, the infant Dimitri, was taken by his mother, using a forged passport, on the slow and painful journey from Moscow through the German-occupied Ukraine to the Crimea, where British ships would provide the means of escape to the West. At Yalta, the old Countess, Ilarion's widow, while admitting Dimitri, banned her granddaughter from the Vorontsov Palace. Apparently she disapproved of her marriage to Dimitri's father. She seems to have been a good disapprover, for in the past she had disapproved of her daughters too – they had been too fond of their father – and had made them wear "hideous" hats. Now she directed her wayward granddaughter to a hotel. Even in the chaos of revolution and the crash of empires, dowagers must stand on *punctilio*.

Dimitri's grandmother Sandra also arrived in the Crimea. So did the Empress Maria Feodorovna, Queen Alexandra's sister. These two had an emotional last meeting there. An unconfirmed rumour from Moscow told of the massacre of the imperial family. Was it true? the Empress asked. Sandra professed ignorance. "An iron curtain," she said, had descended, and until it was lifted nothing was certain. "The Empress wept. I wept with her and knelt to kiss her hand." The iron curtain would not be fully lifted for seventy years.

Sofka and her husband also escaped. Materially they were the lucky ones. Appointed ambassador to Athens in 1912, Elim Demidov had bought a property in Greece which would become their home in exile. He had also inherited, via a great-aunt, Mathilde Bonaparte, Napoleon's niece, the handsome estate of Pratolino near Florence, which had once contained the villa of the Grand Dukes of Tuscany; and perhaps his industrial fortune was well spread. Besides, he was an old Etonian, and they, as is well known, seldom starve.

One member of the family who did not emigrate was Count Ilarion's widowed sister, Princess Paskevich, who emerges as a very attractive character. Driven out of her "magnificent castle" at Gomel in Belorussia, built by Rastrelli, the famous Italian architect in Russia, and stuffed with the antique furniture of which her husband had been a connoisseur, she stayed resolutely on the relics of the estate in a former tenant's cottage with her faithful maid. Her relations, now settled in the West, sent her food parcels and sought to bring her out, but she remained there until her death, ninety years old and quite blind, but "always cheerful and uncomplaining". That indeed is the redeeming characteristic of so many of these Tsarist aristocrats who, in the catastrophic reversal of their fortunes, never surrendered that natural dignity which is independent of circumstances, and cheerfully adjusted themselves to a very different way of life.

The same can be said of Prince Dimitri. After escorting his wife and child to England he returned via Sweden to Russia to fight under General Yudenich against the Bolsheviks on the northern St Petersburg front. He was wounded, but survived thanks to the devotion of his Tartar orderly. But his marriage did not survive. He was supplanted as husband by Count André Tolstoy, who had also fought in the civil war, but on the southern Black Sea front, and had become aide-de-camp to the commander, General Wrangel. His war diary is in this book and documents the last stand of the White Army, which was finally evacuated from Sevastopol.

Prince Dimitri may not have been an ideal husband, but his love of nature, of "the earth and all that grows on it", as recorded in his memoir – his descriptions of elks, wolves and bears, of hunting and forest lore, of peasant life and its problems – has a whiff of Turgenev's *Sportsman's Sketches*, not to mention, occasionally, Chekhov's picture of Russian provincial life. Unfortunately he left no memoir of his life in exile; but as retailed by Dimitri, his picaresque adventures – selling rabbit skins in Normandy, buying rivers in Corsica, serving as night-watchman outside a bank in Paris, growing tulips for old ladies on the Riviera – show a man of irrepressible vitality and humour in adversity.

So we have moved on to the next generation and a very different scenario: no longer imperial courts and palaces, great estates and *douceur de vivre* in Russia but poverty and "bread of exile" in France and Britain. The presentation is different too. Hitherto it has been spectroscopic. The life of the family in Russia has been built up from separate fragments of experience and from separate viewpoints by persons who write for themselves or each other, omitting the connecting background which is already familiar to them all. In this essay I have tried to supply that background. But from now on the presentation is linear and coherent. Dimitri alone speaks directly to the reader and it is not for me to interpose more than a few words of introduction.

Essentially Dimitri's own memoir is an intellectual autobiography, an account of his gradual recovery, in exile, through personal friendship and historical study, of the best and most durable part of his lost Russian inheritance. His early childhood was spent in France – first in Nice and then in Paris – where his stepfather had found modest employment. In both Nice and Paris there were significant Russian communities. Then, by the accident of a trivial episode in Russia before his birth, he found himself placed in an English private or preparatory school in Kent.

Like most of those who had such an experience at that time, he looks back on it with mixed emotions. He still shudders slightly at the memory of those icy rooms, that Spartan discipline, the regular cold "plunge" and the monotonous food. It is inadvisable, even now, to offer him treacle tart. But he remembers with gratitude and some affection the kindly, committed, eccentric headmaster who had once been his stepfather's tutor in Russia and who, though dismissed for an admitted gaffe, had sought out his now impoverished pupil in Neuilly and offered free places at his school for both Dimitri and his half-brother Ivan Tolstoy. It was thus that Dimitri began the English experience which would be resumed, later, after secondary education at two Paris lycées, at Cambridge and Oxford.

But if he thus acquired some familiarity with England, it was in Paris that he was able, among the numerous Russian émigrés, to widen his knowledge of that Russian culture and tradition, literature and religion, which had similarly been driven into exile. In 1937, at the age of 18, he attended at the Sorbonne the centenary celebrations of the death of Russia's greatest poet, Pushkin, an occasion calculated to unite all parties among the exiles, and heard their intellectual leaders declare that, for those who had lost their country, "Russian literature is our final homeland, all that Russia was and will be".

At that time Dimitri had indeed lost his country. He was a full citizen nowhere, provided only with a "Nansen passport" which identified but gave no protection. Even ten years later, when I first knew him, it was thought prudent, when he attended a learned conference in West

Berlin, to provide him with an armed bodyguard, lest he be kidnapped by Soviet agents. But once he had become a British subject, he could travel safely, and he records three occasions when he revisited Soviet Russia. Each of them, in a different way, was dramatic and memorable.

The first, with which he begins his memoir, was in 1958, when he went as a guest lecturer on a privileged cruise in the Black Sea and found himself back in the Vorontsov Palace from which he had left Russia forty years before. There he had a cautious but moving conversation with an old lady who had been a servant there for even longer: she remembered the funeral of Count Ilarion in 1916. Her old masters, she admitted, were kinder than her new. The second occasion was an Anglo-Russian historical conference in Moscow in 1960, when highly charged sparks flew on the subject of the Munich Treaty. After an "acrimonious exchange", which loses none of its fire in the telling, the air, we learn, was somehow cleared and relations with the Russian historians became perceptibly warmer. They were evidently pleased that the truths which they were themselves forced to deny had been vindicated by their guests, leaving themselves unexposed. The last occasion was a Byzantine Congress in 1991, the first ever to be held in Russia. In an appropriately byzantine manner it became – accidentally and indirectly – entangled in the plot to overthrow President Gorbachev and thereby in the events which precipitated the end of Communist rule in Russia and Europe.

These dramatic confrontations make enjoyable reading, but they are not the most important parts of Dimitri's memoir. His more continuous and more fertile contacts with Russia have always been with the Other Russia, the chastened version of pre-1917 Russia represented by the exiles in the West, the true custodians of Russian scholarship and culture – and also with Greece, the original source and continuous home of its religion. These have always been at the centre of Dimitri's professional interest and personal commitment. How fortunate that he was diverted from the sterile "moral philosophy" of Cambridge! Both in his scholarship and in his life he has followed the advice given to him at the Pushkin celebration in

Paris in 1937 and has found in the literature and the culture of Russia – in its language, which the Tsarist courtiers hardly deigned to speak, and in the religion which the Bolsheviks tried in vain to suppress – a new and stronger patriotism than he could feel towards either of its recent political systems. In the first part of this book he has presented, vicariously, a contemporary portrait of the Tsardom in its last phase. In the second, while describing his own life in exile, he has written, incidentally, his *credo*, his *apologia pro vita sua*.

HUGH TREVOR-ROPER

BREAD OF EXILE

Prince Dimitri Alexandrovich Obolensky
(1882–1964)

My father's early life was spent between St Petersburg, where he was born, and the village of Nikolskoe Pestrovka (pronounced "Pyostrovka") in Penza province in south-east Russia, where his father owned and managed one of the major Russian glassworks, established in the eighteenth century. His love of the countryside is movingly described in his memoirs.

In 1900 he entered Petersburg University, but his last years, and especially 1905, were marred by revolutionary disturbances, and the University was closed before he could graduate. After performing his military service, he was elected marshal of the nobility in a rural district of Penza province (see p. 22) and for some years was immersed in problems of local rural administration. The governor of the province refused him permission to enlist in 1914. In 1920 he emigrated with his family, and moved to England where, equipped by the British, he joined General Yudenich's White Army, which narrowly failed to capture Petrograd (see p. 196).

After his divorce from my mother, he spent somewhat restless years as an emigré in western Europe and America, whose more vivid episodes he described to me with genuine humour (see pp. 214–15). He eventually settled down on the French Riviera, where he died.

What I am about to write embraces the period from 1890 or so to 1919, the year of my departure from Russia. I believe that those who left Russia as children, and who know absolutely nothing about our way of life there and our work for the good of our country, as well as those émigrés who still feel themselves to be Russians, will find something here to interest them.

I was born on 11 April 1882 in St Petersburg, in a house belonging to my grandfather Polovtsov, No 10 Sergievskaya Street. Our family – father, mother and we three brothers – lived on the first floor. (My youngest brother, Petrik, was born much later, in 1891 if I am not mistaken.) The second floor housed the Austrian Embassy. Ambassador Wolkenstein, and later on the Lichtensteins, lived there. My father held the post of Chief Procurator to the Senate, until he was appointed Assistant for Civil Affairs to the Governor-General of Warsaw. Prince Imeretinskii and we moved to that city.

The Austrian Embassy often held receptions, and we children, hiding behind the curtains, would peep through the big window in our entrance hall at the guests ascending the staircase, and the lackeys in their ceremonial livery. I remember an Embassy reception for the Emperor Franz Joseph.

The Ambassador sometimes went bear-hunting. The footman, who sat on the box of the Ambassador's coach wearing a hat with white plumes, would bring us bear-cubs to play with. There were many bears in the forests around Petersburg, and in winter peasants would turn up in the city to "sell" a lair, when snow started falling and the bear had retired for the winter. St Michael's Day, 8 November, was supposed to be the date for hibernation. As a rule, beaters would surround the lair and Eskimo dogs would flush out the bear. There was another method, of great antiquity, which called for daring and skill: the bear would attack, rear up on its hind legs, and impale itself on a bear-spear held by a huntsman kneeling on one knee.

We children lived in two enormous nurseries. We became fluent in English at an early age, thanks to our governess, Mrs Thornton (Anna Vasilievna), a rather strict lady no longer young, who efficiently supervised our physical and mental development. Every morning she made us bathe in ice-cold water and eat a great plate of porridge for breakfast, which we hated. Our day followed a strict timetable, beginning with lessons until lunchtime, after which a landau was provided for a drive around Petersburg: along Sergievskaya and Liteiny to the Nevsky Prospect. Or along Morskaya to the Embankment.

We would alight at the Summer Garden for a stroll. Mrs Thornton often called at the English shop, and at a special bakery near the Admiralty, where she bought delicious bread for our tea (I remember its name: "American Graham") and very tasty oatcakes. Between tea and supper we were free, and this was the time for horseplay, games, and gymnastics. We had an enormous sofa with very strong springs, and if you bounced hard enough you could turn a full somersault and land on your feet. Sometimes my brother Alyosha would stand on my shoulders and I would parade around the house, gripping his ankles.

Our parents dined separately, and we would make our way to the dining room after dinner, when their coffee was served, and each be given a lump of sugar. We tidied ourselves up beforehand, because our high jinks would have left us in a state of disarray.

My mother was a good pianist, and our house was a regular meeting place for the finest musicians in Petersburg. Anton Rubinstein was a regular visitor. There were frequent evenings of chamber music, with Auer and Verzhbolovich taking part, and we entertained visiting celebrities from abroad, including, for instance, Isaia Battistini. I heard music constantly from early childhood onwards. I remember the impression made on me by a Schumann quintet, and especially by a Tchaikovsky trio, played by Esipova, Auer and Verzhbolovich. I would give a lot to hear them again.

Father often took us to the rink at the Tavrida Gardens, where there were steep ice-slopes for tobogganing. One of the skaters was Mika Gorchakov who could slide down an ice-slope on skates. We used to put on our skates in the Tavrida Palace, helped by footmen in court livery.

We had another overseer as well as Mrs Thornton – our "preceptor" Ivan Ivanovich Veresov. He was with us throughout our years in Russia, and was like a member of the family. He was a native of Hungary. His father, a travelling salesman, landed in our village with a sick son. The boy was admitted to our hospital, and stayed behind when his father left. He became my father's valet, and married our nanny. In emigration I heard that he had committed suicide in our old home in the country. Thinking of him, I always remembered Old Firs in Chekhov's *The Cherry Orchard*.

Our main dining room attendant was Sergei Savvich who always stayed in Petersburg. The "outrider" Grigory Minukhov, sat on the box of the coach when my mother went for a drive, and stood on the rear footboard of the two-horse sleigh in winter. There were two "pantry men", Vasily Goryachev and Grigory Dyuzhaev and a "kitchen man", Andrei. All three were peasants from our village, Nikolskoe Pestrovka. Alexei Pavlovich, a remarkable cook, was equally talented as a musician – he played the trumpet – and as a raconteur. He had served as a naval volunteer, been shipwrecked and cast away on an island in the Indian Ocean. We were always trying to sneak into the kitchen, where marvellous pies were being made for dinner, but Alexei Pavlovich had strict rules and often just chased us away. He was particularly fond of my brother Alyosha, and indulged him much more than Sasha and myself. When we were in the country Alyosha often absconded to the kitchen, while I would disappear to the stables, so that our parents always knew where to find us if we were missing.

We had an enormous aviary in our nursery, with siskins, bullfinches and goldfinches which we bought from Mityurnikov's shop – he was a noted authority on birds. We had an aquarium, with all sorts of fish, a green parrot that could talk and whistle, and a white pointer called Pirate, who went everywhere with us. Pirate habitually lay under the table at dinner time, and seized any foot that came into contact with him. We had to use the fire tongs to drag him from under the table by his collar. Another of Pirate's characteristics was that he lived in mortal fear of gunshots, and mistook cameras for guns. If he saw one he would panic, and bolt with his tail between his legs. I think he was six, I can't remember exactly, when our tutor, Vladimir Bogdanovich, first appeared in the house. He was a student at Petersburg University when he started giving us lessons. Then he moved in with us, and went on living in our parents' house after all four brothers had left home. From earliest childhood until I left Russia I knew that Vladimir

Bogdanovich was always there, that I could turn to him for advice, and that he would always be helpful. He was so devoted to us that he would do anything in the world to help us.

Winter in Petersburg went by, and spring was on the way. The snow in the streets began to melt. Water dripped from roofs. Yardmen scraped ice from pavements and sanded them. Soon it was carnival time. Showmen's booths and sellers of gingerbread and appeared on Mars field. Crowds blocked the streets. The incessant din from all those pipes, concertinas and tin whistles could be heard a long way off. There were wooden platforms on which clowns dressed up as old men made the crowd laugh. It is difficult to describe all this to anyone who has never seen a Russian carnival . . . Veiki* arrived from Finland in sledges drawn by stout, well-fed horses. They were allowed to ply for hire as cabbies only at carnival time. The horses were decked with ribbons, and the jingling of sleigh bells could be heard everywhere. Samoyeds gave reindeer rides on the Neva.

Then came Lent, with church services twice daily. We fasted in the first and last weeks. My father used to make what he called "tyurya" – mashed potato with grated radish, caviare, gherkins and vegetable oil. We worshipped in the private chapel of Count Protasov-Bakhmetev at No 72, Nevsky Prospect. (My paternal grandmother lived on the top floor of the building.) Our numerous relatives all assembled in the chapel – the Bibikov cousins, Manya Obolenskaya, our aunts and uncles. After the service we dined upstairs with grandma, and that was also where we broke our fast after the morning service on Easter Day.

The days were drawing out, and we could dine without lights. We began taking our usual outing in an open-topped landau. We could go now to the Islands, where the grass was beginning to grow and there were snowdrops under the trees. All this meant that our Petersburg days would soon be at an end and – usually at the beginning of May – we should be leaving for the country. The very thought of it filled us with a sort of solemn joy.

* veiki: cabbies for hire during carnival time.

The long-awaited day of our departure arrived at last. The "heavy baggage" was sent on ahead. Andrei the kitchen man went with it. Then it was our turn. We left by train from the Nikolaevskii Station, changing at Moscow for Penza and Syzran. Father usually booked us a first-class carriage, with room for ourselves and all our luggage. We were accompanied by Vladimir Bogdanovich, Mrs Thornton, Ivan Ivanovich the cook, Grigory the footman, Natasha the chambermaid, our dog, Pirate, and the cook's dog, She-Bear. The journey took two days. We had all sorts of food, and lots of it. I remember particularly the cold "Pozharskii" pork rissoles.

On the morning of the second day our train arrived at Syuzyum, where our wagon was uncoupled and unloading began. Carriages were waiting for us at the station – we still had some 70 *versts** to go to our village, Nikolskaya Pestrovka. Our drivers were from the local *zemstvo* †
station, and fresh horses were provided thirty *versts* along the road.

SUMMER AT PESTROVKA

We usually rode on the box of our parents' carriage, surrendering the reins to the coachmen only on difficult stretches of road. Coachmen traditionally drove hell for leather through villages and hamlets. They would take over the reins, and drive furiously, whooping and whistling. We learned to drive well in early childhood, and could manage a three-horse or four-horse team easily. In one carriage behind us rode the cook with his wife and his dog She-Bear, in the second Grigory and Natasha the chambermaid, and behind them came the carts carrying our baggage with the pantry men Vasily and Grigory perched on top of it.

Ten *versts* from the station we reached pinewoods, with the River Sura beyond them. On entering the woods the whole procession halted, and we all walked to the river on foot, because our horses had

---

* *verst*: a Russian unit of measure, about 1.1 km (0.66 mile).
† *zemstvo*: the elective district council.

difficulty drawing the heavy carriages through the shifting sand. We children rushed through the woods with Pirate, like mad things. To this day I have a vivid memory of the wild joy which this first contact with nature gave me. I remember as if it were today the marvellous sunny morning, the gentle swaying of the pine trees, the white lilies, the tapping of woodpeckers on tree trunks.

But now we have reached the Sura, and crossed the bridge. We climb onto the box again, and drive through two big Tartar villages, Truevo and Latvino, to "Dvoriki", the coaching inn, then onto Empress Catherine's highway, lined with ancient birches, and running from Penza to Simbirsk. There, an old Mordovian woman stands on her porch to welcome us. The samovar is boiling, and there is a pitcher of cold milk on the table. Food is unloaded and we sit down to breakfast. The coachmen change the horses and check the carriage wheels and we go on to Bazarnaya Kensha, where our own coachman Vasily will be waiting for us with horses brought from Pestrovka.

Just outside Bazarnaya Kensha there was a small estate, the home of the elderly Baron Shtakelberg and his wife. A little wooden house in a small park. Flowerbeds around the house. The scent of mignonette and white tobacco flowers. Everything clean and cosy. But there is the jingle of bells and Vasily rides up with the barouche. By now it is getting dark. We still have 20 *versts* to go. Have you ever ridden in a Russian troika? Vasily was a real troika driver, of a kind no longer found. He controlled his team not just with the reins, but with his voice and his whistling. When they heard him whistle, the wheel-horse would break into a round trot, while the trace-horses galloped to keep up. Vasily had three greys. Bobrik ("Beaver"), his wheel-horse, was grey with pink specks, and the two trace-horses were grey mares. Vasily was an enthusiastic wolf-hunter, and all our hunts with wolfhounds took place under his close supervision.

We took turns sitting on the box all the way from Syuzyum to Pestrovka, but the last lap, from Bolshaya Kensha to Pestrovka, with Vasily driving, was something quite special for us. We remembered clearly who had sat next to Vasily last time, and took it in turns from year to year. He had so much to tell us about the year's events, all the horses, all our friends among the village children.

But now we are approaching Pestrovka. We have entered the pine forest. A steep decline, the village lights, our house ablaze with light. Supper, and to bed with the joyous feeling that winter, lessons, life in Petersburg are behind us, and ahead of us from tomorrow the pine forest, and all our friends among the village children. Barefoot in the forest all day long. Fishing in brooks for gudgeon, helping with the horses in the stableyard, the harvest, in short the freedom of which you dream all winter.

In the first few days we were allowed complete freedom. Then lessons with Vladimir Bogdanovich, and others invited by our parents for the summer, began. D. N. Nelyubov taught us science – botany, chemistry, etc. Monsieur Michel was our French teacher. S. I. Korguev, a professor at the Petersburg Conservatoire, was there for my brother Alyosha who had begun learning the violin very young. Summer evenings at Pestrovka. The lilac is in bloom. Nightingales are singing. The strains of the Kreutzer Sonata played by my mother and Korguev reach us from the house. Alyosha comes out onto the balcony of our nursery and plays a Chopin nocturne on his Stradivarius. The sound of an accordion is heard from the village – and it all seems to merge into a single melody: the song of this wonderful Russian summer night!

What with lessons and games, expeditions with the village lads, work in the stableyard, riding out to farmsteads with my father or the bailiff, or with the forester to watch his men at work, the summer went by quickly.

In the afternoon we three children, together with Mrs Thornton and Vladimir Bogdanovich, went for drives in the forest in three carriages – two of them racing droshkies. One of our coachmen was Ivan Truevuev, whose grandmother, as a girl, had hidden in a hempfield during the Pugachev incursion.

Teatime was at 4 p.m. The table was laden with yoghurt, jam, berries, fruit . . . Supper was at about seven.

Pestrovka and the Nikolsko-Bakhmetevskii Glassworks had belonged to the Bakhmetev family, and were left to my father by his aunt, Anna Petrovna Bakhmeteva, who brought him up. The works, established in the reign of Catherine the Great, had been greatly damaged by Pugachev's rabble army. The works stands on a little river, the Vyrchan, in which we caught gudgeon and perch. In the museum attached to the works there were tumblers of blue glass ornamented with gold, and dated 1790, and others with the inscription "Rejoice Moscow! The Russian is in Paris!" commemorating the entry of the Russian army into Paris in 1814.

The village of Nikolskoe-Pestrovka was bordered on three sides by pine forest – I have never seen such towering trees – and on the other lay peasant fields, and the highroad to the town and on to Penza. The River Vyrchan formed two large pools. The lower of the two was surrounded by our garden, and on one bank stood the foundry, in which moulds for the glassworks were cast, and the smithy in which implements and agricultural machines were repaired. The workers were all local peasants.

The glassworks itself consisted of two buildings, with five furnaces. There was also a department that made pots of fire clay and repaired stoves. The works manager, N. I. Protasov, belonged to a family that had worked in local industries for several generations. The total number of workers employed was, if I am not mistaken, 2,000, including women and juveniles. There were outstanding craftsmen among the workers, and our factory was, I think, the only one in which Venetian glass was made.

Our craftsmen won high awards at international exhibitions. There were real artists – Vasily Rogov, for instance – in the cut-glass department. The tableware and chandeliers produced were works of art. The works received many orders for flacons from famous perfumers. Glass was exported down the Volga and across the Caspian to Persia, much of it for hookahs. Lamp-chimneys and pharmaceutical glassware were made, as well as tumblers and utensils for peasant households, and the famous decanters with "cockerel" stoppers. The floor in our church was made from glass blocks. The method of smelting the glass had been handed down through the ages. My father did a great deal for the workers and made the works one of the best known in Russia.

There was in Pestrovka a factory hospital with 30 beds, a doctor and medical orderlies, and a maternity home. The doctor, I. M. Shchegolev, was both a surgeon and a general physician. Apart from his own work he visited patients elsewhere in the district, and was called in for consultation by the zemstvo doctors. Patients suffering from tuberculosis were often sent to Samara province for the kumiss* cure.

There were two schools – the zemstvo school, and a Ministry of Education two-grade school. My mother occupied herself with the hospital, the schools, and help for the poor and needy, both in Pestrovka and in the neighbouring villages. All the farm managers on our estate kept lists of peasants in need, and reported to my mother. She would provide timber for building and help towards the purchase of a horse or a cow. She made it possible for many young people to complete their education after leaving school, either in Penza, or in higher educational establishments in Moscow.

Pestrovka had a theatre of its own, and its own amateur dramatic society of workers and employees, and we took an active part in it. We put on both Gogol's *Inspector General* and Ostrovsky's *Forest*. The Vasily Rogov mentioned earlier was a remarkable actor, as was his brother Sasha. We also had a brass band, and a balalaika ensemble which gave concerts in towns along the Volga. We had our own volunteer fire brigade . . . But much of this came later, when we four brothers were able to take a very close interest in these matters.

My father looked on the works not as a source of income but as an obligation to provide a good livelihood for the workers and raise their quality of life culturally as well as materially. There was a factory

* kumiss: a fermented liquor prepared from mare's milk. See also p. 47.

shop in which the workers bought all their groceries. It had a good turnover, with many customers, landlords as well as peasants, from neighbouring villages. My father gave the shop with its entire stock to the local workers' consumer cooperative when it was set up. He sometimes brought in craftsmen from abroad. We had several Czechs from Bohemia but, I repeat, the main craftsmen in every department were natives of Pestrovka. The workers formed a distinct community, with their own elected headman. They lived in houses of their own, had their own allotments, orchards, hayfields and cattle, which grazed in the forest. Their lives were more comfortable in all respects than those of the peasants. Their cottages were cleaner, with curtains at the window. They were nearly all literate.

The variety of expertise needed in the works made the division of labour rather difficult. Some craftsmen made scent-bottles, others could only make pharmaceutical ware. A market had to be found for all of it. People from neighbouring villages traded in tumblers and other glassware for peasant households. They journeyed with horse and cart round Russia and Siberia, taking our glassware on credit, and would be missing for almost a year at a time, leaving proxies behind in the village to answer for the goods. Several villages felled timber and transported it to the works. The works had gas-generator furnaces to smelt the glass. Four thousand cubic *sazhens** of timber a year were required. We had agents, warehouses, and shops in Moscow, Penza, and Samara. We also had representatives in Persia.

If I am not mistaken the annual turnover of the works in the years immediately before the Revolution was around one million roubles. I. K. Stefanovich, estate manager at Pestrovka for some years, had two sons who were officers in the Cavalry-Grenadier Regiment. They would visit their father at Pestrovka in the summer, and they taught Alyosha and myself the basic skills required by cavalrymen, including acrobatics, bareback riding and jumping.

I must mention one other person, who came to us at Pestrovka

* *sazhens*: approximately 2.13 metres.

on my mother's invitation, and who was my closest friend from my adolescence until his death. This was an Englishman called [Stafford] Talbot. When he first came to us he was a student at Cambridge University, visiting Russia to learn the language. He had for some reason always been interested in Russia, was fond of the country, and later on helped Russian refugees in every way he could. Like most English students, he was first and foremost a sportsman. His specialities were running and boxing. Thanks to him I got good results in both these sports. In the boxing ring I sometimes made his nose bleed, and I could run 2 or 3 versts with ease.

Certain scenes from Russian life made a great impression on Talbot. On one occasion we came across a peasant sitting astride his prostrate horse in the roadway. A cart stood nearby. The peasant was skinning the horse, with tears running down his cheeks. It was difficult to explain to a Cambridge student what was happening.

Like all Englishmen, Talbot was physically strong, all muscle, but he lacked Russian staying-power. I could, for instance, easily go without sleep for several nights in succession. If Talbot missed a night's sleep he was good for nothing. I can remember occasions when I did not sleep or lie down for three days and nights, especially towards Easter at Pestrovka, with late church services, and night hunts. You would get home in the morning feeling fine and not at all sleepy, so you would saddle the mare and head for an outlying farmstead. My favourite farm was seven versts or so from Pestrovka. I set up a stud farm for remounts there, cross-breeds, and I loved lying on the grass in a coppice among a herd of young horses listening to the larks and watching the mares grazing and the foals frisking. But I digress.

Our office manager and chief accountant was Albin Antonovich Inman. He loved driving about in a racing droshky to watch peasants at work in the fields. Once I was riding across a field where the first binding machines were at work, and a crowd of peasants from neighbouring villages had gathered to watch them. When I rode up they were all laughing heartily. I asked what had happened. "Well, he drove up, you know, Belim Antonovich," (that was what the peasants called him) "bent over the machine, and his beard got caught and bound and tossed out in a sheaf."

Ours was a large, stone-built house with no pretensions to style – no pillars, just a big white house with a green roof. In front of the house was a garden running down to a pool, with an island reached by ferry. The lower part of the garden was somewhat neglected. There were old trees – elms, birch, wild cherry. The only flowerbeds were immediately in front of the house, where there was also a fountain and a balcony on which my mother would sit with her book or her needlework. There were lilac bushes all round. In spring nightingales sang in them, and in winter robins found shelter there. Behind the bushes was a gigantic "giant's footstep". My brother Alyosha's fox terrier, "Buika", loved hanging onto the strap with its teeth and flying through the air with us.

On the other side of the house were the orchard, hothouses and a vegetable garden which merged with the pine forest. I have never seen pines like those which surrounded Pestrovka on three sides. These towering trees were never felled. Only the deadwood was cleared away. Under the trees grew ferns and wild strawberries, which could be gathered by the bucketful. In the forest round about there was a profusion of raspberries, stone brambles, and bilberries. Jam and syrups were made from these berries. A special jam made from wild strawberry was sent through my father's brother, a court official, to the Emperor Alexander III, who was very fond of it.

The centre of the house was occupied by a great hall, with a gallery and a fireplace the height of a man. My mother's rooms opened onto this hall, which we used as a dining room – her drawing room, and beyond it her study with her desk and photographs. This room was panelled with polished wood, and there was straw matting on the floor.

There, after her morning tea, my mother dealt with all our pensioners and received applications from those in need. Sometimes she would spend the rest of the morning before lunch visiting the hospital or the schools. She was, as I have said, a good pianist, and she played either alone, or with one of the musicians who regularly visited her. Through one of them, Kosovsky, from Penza, she bought the marvellous grey mare "Yashma" ("Jasper"). She was a good rider, and my mother, father, and we children on our ponies, would go for rides in the forest. My mother read and wrote a great deal. She translated from English. Her translation of *The Garden of Allah* was published, and could be bought at Wolf's bookshop. She liked going for long walks in the forest, often accompanied by one of us on horseback, and always by our dog, Pirate.

There was always music in the evening. As a rule, my mother would be joined by Korguev, or my brother Alyosha, playing the violin. Dr Shchegolev from the hospital adored music, and never failed to appear. Tea would be served at 10 p.m. by Ivan Ivanovich, and then it was time for bed.

Alyosha and I had our own gang, organised on military lines. Our supervisor was Nikita, a one-time Uhlan in charge of the riding horses in our stables. He organised our battles in the forest, with reconnaissance and exchanges of pine-cone fire, according to all the rules of the military art. It always ended in hand-to-hand fighting, torn shirts and bloody noses, with Nikita himself furiously joining in. The bottle of vodka to which he frequently applied himself was probably partly responsible, and the side on which he exerted himself always won. His only duty was to look after the riding horses, and when we were away he did not have much to do. When we were riding home in summer as soon as we neared the village our horses would break into a gallop and pull up at the door of the tavern – as Nikita had taught them to do.

We sometimes went abroad in autumn, usually to Biarritz, but occasionally to Nice. Among my earliest memories is one of seeing Queen Victoria in a small carriage on the seafront at Nice. A trip to Franzbad was made memorable because our parents introduced us to the Iron Chancellor, Bismarck, who was out walking with two huge Great Danes. I remember spending one autumn in the Crimea. We went to the palace in Livadia to play with the Emperor's children, Nikolai, Xenia and Mikhail. But these journeys took us away from the life in Pestrovka which we so loved, and from all our childish interests. I still vividly remember the grief, the infinite despair we felt as our train drew out of the station and we could still hear the bells of the troikas which had brought us there, and the voices of our coachmen.

A great event at Pestrovka was the arrival of the Bishop of Penza, making the rounds of his diocese. He always rode in a closed carriage, even in the hottest weather. An enormous carriage, drawn by four horses abreast, and two others in front, with a postillion on one of them. At the rear of the carriage was a seat occupied by the young monk in charge of the baggage. He also acted as the bishop's valet. Ahead rode various constables and wardens on horseback, and the local police-chief in a troika, while a number of carriages with the bishop's retinue and assorted clergy brought up the rear.

The police always escorted highly-placed persons travelling along our roads. My father had great difficulty in escaping their attentions. When they galloped ahead you had to ride through the clouds of dust they raised. On one occasion when the local police-chief wanted to escort him my father made room for him in the carriage, and the officer took his seat politely. A peasant wagon came in sight ahead of them, completely blocking the road. "Your Excellency," said the policeman, "permit me to raise my voice." Permission was given, and expressions were heard which cleared the way in an instant.

But to continue with the bishop. Tables bearing bread and salt were set before cottages in the village, and the bell-ringer was on duty up in the bell-tower from early morning, so that he could begin ringing a full peal as soon as he saw the enormous dust-cloud in the distance. The bishop and his entourage stayed in our house. Huge carp were netted in the pool in time for his arrival, so that we could feed them all Lenten fare.

HUNTING

Here I must begin by saying something about the man who made me a hunter, and to whom I owe my knowledge and love of the Russian countryside and my understanding of animals and their way of life.

This was Alexei Dorkin, our forest warden. He was a lean old man with a beard and greying hair, a Mordovian, who had spent his whole life from the days of serfdom onwards in the forest. His main duty was to inspect the work of the foresters, supervise timbering and planting and, in addition, supply the "master's table" with game.

When I speak of hunting I have in mind not that well-organised variety with hunt-servants and beaters, to encircle the beast before the gentlemen arrive to take up their allotted positions, but our elk-hunts on skis, for a whole day, or sometimes two, spending the night in the forest. When we came across fresh tracks we circled round so that we could approach the elks from down-wind, when hawk-eyed Dorkin spotted them standing still. Approaching them called for great skill and patience.

We would camp for the night in the huntsman's lodge and after a tumblerful of vodka, and eggs boiled in the samovar, we would sprawl on straw round the stove. Dorkin could drain a cupful of pure spirit without difficulty, claiming that it would be "burnt off on the move".

But ah! The woodgrouse season in the Pestrovka forests! Dorkin would not rush at the woodgrouse while it was making its mating display, as is usual. He would sit in the bushes and imitate the call of a hen grouse. The cock would fly down from a tree and run towards him. I have seen this often enough, but am bound to say that I never killed grouse in this fashion. Dorkin saw no point in hopping about over ice and spring floodwater. In fact, it was easy enough tracking them down by their mating call in the Pestrovka forests, since they usually mated among the pines where it was dry and the ground was covered with dry moss. I remember killing six grouse one sunrise, which was a sort of record.

Elks in the forest were not numerous, and there were few with large antlers. There were woodgrouse, blackcock, partridges, and of course marshfowl. Hares were plentiful. Dorkin knew the forest well – every landmark in it had a name of its own. There were, for instance, "Bakaldina No 1" and Bakaldina No 2". "Balkaldina" meant a deep ditch in which there was water, even in the hottest weather. Elks would go there to drink, and we would conceal ourselves in the undergrowth at dawn and shoot them.

WOLVES

Wolves were simply a plague in winter, and the whole district, including the immense State forests, was at my disposal for wolf hunting. There were so many of them that one of the two constables killed a wolf in the street of the district administrative centre.

We used the Pskov method of hunting – the best huntsmen nearly all came from Pskov. When the hunter, on skis in winter, came across wolf tracks he would ski around in diminishing circles until he reached a spot with inward but no outward tracks, which meant that the beast was cornered. As a rule, the hunter would leave the carcass of a horse, or some other animal, in several places, as bait, and would visit each spot in the early morning to pick up the wolf's trail. The beast is usually inactive in the daytime, and after a morning of walking the hunter has it "encircled". Then begins the "cutting off of the circle", which requires great caution, so as not to arouse the animal.

The hunter's guide strings two lines of red flags from the trees, leaving a conical corridor between them. The hunter stands with his gun at the narrower end of the corridor, and the guide creeps up on the wolf from the other end, then rouses it by yelling and banging. The beast rises, sees the red flags, and – because the colour is unfa-miliar – runs along the corridor, right towards the hunter, who is dressed from head to foot in white (often wearing a night-shirt over his sheepskin). The hunter bides his time and shoots when the wolf is quite near.

For me, the main pleasure was in tracking down the wolf and the preparations. I passed on the skills acquired from the men of Pskov to Dorkin. He was a remarkable mimic of animal cries, and could howl like an old wolf (I acquired this skill myself). This was useful when he and I rode out on autumn evenings to discover where the wolves had their cubs. There might be as many as thirty wolf packs in our district. The old wolves would come out in the evening looking for prey, leaving their cubs behind somewhere in the forest. When they found their prey they would begin to howl, and their young would answer and rush to them. If you started howling before the old wolves left the lair you would hear them growling, chiding the cubs to prevent them answering. The frosty autumn night would be full of a symphony of wolf voices, in which you could distinguish the deep voices of the old wolves and the whining and yelping of their young.

Dorkin and I stalked one old wolf several winters running. We could tell from his tracks that he was very big and went on three paws. It was almost impossible to "circle" him, and if you did he ran towards the man who was howling, not the hunters. None the less I killed him in the end. One of his paws had been amputated. He must have fallen into a trap set by the peasants and gnawed off his paw to escape. He was the biggest wolf I ever saw. I had him stuffed, and he stood on his three paws in the entrance hall of our house.

My last encounter with a wolf was during the war, when I went on leave to Pestrovka for a few days. I was riding to the station in a troika, with my trunk at my feet. Suddenly I saw a she-wolf on the road ahead. My driver glanced at me and the troika took off along the road at a furious speed. I stood up in the sleigh, clinging to the driver's belt and trying with my other hand to open the trunk, in which I had a revolver among my linen. It was difficult to keep my balance, with the sleigh bumping over the ruts. The wolf flew along the road, with us in the sleigh behind her.

Three *versts* away there was a large Mordovian village. There was snow about the height of a horse's chest along both sides of the road. I got hold of my revolver, calculating that the wolf would not enter the village, but would jump into the snow, that we should then overtake her and I would be able to shoot. She did jump into the snow, but realised that it was too deep for her to get away and returned to the firm roadway. We were now much closer to her, but I could not fire because there was a bend in the road and I had three horses in single file ahead of me. So we flew into the village in broad daylight, the wolf ahead, with the sleigh following her.

A Mordovian stood at a sharp turn in the village street. I shouted to him in his own language, and the wolf vanished. I jumped out of the sleigh and followed her track to a barn. I entered cautiously, revolver in hand, but was in time only to see her back legs as she jumped over a fence to disappear into the fields. As we left the village I saw my wolf standing on a distant hillock watching us go by. This was the last wolf I ever saw in the wild. Since then I have seen only the unfortunate rachitic creatures they keep in zoos. They bear no resemblance to real wolves.

* * *

In the year 1900 I entered Petersburg University. My last years there, and especially 1905, when I was supposed to graduate, were a period of revolutionary disturbances. The university was a centre for revolutionary gatherings of every imaginable kind, and those taking part often had no connection whatsoever with it. Disorderly behaviour in the lecture room was common, and lectures might be physically disrupted – by stink bombs, for instance. I took an active part in a student group formed to combat all this. Our watchword was "The University is for Learning" – and not for politics. It ended in fist-fights in the university corridors. These were narrow, and we stationed the strongest of our number in the front ranks, foremost of all a student who was a wrestler and refereed wrestling matches. Next day leaflets were strewn about the university, proclaiming that "the Government has resorted to a new means of struggle: dressing up wrestlers from the circus in students' tunics so that they can beat students". But the university was closed down, and so as not to waste time I decided to perform my military service as a volunteer in Her Imperial Majesty's Uhlan Regiment.

I joined up on 10 October 1905. In the year of the Japanese War, and revolutionary turmoil, the regiment was stationed at Peterhof, but regularly went into Petersburg to restore order. In 1906 we lined the route in full dress uniform to welcome the deputies when the First Duma was convened. Then came the dissolution of the Duma, and my platoon patrolled the city by night. A battalion of the Preobrazhenskii Regiment, standing guard in our barracks at Peterhof, mutinied, and we were called back to Petersburg to drive out with our rifle butts the whole revolutionary crowd, drunken Preobrazhenskii guardsmen among them, from our barracks. We returned to Krasnoye Selo singing, after the Emperor and Empress had thanked us for our efforts and accompanied us part of the way.

One night towards the end of the summer manoeuvres I was out reconnoitring and ran into a company of "enemy" Cossacks. Not wishing to be taken prisoner I retreated at full gallop with my platoon, and collided with a hansom cab in the darkness. I lay on the highway, while the whole company of Cossacks galloped by. I lay still, and the horses jumped over me. My soldiers picked me up and took me to the casualty post. There they tried to set my dislocated hip but failed. When I awoke from the chloroform I saw an unknown lady sitting by me. I suddenly realised that the Empress, as colonel-in-chief of my regiment, had come to visit me. I had badly bruised my spine and dislocated a hip in the fall.

I was on the sick list for almost two years. The doctors made a mistake. They decided that I had fractured my hip, and put it into plaster without trying to set it. I had to undergo several very painful operations later on, before my displaced hip was repositioned. I also contracted uraemia, and almost died in Pestrovka, when I went home after an utterly pointless visit to Karlsbad on doctors' orders. Then I had to undergo an operation on my kidneys in Petersburg where, to cap it all, I caught scarlet fever in hospital.

So I was almost completely cut off from Pestrovka for two years, and returned there, fully restored to health, only in 1912. That was when I began to take part in the work of the zemstvo. I was elected marshal of the nobility for the Gorodishche rural district of Penza province, and remained in that post right up to the Revolution.

The city of Penza is situated on hilly ground, with the River Sura and its water meadows on one side and the pinewoods of Gorodishche on the other. The province of Penza is in the black-earth belt of Russia. Its two biggest rural districts, however, were covered with pine forest, some of it State land, some privately owned. The Gorodishche district was bordered on one side by Simbirsk province and on the other by Saratov province. Its population was mixed. There were many Mordovian and many Tartar villages, the population of which lived quite separately from their Russian neighbours.

THE MORDOVIANS

The Moksha (steppe Mordovians) and the Arzyas (forest Mordovians) differed greatly from each other. The Moksha were short in stature, wore blue smocks and lived mainly in the Moksha region. Our forest Mordovians were mostly very big people, and they wore white smocks. The women wore very distinctive smocks and ornaments.

I was always struck by the heroic build of the men who turned up when I was presiding over the local draft board. They engaged mainly in forest trades – tar boiling, shovel making, cooperage – and were experts in stubbing. Most of them were honest people. A Mordovian from a village 40 *versts* away once came to see me in Pestrovka. He said: "I come to you. My wife has died. Little children are left and the cow has died. Give me money for a cow. I will work it off. I will come to mow." I gave him 30 roubles, the price of a cow, and said "Come on St Peter's Day" (29 June). This was in winter, and I forgot all about it. But when I went outside on 29 June I found this Mordovian waiting with his scythe. He had come to work off his debt. I gave him a good tumblerful of vodka and he went off home on foot. The Mordovians are of Finnish stock, and have their own language. We had an Estonian gardener who could converse freely with them.

A few words about the Tartar villages, of which there were several in the Gorodishche district. The Tartars, even more than the Mordovians, lived separately from the Russian population. There were mosques in their villages, and the mullahs had a big influence on every aspect of their lives. They were abstemious, and good workers. They generally wore red smocks. When I was supervising the call-up I was always struck by their stubborn desire to avoid military service by any means possible. I believe that propaganda from the mullahs had powerfully influenced their efforts. Healthy Tartar youths would report to the recruiting officer with stitches in their legs, and pus-soaked bandages round self-inflicted wounds. Some starved themselves until they were mere skeletons. If they were pronounced fit, a mullah had to administer the oath. If no mullah was on hand, I, as chairman of the draft board, would read the oath to them in Tartar, taking care – following my instructions – that no one should utter the Tartar words meaning "if Allah so pleases", which would invalidate the oath.

To be sworn in they squatted on the ground. I am bound to say that any Tartar who did find himself in the army made an excellent soldier, especially in the cavalry. When I was serving in Yudenich's cavalry and out on patrol, my life was saved by my Tartar orderly, Akhmachin. I was lying on the ground with a broken leg, under fire from an enemy outpost, and about to draw my revolver and shoot myself in the head so as not to be taken prisoner by the Bolsheviks, when he dragged me to safety.

THE TOWN AND ADMINISTRATIVE DISTRICT OF GORODISHCHE

Gorodishche, 50 *versts* from Penza, stood on the banks of a little river and was surrounded by forest. In appearance it was just a big village, and its whole population was some 4–5,000 souls. It only had three stone buildings: the prison, the recruiting office, and the local administration offices. The great "Catherine Highway", which ran from Penza to Simbirsk, lined with ancient birch trees, passed through the town. It was probably once a small fortress, guarding against Tartar and other raiders: the old fosse and rampart were still there, and I dare say that excavation would produce much of archaeological interest. The railway line was 20 *versts* away. Local people have told me that when the line was first discussed the town's merchants went to plead with the chief engineer (probably giving him a substantial bribe) not to run the railway through the town, believing that it would ruin their trade!

In the middle of the town were the market place, on which stood several taverns and shops, and the cathedral. The streets were unpaved, and had wooden sidewalks. In autumn the mud on the streets was knee-high to a horse.

ZEMSTVO

The *zemstvo* was quite separate from the state administrative agencies under the provincial governor. I will go so far as to say that all of Russia's intellectual and cultural forces was either engaged in *zemstvo* work or connected with it in one way or another. What, then, was the *zemstvo*?

Every *uyezd** in Russia had its *zemstvo*, an elected assembly representing all levels of the population: big landowners, small landowners, townsfolk, peasants. They met three times a year to elect a *zemstvo* board, which disposed of funds raised by local taxation, and was responsible for the upkeep and supervision of schools, hospitals, roads, and the telephone network. It also employed agronomists, organised centres for the improvement of stock farming, libraries, and so on.

The *uyezd zemstvos* elected delegates to the provincial *zemstvo*, which was their link with the government. As an example of the *zemstvos'*

---

* *uyezd*: an administrative area, smaller than a *gubernia*.

activity I may mention their role in the implementation of the government's plans for universal education, adopted some years before the First World War. In each *uyezd* the local *zemstvo* covered one quarter of the cost, the provincial *zemstvo* another quarter, and the central government the other half. True, the primary school did not provide much of an education, but at least children learned to read and write.

What Russia most lacked was educated and honest people. Those with any pretension to culture found life in the provinces unbearable and aspired to live in the larger towns. Russian provincial life has been so vividly and accurately described by Chekhov and Leskov that it would be superfluous for me to talk about it.

Even among the peasantry the ablest did their best to escape to the towns as soon as they left the village school, and to find a place in trade schools or schools for medical auxiliaries. Only the illiterate and ignorant remained in the villages.

Our district *zemstvo*, as far as I remember, consisted of twenty elected deputies, nine from the gentry, and eleven peasants. The peasant deputies often completely failed to understand the subject under discussion, and resented having to leave their villages and spend a week or more in town listening to interminable reports.

CONSEQUENCES OF STOLYPIN'S REFORM

[My father took an active part at the local level in the implementation of Stolypin's agrarian reform: an attempt to break up the peasant commune with its practice of periodical redistribution of land, and to convert the peasant into an independent smallholder. My father regards Stolypin as a great statesman and believes that if this man had not been assassinated the whole subsequent history of Russia would have been different.] In the few years during which the law was operative a completely new class of peasant smallholders appeared. It was of course mainly the most efficient and prosperous peasants who left the commune – the so-called "kulaks" who were so violently hated by the Bolsheviks, and who suffered so dreadfully in concentration camps and in Siberian exile. The peasant did not have the right to sell his allotment. If he went away to work in a factory he could assign it to someone else in his village, but he was secure in the knowledge that he could return and take back his holding whenever he wished. Nowhere else in the world, I think, is it the case that any peasant who loses his job in the town can go home and resume possession of a plot of land. In fact the "employment problem" as it is understood in Europe was non-existent in Russia in my time, since every factory worker was a peasant from a particular village in which he could claim a piece of land.

PEASANT COOPERATIVES

Our whole district was covered by a network of cooperatives and consumers' associations, which freed the peasants from dependence on brokers and speculators. On the debit side, nearly all *zemstvo* agronomists were people of extreme leftist views, so that these cooperatives served as centres of vigorous revolutionary propaganda. Only the estates of the landed gentry were efficiently farmed: only there would you find the land manured, tractors and reaper-binders at work, and a proper system of crop rotation in being. At Pestrovka we had a nine-field system, root crops alternating with cultivated grasses. Nearly all the cereals (wheat in particular) which fed the rest of Europe used to come from landowner estates in Russia, and especially the Ukraine. This was good quality wheat. The wheat on peasant land was usually stunted and full of weeds.

ZEMSTVO TEACHERS

They sometimes endured great hardships, especially the women teachers. They received very small salaries and lived as a rule in benighted villages, remote from any urban centre of civilisation where often enough the only more or less educated person was the priest.

They often had to negotiate deliveries of wood for fuel, and other necessities, with the local peasants. Life was particularly hard for women teachers, fresh from school themselves, suddenly landing in midwinter in a remote village, snow-bound and with a blizzard raging. It took great strength of character to endure such an existence.

MEDICAL SERVICES

There were four *zemstvo* hospitals, and one belonging to our factory, in our *uyezd* besides a number of clinics manned by medical orderlies. I should like to say something about the difference in ethics and traditions observable then, and perhaps even now, between our Russian doctors and their colleagues in Europe and in democratic countries generally.

A *zemstvo* doctor, in charge of a hospital and a number of clinics, had to be an all-round specialist. A patient needing a complicated operation would, of course, be sent to a hospital in the provincial capital, but I believe that our *zemstvo* doctors, after many years dealing with a great variety of cases, were the best in the world. I cannot imagine a Russian *zemstvo* doctor refusing to answer a call in the middle of the night from a patient living many miles away – without, of course, any fee at all. This was in old Russia. There was nothing like it anywhere else in the world: every peasant had his piece of land, was educated gratis in elementary school, and received hospital treatment and medication also without payment. (Some *zemstvos* did introduce a charge of five copecks for a bottle of medicine.) This is supposed to have been something first organised by the British government, but Russia's tsarist democracy had organised it long, long before.

Everyone, of course, paid the *zemstvo* levy, but this was an inconsiderable sum. I have no figures to support this statement, but am bound to say that the Russian peasant, like everyone else, did his best to avoid paying taxes. Disorderly scenes were common in the villages when tax collectors tried to carry out their task with the help of the village constable. But as soon as the constable laid hands on the samovar the tax would be paid.

For the most part, *zemstvo* employees were motivated not so much by the salaries they received as by concern for the well-being of the Russian peasantry. This was what we were all working for – the *zemstvos*, we marshals of the nobility, and all Russia's cultural forces. But our work came up against insuperable obstacles, and was hampered by the absence of people who were honest, civilised and educated from provincial Russia. I knew people who would have liked to take a hand in our *zemstvo* work but, knowing how things were, said "there's no point in it, you can't get anything done". Yet, in spite of difficult conditions, obstacles which sometimes appeared insuperable, and the apparent hopelessness of it all, I am convinced that nowhere in the world would you find such selfless, idealistic people as our *zemstvo* employees. This was where the Russian democratic ideal was to be found – not an abstract idea but one realised in practice in everyday Russian life.

THE GENTRY

Distinct social "estates" still existed in Russia. Every Russian was either a gentleman, a merchant, a townsman, a peasant, or an ecclesiastic. Every class had its own elected representatives and its own professional organisation. Of old, the gentry had been servants of the State, in a military or civil capacity, and had been given estates in return. After the abolition of obligatory service, the gentleman was still honour bound to perform duties for the Tsar. Hence the marshals of the nobility carried out their often onerous duties without payment in any form. The marshal of the nobility in each district presided over *zemstvo* assemblies, and in general over all local bodies, including the draft board, the district court, the schools council, and prison committee.

Every Russian province kept a genealogical register, in which gentry children were entered at birth. Membership of the gentry class was a sort of guarantee of honesty and propriety – all that is meant by the English word "gentleman". A marshal of the nobility was unpaid, was not a civil servant, took orders from no one (not even from the provincial governor or the Minister of the Interior), and could, I think, be indicted only by the Senate. The marshal's powers were extensive. He could overrule the local draft board, doctors included, if he considered fit someone whom they had rejected. A district peasant assembly could banish to Siberia an undesirable element in their midst, but the sentence had to be confirmed by the marshal. I overturned one such sentence as unfair, knowing very well that for a few pails of vodka you could get any decision you liked in a village assembly.

Civil servants and policemen could be bribed, but everyone knew that we could not, and so the peasants respected us and valued our opinion. That, at any rate, was the theory. Many nobles of course did not live up to it.

RUSSIAN BUREAUCRACY AT WORK

[*Peasants who left the commune under the terms of Stolypin's agrarian reform received a consolidated landholding instead of strips of land in the periodically redistributed communal fields. Land tenure commissions were appointed to carry out the work of consolidation. My father presided over such a commission and here recalls an episode which shows how remote the central power and members of the government were from reality.*] The secretary of the local land tenure commission reported to me in uniform and showed me an order from the provincial commission: we were to load all the documentation of our commission onto carts, and take it to Penza, some 50 *versts* away, because a "general" was coming from Petersburg to "inspect". The secretary had already loaded two files, and was awaiting permission to continue.

"Get your uniform off and take the files back inside," I said. "You're going nowhere."

I had never before heard of an inspector asking for the files to be brought to him instead of coming to examine them on the spot. Some days later the secretary came to me again and showed me an order from the Provincial Commission signed by the Governor. "His Excellency" (the visiting inspector) was on his way, and a reception should be prepared for him at farms en route. I quote verbatim: "A light repast should be prepared at these farms – milk, eggs, etc., as His Excellency is trying to keep to a diet."

Then the local inspector of police arrived with orders from the governor to provide a comfortable carriage, preferably from one or other of the local landowers, for his excursions. I immediately got the secretary to make three copies of this order. One I sent to the Minister of Agriculture, Krivoshein, the second to the governor with my reply, and the third to a Duma deputy from our district, who published it in the newspaper Novoye Vremya [New Times]. Gogol's Inspector General is not yet extinct in Russia!

PEASANT PATRIOTISM

For some reason the first to be called up in 1914 were elderly ex-soldiers. And Gorodishche, with not more than 5,000 inhabitants, was to be the assembly point for 5,000 reservists. We had to arrange accommodation and food for them all. They started arriving, and we began registering them at the recruiting office. Men from 27 of the 29 rural districts in the uyezd arrived in good order, but the other two contingents were missing.

Since my work was nearly over I had telephoned home for horses. When my coachman arrived he told me that a mob of reservists was on the way, wrecking all the liquor stores as they came, drunk and disorderly to a man.

"If you let that mob into the town," I said to the police inspector, "it'll be just the same here. Send the rural constables to meet them, take the vodka from them, and keep them in the forest."

He said he couldn't, he had only ten village constables and two regular policemen. But I managed to persuade him, and telephoned Penza to inform the Governor of the situation.

Next day the two missing contingents turned up and we were able to complete the registration. Two ensigns had arrived from Penza to take charge of the draftees. Once the count was over a farewell service was held on the market square. An aged archpriest, the recruiting officer, and I myself, with a handful of rural constables, stood in the midst of the 5,000 draftees. The archpriest made a speech, and instead of trying to raise the spirits of the draftees, spoke roughly as follows:

"So here we are at war again. Once again your families will be left alone. Pray to God. Pray to the Mother of God. Above all obey your officers, and follow where they lead you."

In the dense crowd around us there was laughter, and men shouted: "We know where they'll lead us! We followed them against the Japanese."

The two ensigns sent to take the draftees to Penza were standing with us. I saw them turn pale and clutch their revolvers. The crowd started yelling, and the mood was ugly. I plucked the priest by his cassock and said: "Begin the service." They all calmed down a little, but I felt that I must do something – there was no knowing how it might end.

These men, the first to be called up, were mostly veterans of the war with Japan. They didn't even know who was at war with us this time. Luckily I had a recent newspaper in my pocket, with the first news of military actions, and the new law on assistance for the families of conscripts (an excellent law which hardly anyone yet knew about). When the service ended, I took out my newspaper and without preamble read out the first news and explained what was happening. As soon as I said that the Austrians were shelling Belgrade the crowd instantly fell silent and I felt that I had their attention. There was complete silence. Then I went on with the law on assistance to their families, and was bombarded with questions as to which family members would receive help and how much. This went on for some time, and then there was a display of patriotism, with new shouting "Hurrah!"

As I turned to leave the crowd parted before me and there were shouts of "Make way for our prince!" When the police inspector came to see me that evening I asked him why the news that Belgrade was being bombarded had had such an effect on them. He answered that "They thought you were talking about Belgorod near Kharkov where the relics of Saint Ioasaph are."

THE 1914 WAR

Because of my duties as chairman of the draft board I was not called up but "embodied" on the spot. Orders to mobilise men and horses, and to requisition sheepskin coats and felt boots in winter, and much else, followed in quick succession. Land captains were called to the colours, and there were far too few people available locally to do all this work. I spent whole days at a time in the overheated recruiting office, and sat through the evening and into the night making and checking lists of men called up, and their families.

The government, in my view, had made a mistake in calling up such a huge number of reservists. The towns were all full of reservists with nothing at all to do, and there weren't even enough rifles to go round. One of the two companies in our town was commanded by the local land captain, a man no longer young, and rather corpulent. As company commander he had to parade on horseback, but he was originally an infantry officer, and could only walk his mount. In due course the unit was sent to the Turkish front, near Erzerum. A few months later I met one of the soldiers and asked him what had happened to them all. He said that the Turks had thrashed them in battle and very few had escaped alive.

"What about your commanding officer?" I asked.

"Oh, he just left his horse behind and legged it faster than the rest."

Our work on the home front was very difficult. There were so many orders which it was simply impossible to carry out. We were ordered, for instance, to re-register all those who had been discharged from the army, and all the wounded, and to do this in Gorodishche – in other words these people, some of whom had lost legs, would have to travel as much as 40 miles at their own expense. I wrote to my father in Petersburg, he went to see the Minister of War, and the order was cancelled.

I was young and healthy, and longed to be at the front instead of sitting around at the rear, although I realised that my work there was perhaps much more important than what I would be doing as an ensign in some cavalry regiment. But in the end I could stand it no longer, and I sent a telegram to my uncle, P. Polovtsev, commander of the "Wild Division", which was at the front. He replied: "Come. The Tartar Regiment will take you." But I needed the Governor's consent, there was no one to take over from me, and the Governor refused me permission. I had to obey, and immerse myself in my work.

We in the rear sensed from the mood of the wounded and the draftees that there was some sort of breakdown. (When I did finally get to the front I found that morale was quite different in spite of horrifying losses and the shortage of shells and rifles. Some of our infantry regiments had lost two full complements and were only able to fire two or three shells a day. No army in the world could have stood that, and yet, although we had begun to retreat, and although our best soldiers and our regular officers were suffering horrifying casualties, the retreat proceeded in good order and morale at the front was higher than in the rear.)

German and Austrian subjects expelled from the big towns began to appear in Gorodishche, and we were sent Austrian prisoners to be distributed around the *uyezd*. The sergeant-major in charge of the whole batch began by asking me to separate its two components – half were Serbs and half Croats, and they were continually quarrelling and fighting. I stationed the Serbs near Pestrovka, arranged accommodation for them and put them to work on one of my farms.

When the news came that Russian troops had taken Przemysl, the farm manager telephoned to say that the prisoners wanted me to attend a service of thanksgiving. I went along with the priest. I asked the priest to say a few words to the prisoners, but when I saw that he was at a loss, spoke myself, roughly as follows, with the sergeant-major translating my words into Serbian. I said that "as a Russian I am delighted that you, Austrian soldiers, should want to celebrate today the capture of Przemysl from the Austrians by Russian forces. Long live Great Serbia!" The effect was tremendous. There were loud cheers, the prisoners threw their caps in the air, and started shaking me by the hand. Some even wept. I stood them a keg of vodka and went home feeling that although it was only a small thing I had done something good for Russia.

These prisoners worked on our farms for about a year. They were good workers. They made many acquaintances, and quite a few little Serbs were born in villages round about.

I often visited the recruiting officer in the evening. One of his duties was to read letters written from the front. He showed me one which is embedded in my memory. It read as follows:

How are things with you? Let me tell you our news: they've found an underground passage in the palace, through which the Empress can talk to Wilhelm, and Nikolai Nikolaevich has arrested her and sent her to the island of St Helena off Libau (!)

* * *

[*After serving on the Northern Front . . .*] When I got back to Pestrovka after the [*February*] Revolution, under the Kerenskii government, the office of marshal no longer existed, and an appointed commissar, assisted by an elected committee of peasants, was in charge of the *uyezd*.

The commissar told me of an incident in his dealings with the local peasants. A few months after the elections a few of them came to him and asked whether they could replace some members of the committee. He said that this was impossible, since they had been elected for three years. Why, he asked, had they elected these men?

"Well, to be honest", they said, "we thought we were electing like in 1905" (during the first Revolution, when all the revolutionary committees were arrested) "so we elected all the crooks and horse thieves, and now they aren't in jail but ruling us."

Of course this was all long ago and the psychology of the Russian and the Russian peasant mass may now be different, but it still seems to me that our Russian understanding of democracy is quite different from that of Europe and America, and that those Western governments which try to implant their concept of democracy in other European and in Eastern countries are making an enormous mistake.

Countess Maria Shuvalov
(1894–1973)

My mother was eleven years old when her father, the City Governor of Moscow, was assassinated by a terrorist. After a brief and unhappy marriage to my father, who accompanied us to Malta and England in 1920, she married in 1922 Count André Tolstoy, General Wrangel's former aide-de-camp.

They lived in Nice, Paris, and New York, where they moved in 1946. After André's death in 1963 she lived in San Francisco, and from there moved to Oxford, where she died.

On 19 March (1 April, New Style) 1918 at 12.20 p.m. a son was born to us, whom we called Dmitri,* in memory of Dmitri Vyazemsky.† He was 56 centimetres long at birth and weighed 8.9 pounds. When they had washed him and brought him to me I was immediately struck by his eyes, which were amazingly clear and a brilliant light blue. From the moment I saw him I thought he was very sweet – his head was covered with dark hair, he had big eyes, and his mouth, ears and nose were tiny. For the first few days he was terribly hungry and cried a lot. Because he wasn't getting enough food he lost weight in the first two weeks, but after that all went well.

Dmitri was christened on 7 April. Uncle Sasha Polovtsev [my paternal great-uncle] was his godfather and his Mama his godmother in absentia –

* Dmitri, the Russian vernacular form of my name, corresponds to the more formal Dimitri, derived from Greek and Church Slavonic, and now in general use in Western Europe. In about 1950 I began regularly using the form Dimitri.

† Prince Dmitri Vyazemsky was my mother's brother-in-law. He was killed by a stray bullet while accompanying Alexander Guchkov in St Petersburg in March 1917.

Maria Pavlovna Rodzyanko acted for her. Dmitri was relatively quiet to begin with, until the priest plunged him into the water clumsily, causing him to choke and cry lustily. Uncle Sasha gave Dmitri a chain, and Maria Pavlovna Rodzyanko blessed him with an icon of the Saviour. Of our older relatives Aunt Paskevich was present.

On 20 April, aged one month and one day, Dmitri smiled for the first time – I saw it myself. When the warmer weather arrived we took Dmitri to my father-in-law's sister, Elizaveta Dmitrievna Novosiltseva, who blessed him with an icon that had belonged to his great-grand-father, Prince Dimitri Alexandrovich Obolensky.

Afterwards Dmitri and I visited my father-in-law's other sister, Varvara Dmitrievna Bibikova.

At the end of May we moved to Count Gudovich's dacha at Tsarskoye Selo, 20 Volkonskaya Street which my mother had rented. Dmitri was very happy there. He had a balcony of his own, on which he could lie all day long, more or less naked when it was warm enough. In mid-June he began laughing loudly. It first happened in the bath, when his nanny tickled his cheek with the sponge. His laugh was so loud that he frightened himself and was silent. But after this he began laughing in the bath every day.

In mid-August we joined Mama in her Moscow apartment at 44 Sivtsev Vrazhek. Dmitri was beginning to crawl, and in general becoming much more mobile, when we left Moscow for Kiev, on 8 September (1 October), in a Ukrainian hospital train. This journey was a nightmare – there is no other word for it. We had to travel in a jam-packed, dreadfully filthy fourth-class carriage – and the journey dragged on for ten days!

Imagine my surprise when on the fifth day of this horrible journey Dmitri cut his first tooth. He behaved very well after the first evening, when he cried terribly. In those days I kept trying to teach him to say "Papa" – and he pronounced this word, without of course knowing what it meant, several times, with his lips, rather than his voice – but even this was enough to show how precocious he was.

After a week on the train Dmitri's stomach was upset and he looked pale. The senior nurse on the train had seen that, one by one, those in our carriage were going down with Spanish flu, and she gave up her own compartment in the best part of the train for Dmitri. He had become a general favourite on the train, and all the passengers came along to admire him.

We arrived in Kiev on the evening of 28 September [Old Style], left for Odessa on 6 October and sailed from there to Yalta on the following morning. We arrived at Yalta on the evening of the 8th, and spent the night with Lyuba and Alyosha [her brother and his wife]. Next day we moved to Alupka, in which Asya [her sister] was living. On 16 October we moved to our present quarters, in the Blinova pension. Dmitri has a wonderful room on the lower floor, with a balcony, and its own door into the garden.

[Memoir resumed in 1919 . . .]
27 MARCH (3 APRIL) 1919

We were among those hastily evacuated from the Crimea.

I had engaged a new nanny for Dmitri, because Ekaterina Eduardovna had hoped to get through to St Petersburg. Nothing came of it, of course. The new nanny, who had a family in Odessa, did not much want to leave for parts unknown, and Eduardovna begged me not to leave her behind, so she went with me. We spent the night with Lili and her mother-in-law, to be near the embarkation point. But in the morning the waves were so high that the English launch could not put in to the shore, and we were all told to go to Yalta and embark there.

At Yalta there was a long wait on the pier, and we decided that it was time for Dmitri's feed. We sat down, opened the basket which held his feed and were just beginning to prepare it when a huge wave washed over the pier, drenching Dmitri and all of his food. The poor little thing was terrified, of course, and began crying. We dashed into the hotel, undressed him, put clean clothes on him, fed him, and laid him down to sleep.

He had just fallen asleep when someone rushed in to tell us that it was time to embark. Dmitri had to be bathed, fed and put down to sleep in the open, on the deck of the boat. The English sailors made a great fuss of him, carrying him around the ship all day long. To my surprise he was not in the least afraid, and was reluctant to let me hold him when I called him.

It was evening when we transferred to the *Princess Ena*, where the elderly and the children, Dmitri among them, were given cabins. We sailed almost at once. There was a heavy swell, and, although he slept on, Dmitri felt sick. At dawn we reached Sevastopol, where Mitya* joined us. We left Sevastopol on the evening of 28 March (10 April), arriving in Constantinople on 30 March (12 April).

Next morning we left for the Princes' Islands, where we disembarked, and moved in with Grandmother Vorontsova. On 4 April (17 April) we were taken back to Constantinople, and embarked on the SS *Bermuda*, a British troop-ship. It was terribly crowded, but a senior officer gave up his cabin to Dmitri.

On 8 (21) April, the second day of Easter, we sailed from Constantinople. The sea was rough, and Dmitri was seasick – he looked quite green. And this was when he began to walk – with assistance. He could not have chosen a worse moment – the rocking of the ship made it very difficult to keep up with him. In March, in the Crimea, he had moved around a bit in his playpen, but slowly and unsteadily. Now he kept trying to run.

We put in to the harbour there on the evening of 24th but were not allowed ashore until the 26th.

Eduardovna spoiled him, and he took advantage of it. It was impossible to quarrel with her, and we decided to put up with it all until we got to England. Dmitri owed a lot to her as far as his physical well-being was concerned.

---

* "Mitya" in my mother's memoirs is a common Russian diminutive of Dimitri, and refers to my father. The children are two sons and the daughters of my father's first marriage to the Countess Helen Bobrinsky.

On 30 May (12 June) we left Malta for Italy, and after a week in Rome, where the heat was savage, we went to Paris, and put up in the Hotel Metropolitain.

Paris did not seem to suit Dmitri, and I called in a doctor, who pronounced him absolutely fit, but naturally rather weak after so much journeying. When we got to England we should on no account settle in a big town. The best thing would be to take Dmitri to the seaside, but, failing that, to live in the country.

We left Paris for England on 6 (19) June, and settled in Southborough, between Tonbridge and Tunbridge Wells. Southborough is high up, and is considered a very healthy place for children. We put up at the Hand and Sceptre. The hotel had a very nice garden, so that Dmitri could get some fresh air.

At the beginning of August I hired another nanny, Miss Stokes, a young and energetic Englishwoman. Unfortunately she finally left for Finland on 16 (29) August. I am bound to say that she did a lot for Dmitri. I don't know what I should have done without her on my travels, in that dreadful situation, and when he was a little boy it was thanks to her that he became so strong and healthy. But it would have been impossible to keep her any longer.

31 AUGUST (13 SEPTEMBER) 1919

Dmitri and his nanny moved from the Hand and Sceptre to the boarding house, also in Southborough, in which Asya and her children were staying. We followed a week later. The rooms there were much cleaner, and it was a lot cheaper.

Miss Stokes was a very good nanny and after a month Dmitri was much more obedient, and hardly ever naughty. Her one mistake, as I saw it, was that she made him eat too much, trying to fatten him up. The result was that he began misbehaving at mealtimes. I could do nothing with him – he knew that if he played the fool I would burst out laughing. Mitya and Miss Stokes could make him behave.

2 (15) OCTOBER 1919

Mitya left for the north-western front.* Dmitri and I stayed on until 18 October. Miss Stokes left me on the 13th (26th), not wishing to go with me to Sweden. I changed my mind several times about a possible replacement, but finally settled on Miss Clegg, who had good references and enormous experience. I was very sorry to part with Miss Stokes. Miss Clegg's experience showed an attention to the child's physical needs, but she was much less effective than Miss Stokes in character-building.

18 (31) DECEMBER 1919

Dmitri and I left Southborough and went to stay in London for two days with Mr Talbot's† sister, at 1 Barton Street, Westminster. There was no cot in the house, so Dmitri slept in an improvised bed borrowed from a chest of drawers.

20 DECEMBER (2 JANUARY) 1919

We caught a train at King's Cross, arrived in Newcastle in the evening, and immediately boarded the SS *Thule* which was due to sail at 6 p.m. Throughout the following day we were troubled by the rolling, pitching and tossing of the ship. Dmitri was green and miserable, and was sick twice. Luckily it did not prevent him sleeping.

22 DECEMBER (4 JANUARY) 1919

We arrived in Gothenburg, where to my great joy we were met by Segi and Sonia Shuvalov. We went at once to the Palace Hotel, where Dmitri was bathed, fed and put to bed. He could not sleep for long, since the

---

* This "north-western" front which my father joined in north-west Russia was commanded by General Yudenich.

† For Stafford Talbot, my father's friend in Russia, see pp. 13–14.

train to Stockholm left at 10 p.m. He cried at first when we woke him, but fell asleep at once when we got into the compartment.

We got to Stockholm early in the morning, and were met by Irina Mengden, Praskovya Sheremeteva and Pavlik Shuvalov (Segi's son), who took us to my new apartment at No 5 Jungfrugatan. We were very comfortable there. Dmitri had his own bedroom, and a day nursery, in spite of which he always stayed with me when I was at home, and was in general very attached to me. Miss Clegg's softness has had one good effect – it has greatly enhanced my authority in Dmitri's eyes, and he has begun to obey me almost unquestioningly.

4 (17) JANUARY 1920

Dmitri was visited today by Alek Lieven, who is two months his senior. It was very amusing: they took very little notice of each other, but at the same time were not a bit shy.

We went to Segi and Sonya's Christmas party – Murza and Natasha Bobrinsky's children are living with them. Missy is a year and a month older than Dmitri, and Lev six months younger. Segi and Sonya gave Dmitri a big elephant on wheels and some building bricks with pictures of animals. These are now his favourite toys.

The air here evidently suits him – his appetite has greatly improved. He has also started talking more. He understands absolutely everything, in Russian and in English, but speaks a mixture of the two languages, with additions of his own invention.* He comes to wake me every morning, banging on the door until I open it.

Something awfully funny happened this morning. He was sitting on my bed and I was reciting nursery rhymes from memory. At one point I forgot what came next, and he looked at me quite sensibly and said "moon" – which was indeed the word I needed. This shows how advanced he is, and what a good memory he has. After all, he is only one year and nine-and-a-half months old!

* My capacity for mixing different languages in my early years caused general amusement.

Dmitri was taken to see the little Bobrinskys this afternoon. He was quite cheerful and not a bit shy. When we were getting him ready to leave he suddenly pointed at Mikhail Konstantinovich Zografo, an old man of 70 who was among those standing around him and said "Papa". Everybody burst out laughing, of course, and when he saw this Dmitri repeated the word four or five times.

Countess Sandra Shuvalov
(1869–1959)

My maternal grandmother, née Alexandra Vorontsov-Dashkov, was in her young days a close friend of the heir to the throne, the future Emperor Nicholas II. In view of the warm friendship that existed between their fathers, it is hardly an exaggeration to say that the children of Vorontsov and Alexander III grew up together. On Nicholas' part at least, it seemed at times to be une amitié amoureuse: see pp.60–61. Sandra was also a life-long friend of his sister Xenia, while their mother, the Empress Maria Feodorovna, repeatedly stated that she regarded Sandra as a daughter.

In 1890 Sandra married Count Paul Shuvalov, my grandfather. During the Khodynka affair (see pp.70–75) he supported her father Vorontsov-Dashkov, the Minister of the Court, against his own superior the Grand Duke Sergei, Governor-General of Moscow. This led to a lengthy and somewhat acrimonious dispute between Sandra and Sergei's wife, the Grand Duchess Elizabeth.

From 1896 to 1898 the couple lived in Odessa, where Paul was City Governor. A few years later he became City Governor of Moscow, where in June 1905 he was assassinated by a terrorist belonging to the Socialist Revolutionary party. The same year witnessed the assassination of his immediate superior, the Grand Duke Sergei. Sandra, who never remarried, emigrated after the Revolution, and died in Paris.

My children and my friends have often told me that I should write down all that I have seen and heard in a life full of interesting and, I may say, historical impressions. I have long hesitated, and am still hesitant, because I am afraid of falling into the common error of memoirists – inability to remain impartial. But since I am writing only for my family I have resolved to make a beginning today, and to write down all that I remember, without strict observance of chronological order, and asking forgiveness in advance for departures from impartiality.

From my earliest childhood I remember my Father's love for me and mine for him. I knew that my brother Roman and I were his favourites. He called me "my old woman" and I called him "my old man" – and stopped calling him that only when he did begin to show his age. I remember the telegram he sent me on my sixteenth birthday: "Birthday greetings on this day so dear to me." I remember his letters to me, still a girl 13–15 years old, telling me about things he disliked in one or another of my brothers and sisters, and saying, "Help me to put this right."

When we first began to hear about assassination attempts in 1880–81 (I was then twelve years old), I used to hurry to Father's study before breakfast to make sure that there was no bomb under his desk. I made a habit of going into his study if he was alone, to spend the ten-minute break between lessons with him. On one occasion my mother caught me and made me leave. As I closed the door I heard her say, "Tu gâtes la petite." For some time afterwards I did not visit him between lessons. When he asked why, I mentioned mother's disapproval.

"Well", he said, "you and I will just have to keep our ears open."

Everyone knew how I loved my Father. When I was presented to Empress Maria Feodorovna, she told me that she had read that very day in Alexander III's diary: "Dear Ilarion Ivanovich was here today. Whenever I see him I feel happier and calmer."

"Je te le dis car je sais que ça te fera plaisir," she said. Mother was jealous of my father's affection for me, and I lived in constant expectation of some critical, often unjust, remark from her. I believe that my character was formed by the difference in their treatment of me.

Looking back, I often feel sorry for my mother. Her suspicious nature made her life less pleasant than it might have been and spoiled her relations with the people closest to her. Yet she had everything she needed to make her happy – a marvellous husband, good children and grandchilden, wealth and social standing. I once said this to her, adding, "*Les présents sont toujours exclus, ainsi je m'exclus.*" We thought that my Father, who was sitting at the other end of the room reading documents, could not hear us, but he joined in and said: "I don't exclude Sandra. I love my family and am proud of them."

My older brother Ivan was very sickly as a child. The doctors forbade him to live in Russia, and my sister Sofka and I also lived abroad to keep him company. We spent the winter at Menton or Nice, and the summer in Switzerland, at Vevey, Montreux, or Merano. When the doctors decided that my brother could spend summer in Russia, Father bought an estate at Berghof in Courland (which, to our sorrow, he later sold), and in 1877 we returned to Russia for good.

At Merano we used to drink *kumiss* – my Father believed in its curative power. A Tartar "kumiss-man" was brought in from Russia. Two mares selected by him were bought in Merano, and a meadow was rented for them. One day two ladies came to see us. One of them was tall and beautiful, with hair down to her waist, braided, and with each braid tied with a strand of red wool. She was holding a fan, with which she hid her face. This, the other lady told us, was Empress Elizabeth of Austria, and she wished to talk only to us children. The Empress told us that she wanted to try the strange beverage that we drank. She liked the *kumiss*, and came to drink it every morning while she was in Merano.

Shortly afterwards we went to Vienna to see a famous paediatrician. The Empress evidently heard about it, and we were invited to Schönbrunn to play with the Grand Duchess Marie Valérie, the Emperor's younger daughter. We played tag in the palace grounds, and Marie Valérie, who was older than us, tried to catch me. I dodged her, she fell down, and her nose started bleeding. A lady-in-waiting scolded me – "One should be more careful when playing with an august personage". At that moment the Empress emerged from a clump of trees, and said that it was not my fault, but her daughter's – she did not know how to play tag.

In 1896 Nicholas II and his young Empress went on tour and visited Berlin, London, Paris, Vienna, and Copenhagen. As Minister of the Court, Father accompanied them. The Empress of Austria, who had by then ceased to take part in court ceremonies, made an exception on this occasion. After the palace banquet she remembered the three Russian children that she used to visit to drink *kumiss*, asked Father about us and sent each of us a sweet. The Austrian and German courts both had special sweetmeats for formal occasions – bars of chocolate or peppermint wrapped in silver paper tied with a lacy ribbon, with a knick-knack of some kind attached to it. It was considered a signal honour when your royal hosts gave you one of these.

When Empress Maria Alexandrovna was living in Menton, and we in Nice, she used to send a landau, harnessed *à la* Daumont, to fetch us. The horses had white ostrich plumes on their heads. Two of my sisters, later to be the wives of Count V. V. Musin-Pushkin and Count D. S. Sheremetev, were with us.

The future Countess Pushkina was naughty and started jumping onto tables, chairs, and sofas. Our governess wanted to stop her. At first the Empress said: "Let the little girl romp a bit." But at last she grew tired of it and said: "That's enough running around, you naughty little thing, come here!"

To which my sister replied: "You just be quiet, you naughty old thing!"

I too disgraced myself. The Empress's present for me was a doll, but I made her give me a little mother-of-pearl basket with a golden handle, from which hung ivory fuchsias painted mauve.

In the summer of 1874 we were staying at Vevey, and my brother Ivan received a birthday telegram from Father: "Congratulations on your birthday and on your brother." This new-born brother was Roman, the favourite of the whole family, who died in 1893 of typhus, caught at the Naval College a few months before he was due to be commissioned. Before his birth our family consisted of Vanya, born 29 April 1868, myself, born 25 August 1869, Sofka, born 9 August 1870, Maya, born 6 September 1871, and Ira, born 8 December 1872.

Then came Roman, and after him Lari, born 12 May 1877, and Sasha, born 10 April 1881. Only Sofka [Demidova], Ira [Sheremeteva] and I are still alive.

We finally returned to Russia in the spring of 1877. I still remember our arrival at Tsarskoye Selo, the joyous meeting with our younger sisters and Roman. They had difficulty getting us to bed after supper. There were four beds in the big nursery, mine nearest to the door. No sooner had we settled down than my mother appeared carrying a candle, and behind her a young lady with wonderful eyes who said: "*Ne me les nommez pas, je veux les reconnaître moi-même.*"

She came close to me and said: "I know you, you're Sandra."

I of course answered: "But I don't know you, who are you?" The lady answered that she was an "auntie". She talked to me a long time, I wouldn't let her go. My mother told her that I spoke French,* and she asked me several questions in that language. As she moved on to talk to my sisters, I made her promise to come and say goodbye. She came and tucked me in and went out with my mother. Next day I was told that that was no way to behave when the Crown Prince's wife [the future Empress Maria Feodorovna] was talking to you. In my mind the "Crown Princess" [Tsarevna] merged with the "Tsarevna" in Russian fairytales – and all through my life Empress Maria Feodorovna remained a fairy-tale "Tsarevna".

We often met Emperor Alexander II strolling on the Embankment, with a black and yellow setter running before him. When we drew level with the Emperor, my sisters and I bowed to him and he would say, "Good day, little Vorontsovs."

In 1881 my older brother and I were having a lesson when our footman, Andrei Yuzefovich, came and told us that a messenger had brought an invitation to the Winter Palace. As soon as she returned we took advantage of the first break in our lessons to run and ask her who exactly was invited and for what day. Mother told us that she

* Sandra's mother, née Shuvalov, was one of the comparatively rare Russians of her class who spoke French better than Russian.

didn't know yet whether we would be going or not. She had written to the Tsarevna, and was awaiting her answer.

I learned afterwards that we were supposed to meet the Yurevsky children, and my mother did not know whether to let us go or not, so she had written to ask the Tsarevna's advice. The Tsarevna replied that her own children were also invited, that for family reasons she could not refuse on their behalf, and would my mother please let us go, so that they would find someone they knew among the guests. So we went.

Those invited included the Tsarevich (the future Emperor Alexander III) and his three older children (the future Nicholas II, Grand Duke Georgii and Grand Duchess Xenia). Grand Duke Mikhail Nikolaevich, Viceroy of the Caucasus, was also present, with his five children. I was hopping upstairs on one foot, when I heard my father say, "Sandra, you're in the way."

Grand Duke Mikhail Nikolaevich halted and asked me my name.

"Sandra Vorontsova," I said.

He pointed to one of his sons and said: "Well, let me introduce you – this is Sandro."

And that's how I met Grand Duke Alexander Mikhailovich. When all the guests were assembled in the Great Hall, the door to an adjacent room opened, two footmen and a black page took their stand there, and Emperor Alexander II entered with a lady on his arm, followed by two little girls and one little boy. There was a "no losers" raffle, and I won a doll (which I kept until the Revolution). On the way home in the family landau I asked my parents: "Who was the lady who came in with the Emperor?"

"His wife," they said.

"The new Empress?"

The answer was "no", and they explained why.

"And who are those children?"

After a minute's silence I was told that the Emperor had married a widow, and that they were her children from her first marriage. I of course believed it. But I was taking English lessons with Nellie

Meshcherskaya, whose mother was Princess Yurevskaya's sister. The Emperor sometimes appeared during our lessons, and once, on Nellie's birthday, he arrived with Princess Yurevskaya and a present, and said that the children would be there shortly. As soon as they went off to see her mother, I asked Nellie who Princess Yurevskaya had been married to before.

"Nobody," I was told, so then I asked about the children, and Nellie answered that all three of them were the Emperor's children. When I got home I repeated this to my mother, after which lessons with Nellie came to an end.

In February 1881 we were invited to an afternoon fancy dress party at the Winter Palace. His Majesty had provided costumes for everyone. The Yurevsky children arrived already wearing new costumes specially made for them. For the rest of us there were two dressing-rooms. Grand Duchess Xenia, Vera Naryshkina, Nellie Meshcherskaya, my sisters and I changed in one dressing-room. Grand Dukes Nikolai and Georgii Alexandrovich and Alexander and Sergei Mikhailovich, Kira Naryshkin and my brothers Vanya and Roman in the other.

We were all told to put on costumes like those worn by children in the chorus at the opera. The costume meant for one of my sisters was so dirty that she refused to wear it, and they dressed her in boys' clothes. When we were ready we were called in to see Princess Yurevskaya, and we found her in a room with a bed, and there was an icon propped up on a pillow. There were masks in a big basket on the floor, and we laughed a lot as we made our choice.

The door opened, the Tsarevich, Alexander Alexandrovich appeared, and summoned his daughter. Shortly afterwards my mother was at the door, calling my sisters and myself. Out in the corridor my mother began scolding us, but the Tsesarevich cameover and said: "Don't scold them, it isn't their fault."

I learned later that, enormous as the Winter Palace was, Princess Yurevskaya had chosen to distribute the masks in the room in which Empress Maria Feodorovna had recently died, and that the Tsarevich had come there to pray when he chanced upon the scene I have described.

On 1 March 1881 my two older brothers and my sisters had gone to a birthday party. I had stayed at home, because I had not quite recovered from a sore throat, and Nellie Meshcherskaya had come to see me. We heard two loud bangs, and asked our nanny, Marie Antonovna Isaeva, to find out what they were, because in those terrible times even children had learned to fear attempts on the Tsar's life.

Maria shortly returned, and said that the bangs were probably the noise of the gates from the English Embankment to Galernaya Street being closed. But after a while she said, out of Nellie's hearing, "Tell the Princess to go home. I'll take her. The Emperor has been gravely wounded."

The Tsesarevich's butler, who had previously served my parents, had come to tell Father, and hearing that he and mother were at the race-course had gone on there. My brothers and sisters came home soon afterwards, followed by my mother. Father had gone straight to the Winter Palace, and my mother had come home to put on a grey dress. She was in mourning for her mother, but black could not be worn at the thanksgiving service that had become a regular ritual after one of the frequent attacks on the Tsar's life from which until 1 March 1881 he had, thank God, emerged unscathed. After changing my mother left, taking with her my oldest brother. In spite of my pleas she would not take me, fearing that I might catch a chill.

When they reached Palace Square, it was completely blocked by the crowd, and they had to leave their carriage and proceed on foot. Before they had taken more than a few steps, people on the square sank to their knees, and they too knelt. The imperial flag over the Winter Palace was lowered. Father told me that as soon as he entered the palace, the staircase and corridors of which were blocked by high ranking officers and functionaries, he realised that there was no hope for the Emperor. Those assembled there made way for Father to pass. He was one of those closest to the Tsarevich.

Princess Yurevskaya disliked the circle to which my parents

belonged, and Father had learned shortly before 1 March that there was a plan to appoint him Governor-General of Siberia. It was an honourable appointment. (Father was 44 and at the time in command of the Second Foot Guards Division.) It was, however, meant not as an honour, but as a means of separating him from the Tsarevich.

When he reached the room adjoining that in which the Emperor lay dying he was told that the Tsarevich had been asking for him, and remained at his side until the Emperor died. Before his father died the Tsarevich had ordered his adjutant, Count S. D. Sheremetev, to bring Grand Duke Nikolai Alexandrovich to the Winter Palace. The sledge in which he rode was surrounded by a large escort, but the future Nicholas II dismissed them and arrived at the Winter Palace unguarded.

We were taken to one of the first memorial services, before the Emperor's body was moved to the Peter and Paul Fortress. The coffin stood on a catafalque, and you had to go up at least five steps to make your farewells. When I got to the top of the steps and saw the Emperor's face covered with dark blue bruises, I turned back and started to run out of the church. My mother stopped me and made me approach the coffin. The Emperor was the first dead person I had seen, and long afterwards I still had a horror of dead bodies.

Shortly after 1 March, Maria asked us to find out the patronymic of the nihilist Isaev, who had a hand in the assassination, and I asked Father to enquire. To Maria's great joy it was not "Antonovich". Maria had been bought at an auction by Grandfather's steward before the serfs were emancipated. She had many brothers and sisters, all of whom had been sold to various purchasers, and Maria did not know where the others had got to.

We spent the winter of 1881–2 at Gatchina, because Father thought that he should be near the Tsar, and Maria discovered one of her sisters, who had married well and had a little house there. Her joy knew no bounds, but her sister died in spring 1882. We shared her grief for the kind old lady, whom we had often visited, and went to her funeral.

In 1877 I caught typhus, and seemed likely to die. Father had left for the theatre of war. My mother set out for Vienna, to be with him when the news of my death arrived. But I recovered. Not, so Professor A. Y. Krassovskii said, thanks to the doctors, but because, in my delirium, I had drunk a hearty draught of old wine from a bottle that happened to be standing on my bedside table. Extraordinary things began happening to me. I was thrashing about and yelling. The doctors were called, and could not understand what had happened to me. But Professor Krassovskii, who liked a drink himself, realised at once.

"How often is she given wine, and how much?" he asked. "Because," he went on, "she's simply drunk."

"Don't believe Dr Rauchfuss," he used to say, "when he says he cured you. You cured yourself."

But Rauchfuss was very fond of me, and considered my recovery one of the greatest successes of his career. When he was already an old man, and I was living with my children at Tsarskoye Selo, he used to invite me to join him for a walk in the palace grounds, and tell me his theory that in every human being's heart there is a ruby, given to him so that he can help his fellows, with particles large or small.

"Sometimes a smile is help enough." And he assured me that the Lord had given me a large ruby, and that I knew how best to expend it.

From 1881 to 1884 our whole family spent the summer at Peterhof. Our visits to the Grand Duchess Xenia at Alexandria began in the summer of 1881. We spent our time there playing games, mush-rooming, and taking boat trips on the sea. One day our governess complained to my mother about my behaviour, and she reprimanded me. When I replied that I did not consider myself at fault she said that I was getting out of hand and that she would ask the Empress to speak to me. A few days later we (the Tsarevich, Grand Dukes Georgii and Sergei, and Grand Duchess Xenia) were sauntering around the grounds at Alexandria and the Tsarevich suggested a boat trip.

Grand Duchess Xenia said that she would be given a "boring chaperone", and it would be no fun. The Tsarevich (whom we called "Nikolai Alexandrovich") said: "Sandra can chaperone you – we'll ask Maria."

I was living in fear of "being spoken to" by the Empress, and asked him not to raise the subject, but not knowing my reasons he demurred. As always, we joined the Empress before afternoon tea. From the far end of the room I saw the Tsarevich talking to his mother. When the Empress called to me I stayed just where I was. The Tsarevich then came over and said: "Come on – Mama wants you."

She called to me again, but I told the Tsarevich, "I won't go."

He didn't realise what I was going through, and kept trying to persuade me.

"Mama wants you to take charge of Xenia."

When at last I obeyed her call, I could see that Her Majesty understood my feelings. She did not scold me for not coming to her at once, but asked me kindly, "Will you please chaperone Xenia, Sandra dear? I have confidence in you."

It was so unexpected that tears came into my eyes. The Empress embraced me and said: "I trust you, there's no need to cry."

When I got home Mother asked me what the Empress had said to me and I told her the whole story.

* * *

When Father took over the Ministry of the Court he discovered, quite by chance, that a great deal of furniture from the royal palaces was being sold by Petersburg antique dealers. It emerged that any piece of furniture, damaged however slightly, was not repaired but set aside in one of the palace rooms from which the servants would sell it. This came to light because my parents needed to furnish the house at Novo-Tomnikovo,* and my Mother and Uncle Paskevich†

---

* The Vorontsov-Dashkovs' country estate in the province of Tambov.

† The son of Field Marshal Ivan Paskevich, who crushed the Polish insurrection of 1830.

(sometimes taking me with them) made the round of the salerooms and antique shops.

Just as Father was about to take over the Ministry there was a fire in its offices, all the relevant documents were destroyed, and the safe was empty. Father reported this to Alexander III, who said: "Wipe the slate clean. Adlerberg was my father's friend, and I don't want him to be made to suffer for what has happened."

In 1888 Father submitted to the State Council a proposal to abolish the *obshchina* [*peasant commune*]. The plan was rejected, thanks to S. Y. Witte, then a young minister. In 1905, when the peasants were burning manor houses and plundering noblemen's estates, Witte asked me if I wrote to Father, and when I answered in the affirmative, he said: "Tell Ilarion Ivanovich that I realise how right he was, and acknowledge my mistake. If the commune had been abolished there would have been no fires."

Father's reply when I wrote to him was: "Tell S. Y. it is a pity it has taken him so long to realise his mistake."

*   *   *

I came out in 1888. My mother would not let me go to any other ball before the court ball. For some reason I was introduced to the Empress together with the other debutantes, although I had been skating at the Anichkov Palace and had seen Her Majesty the day before. We were first in line, because of Father's position.

I was wearing a white dress with a train, and a rose in my hair. When the Empress came up to us she was seized by a *fou rire*, and said to my mother: "*Dites quelque chose.*"

"*Mais, parle donc,*" my mother said to me.

After the presentation I went to tea with Grand Duchess Xenia. "The Potato Society" met in her quarters daily. Its members were the Grand Duchess herself, my sisters and I, the Tsarevich, his brother the Grand Duke Georgii, the Grand Dukes Alexander and Sergei Mikhailovich, my brothers Vanya and Roman, and Dimitri and Pavel Sheremetev. The "Potato Society" got its name from an occasion at Novo-Tomnikovo, when we organised a paper chase. Dimitri Sheremetev and I asked some peasants whether they had seen my sister, who was acting the part of the fox, and we were told "*they*'ve shot into the potatoes". ["*They*" – *honorific plural*]. Every member of the club carried a golden charm shaped like a potato.

There was also a "Gatchina Society". Its badge, presented to a number of his young friends by the Tsarevich when he came of age, was golden, with his monogram on one side, and the inscription *Anichkov and Gatchina* 1881–1885, together with the owner's name. We presented him with an ornate blotting pad, with the same inscription in silver letters round the edge and, inside the upper cover, photographs of each of us: the Grand Duchess Xenia Alexandrorna at the top, we four in a row below her, then all the other members of the Society.

Those of us who lived in Petersburg took the train to Gatchina after lunch every Sunday. We rode in a private compartment. Coaches from the palace would be waiting at Gatchina. On arrival, my sisters and I would join the Grand Duchess, while the male members of the party were received by the Tsarevich. Both groups then went down into the garden and stood by the white stone terrace, waiting for the Emperor to appear. After greeting us he would walk on ahead, usually inviting one of us to come and talk to him.

I remember him once summoning me, and after asking how my lessons were going, saying, "My position is a difficult one." I assented. I could imagine how laborious his way of life must be , and how heavy a responsibility the sovereign bore. He went on: "I've found a good Governor-General, but his wife is a cook, she goes to the market and examines barrels of butter, to see whether the butter goes all the way down, or whether there are stones underneath. If she finds stones she lodges an official complaint."

I asked who she was. The Emperor named Count Alexei Pavlovich Ignatiev, and his wife Sofia Alexeyevna [née *Princess Meshcherskaya*].

After a long walk we would return to the palace for tea. Sometimes, we would drive in sledges to the Menagerie. Occasionally the Empress would bring guests of her own to join us for tea in the Huntsman's

Lodge there. Sometimes, when the Emperor did not go walking with us, we would spend our time tobogganing. The runs were steep, with a narrow channel.

We would link several toboggans together in a chain, each of them attached by a rope to a ring in the rear of the car in front. When you reached the bottom of one slope, your impetus would carry you up another. At the top, you would turn, descend a slope parallel to the first, shoot uphill again, and arrive back where you had started.

On one occasion, three of us were gliding downhill when the ring jumped out of the toboggan in which my sister was sitting, and it began swinging from one side of the channel to the other. I struggled to stop our descent using my elbows as brakes, but if the sailors posted on the slopes had not rushed to help us, our descent might have ended tragically. My elbows were bruised all over, and my sister paid a still heavier price. Her foot was cut to the bone, and she lay with her leg in splints until the spring.

On New Year's Eve 1888 the Empress sent for my mother and gave her a monogram for me. I was to put it on at the stroke of midnight. So at the reception on 1 January, I did not walk behind my mother, as a debutante, but behind the ladies-in-waiting, with others newly appointed following me. When I had made the required curtsies – one in the doorway, one ten paces from the Empress, and a third as I kissed her hand – I saw a group, including the Emperor, standing by the door to the next room. The Tsarevich and the Grand Dukes Georgii Alexandrovich and Sergei Mikhailovich were watching me closely and nodding happily. They told me later that I had curtseyed nicely.

* * *

At one of the court balls we attended in that year (1888) my mother and I were in the cloakroom at the same time as Countess V. (later L.). Her footman, helping her off with her fur coat, accidentally disturbed her coiffure, and she loudly called him a fool. My mother always ate at the Emperor's table on these occasions, and she told him about this disgraceful incident. A few days later, on the rink at the Anichkov

Palace, he asked me whether I had heard V. call her servant a fool. I said that I had, and was scandalised.

"Are you polite to servants yourself?" he asked.

I said that it had been drilled into us from early childhood. "So you don't call them fools?"

"Of course not."

"Why?"

I replied that you could call someone a fool only if that person could answer in kind. Or else if it was someone superior or older – so that you would be punished.

"Quite right," said the Emperor.

A little later, at the Concert Ball, I danced a mazurka with the Tsarevich, and, as his partner, was served first at table. I was offered fish, and said: "No thank you." The waiter – as I thought – would not go away.

"No thank you," I said again, "I don't want fish." Still the dish would not move. When, after my third refusal, it still had not moved, I said to the Tsarevich "Il veut me forcer de prendre de ce plat." I was struck by the whimsical look on the face of the Grand Duke Sergei Mikhailovich, as I said it. He was watching these proceedings with pouting lips, a habit of his when something intrigued him – and looking not at me, but over my head. I turned to look, and saw that the "waiter" holding the dish was the Emperor himself. I jumped up, and the whole table rose.

The Emperor said: "Sit down, and take some fish. You've made me wait long enough! But you are polite." I had seen Father whisper something in the Tsarevich's ear a little while before this. I had asked him what it was about.

"Just something Father wants me to do," he had said. Everyone at the table had been asked not to rise, as they normally would, when the Emperor approached.

That same winter Grand Duchess Xenia caught typhus. When she began to recover I went every day to chat and read to her. Sometimes we cut out paper patterns. The Emperor and Empress came every day, and the same question was raised every time: should the Grand Duchess's beautiful hair, which was falling out, be cut short? The Empress thought it should, the Emperor was against it.

On one such occasion the Emperor said: "Let Sandra decide."

"Come on," he said, addressing me, "what do you say: to cut or not to cut?"

"I really don't know, Your Majesty," I said, "but when I had typhus they shaved my head and my hair grew again splendidly."

To which the Emperor said: "Ah, but when I had typhus they didn't shave my head at all, and look how my hair's grown." He bent down towards me and quickly raised his head again. "You are well-mannered," he said, "you didn't even smile. I won't tease you any more." Emperor Alexander was, of course, very bald.

When my husband proposed to me my parents went to the Anichkov Palace to announce my engagement. The Empress congratulated them, and asked them to congratulate me, but the Emperor said that he wanted to speak to me before offering congratulations. While my sisters were skating at Anichkov, I had tea with Grand Duchess Xenia. She informed Their Majesties as soon as I arrived, and they summoned me upstairs to the Empress's drawing room. She was alone. She congratulated me and embraced me.

"L'Empereur veut te parler," she said. After a while the door to the adjoining room opened and the Emperor called me in. He was wearing his grey-blue Austrian jacket. (I learned later that the Queen of Denmark sent him two such jackets every Christmas.)

"You aren't leaving anyone behind?" he asked. I said no, asked whom he had in mind, and listed those whom I had refused. He still wasn't satisfied, so I asked whether he thought that I had accepted Shuvalov's proposal only because I knew that Father had always wanted me to marry him, and said that although I had long known my Father's wish I had come to love Shuvalov and was marrying him of my own free will. At my wedding the Emperor gave me away, and kissed my hand. I am proud of that to this day. The Emperor never kissed hands. [This rather equivocal exchange between Alexander III and my *grandmother will become clearer in the light of an earlier conversation that took place between his son Nicholas, then heir to the throne, and my grandmother, which I know from oral evidence. Nicholas asked her: "Sandra, would you like us never to part?" to which she replied: "What a good idea! I will marry Paul Shuvalov, and you will appoint him your equerry: in this way we won't part."]*

He treated all of his children's regular visitors like members of the family. We all loved him and were not the least bit afraid of him. In our teens we used to make up verses about each other. Once, when we were out walking, the Emperor overhead a few lines of one of these teasing poems, and asked Pavel Sheremetev what it was. When Pavel explained, the Emperor said that he would like to see all those poems. Pavel said that he could not produce them himself, without the permission of the Gatchina Society.

"Very well then," the Emperor said, "hold a meeting and discuss it."

We "discussed" it in the train on the way home, and decided that the Emperor could be given the verses on condition that it remained between him and us. My handwriting was good, so I made copies and, on behalf of the others, handed them to the Emperor on the following Sunday, telling him that we fully trusted him not to show them, or even mention them, to anyone else. He thanked me graciously for our confidence in him, and said he would keep the secret. He never afterwards mentioned those verses if any outsider was with us on our walks. But when we were alone with him he sometimes quoted from them to tease one or another of us.

When Their Majesties were in Petersburg we ("The Potato Society") at first went out to the Anichkov Palace only on Sundays and holidays, but later on we went every day after lunch to skate, and take tea with Grand Duchess Xenia. The Emperor never wore skates. Sand was strewn on the ice where he stood. We were all on skates and had hooked sticks, with which we could send a ball flying over the Palace. In 1889 Princess Alix of Hesse (later to be Empress Alexandra Feodorovna, wife of Nicholas II) was staying with her sister, Grand Duchess Elizaveta Feodorovna. She came along to the rink, and then took tea with Grand Duchess Xenia. We all knew that the Grand

Duchess had invited Princess Alix, unknown to the Empress, but of course said nothing about it at home.

One day the Empress came into the room when the tea-drinking was in full swing, and the secret was discovered. After she left we were all rather subdued. The Princess left at once, and we began getting ready for home. Just as we were leaving someone came to tell the Grand Duchess that Her Majesty wished to see her.

"I'm in for it now," she said.

When we got home we were told that Father wanted us, and that Mother was going to the Palace at Her Majesty's request.

"What happened at Anichkov?" Father asked.

We said that the day had gone as usual.

"Why has the Empress sent for your Mama?"

We professed ignorance, and indeed did not know that there was any connection between the Empress's summons and her discovery that Princess Alix had taken tea with the Grand Duchess. When Mama returned, I and all my sisters were summoned by my parents, and Mother asked, "Pourquoi vous ne nous avez jamais dit que la Princesse Alix prenait le thé chez Xenia Alexandrovna? Saviez vous que ça se faisait sans l'autorisation de leurs Majestés?"

We answered that we did know, but remembering Father's instructions, when we first started going to the Palace, not to repeat anything that looked like court gossip, we had said nothing. I remember telling Father: "You have said to me more than once that we should treasure the confidence placed in us, behave with dignity, and not wash dirty linen in public. That it is a great honour to be so close to the imperial family, but that we shouldn't get conceited, or toady to them, but should justify the confidence placed in us." My sisters said the same. Father turned to Mother and said: "Elles ont raison."

When we went to Anichkov next day the Grand Duchess told us that she was forbidden from then on to invite Princess Alix to tea, and that Grand Duchess Elizaveta Feodorovna would be so informed when she came to tea with Their Majesties at 5 p.m. – but what were we to do today? We suggested cancelling tea, but the Grand Duchess wouldn't agree to that, so we decided that all four of us would escort the Princess to the entrance hall, pretending that we also were leaving, and then when her carriage was brought, and she left, we would remain behind. Permission to invite the Princess to tea was given only on the eve of her departure. After tea, she asked me for photographs of my sisters and myself, and I asked her for photographs of herself.

On the *"folle journée"* (the last day before Lent) in the same year (1888), I was the Tsarevich's partner in the mazurka at Tsarskoye Selo. Before we danced, he told me which was his table, and said, "Invite anyone you like to join me there." I said that I did not know whom he wanted. "Think a bit – and don't pretend you don't understand," he said.

I realised whom he had in mind, and began by asking Princess Alix, who was dancing with V. N. Voyeikov, then an officer in the Horse Guards, and subsequently Palace Commandant. All those who dined at that table wrote their names on the back of the menu, which is reproduced in Voyeikov's memoirs. In spring 1907 I was the guest of Princess Alix, by then Empress Alexandra Feodorovna, at the Alexandrov Palace, in an extremely ugly drawing room.

"Do you recognise this room?" she asked [in English in the original]. When I said no, she told me that the dining table which I have just mentioned had stood there. She had divided one of the palace's great rooms into two, and one of them had held the table for "this nice and gay supper" [in English in the original].

I remember a picnic in the woods near Martyshkino in 1885. The Empress and her guests arrived in a large brake, and the Emperor in a wagonette with Grand Duchess Xenia, the Tsarevich, Grand Duke Sergei Mikhailovich, Vanya and myself. I was wearing a hideous hat with an enormous brim. The Emperor teased me about it.

"Take a bow," he said, whenever somebody stood to attention for him, "they're saluting your hat." I took advantage of his critical remarks and asked him to tell my mother that the hat was very ugly. When we reached the forest the carts carrying food for the picnic were not in the appointed place, and were a long time coming. The Emperor approached my mother and suggested lighting a bonfire to roast my hat, which was really a fungus, and when my mother said she thought it was beautiful, the Emperor replied that it was horrible. To my great joy I was allowed not to wear it from then on. For some reason my mother always bought us dreadful hats.

On one occasion, after my wedding, the Empress praised the hat I was wearing, and said how glad she was that I was able to choose becoming hats, because "*Il faut avouer que ta mère vous achetait des pots de chambre au lieu de chapeaux.*"

I was born on 25 August 1869 at Gomel, on my Uncle Paskevich's estate. My brothers and sisters used to tease me about it: "We know who was born at Gomel." I should have been born at the end of June, when my mother first went into labour. But there was an interruption. Labour had to be artificially induced, and I was finally delivered two months later. So I was an eleventh-month child, and the story of my birth (without my mother's name) was told in a medical journal; as was my recovery from typhus, after my temperature had reached a level which the human organism cannot as a rule survive.

Aunt Paskevich was small, very well educated, extraordinarily kind, but very plain. We were all very fond of her. She translated Count Tolstoy's *War and Peace* into French, modestly withholding her name: the reader is told that it was "*traduit par une Russe*". She and Father were great friends. Whenever we arrived in Tiflis from Petersburg the first thing he wanted to know was when we had seen his sister.

My grandfather came to Gomel for my christening, and as a christening gift had a cross of pure gold made for me by a Jewish jeweller in the city. I still have it, and am leaving it to my grandson, Andrei Shuvalov.

I vaguely remember hearing that my grandfather had died suddenly. My mother herself was recovering from an illness which had seemed likely to prove fatal. She had taken communion with all her family and all the servants around her, but suddenly expressed a wish to go and see her sister Ekaterina Andreevna Balashova in Podolia, come what may. The other doctors were against it, but Anton Yakovich Krassovskii said that "If a dying man asks for an orange it must be given to him, however harmful it might be." So my mother set out by train, in a private coach, with a nurse in attendance. Whether it was from the jolting of the train, or because its time had come anyway, the abscess burst during the journey, the pus came away via my mother's throat and she was saved.

At Rakhny [the Balashov estate in Podolia] my mother lay recuperating for days at a time, on a couch under a great oak tree. I climbed to the top of the tree, unnoticed, could not get down again, and called out to mother for help, which of course gave her a fright. Dear D. Balashov heard her call out, came running, climbed the tree and lowered me to the ground.

One day, when I was out walking with Aunt Kitty and her children we came to a patch of wasteland overgrown with nettles. My Balashov cousin (Pyotr, later a member of the Duma) and Andrei (who died of typhus, caught at the front, in 1915), were terribly afraid of nettles, and wouldn't go near them. I said: "Nettles are nothing to worry about." (We were wearing socks, not stockings.)

My Aunt said: "If nettles are nothing, why don't you walk through them?" I walked through them. My legs swelled up. My Aunt asked whether it hurt, and I said no. So she told me to go once more. And again I said it didn't hurt. Auntie was afraid to make me go a third time – my legs looked terrible. When Father got to Rakhny, my Aunt told him what had happened. He asked me whether it was painful, and I confessed that it was. Why then, he asked, had I said "Nettles are nothing"? I said I didn't like mollycoddles, and the Balashovs were mollycoddles. Father praised me for bearing the pain without complaining.

Father was very nimble: as a young man he once leaped over a card table at which four players were sitting. He was a wonderful rider, and an excellent driver. He trained us to be agile and indefatigable. My Demidov and Sheremetev sisters were the best riders, my Pushkin sister was considered the best troika driver, and I drove a pair of horses better than any of them. I could jump my own height without a run-up, and was the fastest runner – I beat the best runner in the Gatchina Orphanage (the nephew of our *zemstvo* doctor, Butchik) over half a *verst*. My brothers Roman and Ilarion, as well as Father, were good riders.

*　　*　　*

8 November, the Feast of St Michael the Archangel, was the church festival at Novo-Tomnikovo, and there was always an enormous number of weddings in the village church. I remember convincing my two younger brothers that everybody had to marry on that day – even those who didn't want to would be grabbed, taken to the church, and married off. Ilarion, who had been saying since he was very little that he wanted to marry and have a lot of children, strolled outside the house and the church all day long, looking important, but no one, of course, grabbed him and married him. While Sasha couldn't be persuaded, try as we might, to leave the house.

In autumn 1886 Father said that, as I was always a good pupil, it would give him pleasure if I took the examination for a private teacher's diploma. I was not to take this as an order, but to decide for myself. In March 1887 I passed the exam with full marks in all subjects. I chose as my main subjects geography and arithmetic (with algebra and geometry). My examiner in mathematics was Vereshchagin (author of a number of manuals). He kept me there for an hour. Vereshchagin took two girls at once, and my mother, sitting in the boys' school hall, was horrified to see girl after girl leave, to be replaced by another, while I was kept back. She was convinced that the others had all passed, and I had failed. The opposite was true: they had all failed, and Vereshchagin had got interested in me.

Meeting I. V. Meshchersky, who had coached me for the exam, later on, Vereshchagin told him that he had never met such a head for mathematics on a woman. When he heard that he was to examine me he had thought at first that the daughter of Count Vorontsov-Dashkov, Minister of the Court, would expect to be let off lightly, so he had confronted me with a difficult problem. When I had solved it quickly and correctly he set me another, still more difficult. That too was solved quickly and correctly. Then he began examining me orally, and finally said: "What I'm going to ask you now won't affect your marks, I'm just asking you out of curiosity." I don't remember exactly what it was, but I know that it had to be solved geometrically, and when I began drawing the diagram for Pythagoras's theorem he said "Right, you can go," and when I asked whether I'd passed he said that I had.

We were invited to the palace at Gatchina at Easter. "Eggs", made from wood or straw, and containing presents, were hidden in some of the downstairs rooms. Whatever you found became your property. We were told the night before that little Sashka would be coming with us. I wanted to explain to him that the Emperor and Empress did not wear crowns and robes all the time, like the Tsar and Tsaritsa in a fairytale, but mother said she would tell him herself. We had just started looking for eggs, and I had made a bet with the Tsarevich that I would find more than anyone, but had to cancel it, because I was told that Her Majesty was asking for me. I found Sashka on the floor of the large reception room, howling, with Their Majesties, my parents and other guests watching him from a distance.

Mother told me that she didn't know what had happened, but Sashka had refused to kiss the Empress's hand and started bawling. It was just as I had feared. Sashka had taken offence because he thought that he had been lied to.

"Mama said this ordinary woman was the Empress." I explained somehow that it was a great honour to be received by Their Majesties informally, and that they wore crowns only on grand occasions.

"Do you believe me?" I asked.

"You've never told me a lie," he said. I took him to the Emperor and Empress, then made him say sorry to our parents. When I went back to look for eggs I found among those I had previously collected some of unknown origin. It turned out the Tsarevich had put them there for me.

When my future husband's aunt was presented to the Empress

shortly afterwards, she said: "*Pourquoi votre neveu ne se décide pas – vous ne savez pas ce qu'elle est gentille avec ses petits frères.*"

* * *

Every morning at Tomnikovo Father was accessible to petitioners. The request might be for timber to enlarge a cottage, or for a loan, or simply for advice and protection. We – his daughters – used to go outside in advance, question them all, and then report the names and needs of those waiting to see him.

Once, when I was on duty, I saw a group of elderly peasants completely unknown to me standing apart. When I had questioned the firstcomers, I went over to the strangers and asked what their business was. The answer I got was: "We'll tell him, we won't tell you."

"I'm his daughter. Tell me and I'll pass it on," I said, but they repeated that they would tell me nothing. Peasants I knew said that these others were "strange". When Father had dealt with each of the firstcomers he approached these strangers. Every man of them fell on his knees. Father made them stand up. It turned out that they were envoys from Father's Saratov estate, sent to beg him on behalf of all the settlements on the estate to take them back into bondage.

"With you we lived well, take us back. We can't cope with our young folk, they've got right out of hand." This was either in 1886 or 1887 [*about 25 years after the Act of Emancipation*]. We always had good relations with our peasants. Before the Emancipation, Father used to endow every village with land, or present it with a market place, gratis, and never made use of seigneurial rights which could impair the human dignity of the peasants. He was greatly loved. Us children they used to call "*our little ladies*", or "*our little gentlemen*".

In the winter of 1890, Count Alexei Tolstoy's play *Tsar Boris* was put on at the Hermitage theatre. I, with two of my sisters and others, had non-speaking parts as boyars' wives, whose role was to walk in pairs before the Tsaritsa (played by M. A. Vasilchikova). In the scene in which she confronted Boris, she said to us, "You, my dears, go out into the antechamber and wait there." There were endless rehearsals – we entered, made our obeisances, and exited over and over again. At the dress rehearsal (in the presence of Their Majesties) we told Vasilchikova immediately before our entrance that we were sick of silence, and when she told us to go into the antechamber we would reply in chorus: "We won't go."

She took it seriously, and muffed her role: instead of turning to us she spoke over her shoulder and told us to go away. We, of course, exited without a word. When Grand Duchess Elizaveta Feodorovna came behind the scenes in the interval and made a critical remark, Vasilchikova said that it was our fault. The Grand Duchess asked us not to play any more dirty tricks, to which we said that we had never expected Vasilchikova to be so stupid as to believe us. When the foreign envoys came to congratulate Boris on the day of his coronation, the last in line was the Papal Nuncio (played by Prince S. M. Volkonski). We (the boyars' wives) came behind him, followed by the Tsaritsa. Dmitri Borisovich Neigardt, who was announcing the ambassadors, instead of "Nuntsii Papskii" (Papal Nuncio), said "Puptsii Nanskii" (Napal Puncio). Such a roar of Homeric laughter arose on stage, behind the scenes, and throughout the auditorium that the play had to be halted and the curtain lowered.

After the final performance, a dinner was given for the whole cast, with the Grand Duchess Elizaveta Feodorovna presiding – but we were not allowed to attend. We were not on stage in the concluding scenes, and I sat in the body of the theatre beside my future husband. Next day his sister, Countess Stakelberg, arrived while I was having a music lesson, and asked if she could formally ask my parents for my hand, on behalf of her brother. I became officially engaged on 6 February 1890.

We were married on 8 April that year in the chapel at my parents' house, No 10 on the English Embankment. All Petersburg was present. The chapel was small, and inside there was room only for Their Majesties (who acted as sponsors for my parents), my husband's father and stepmother, our nearest relatives, and our attendants. All the other guests stood in the so-called Church Hall (a replica of one of the halls in the Palace of Versailles, so that, to enter, I walked, on the

Emperor's arm, along a sort of corridor through a throng of guests. When I saw them from afar I felt embarrassed and said to the Emperor: "They've all come to gawk!"

He smiled and said: "Don't blame them – they were invited."

My bridesmaids were my three sisters, my Balashov cousin (she died aged 18 in 1896), the two Dolgoruky sisters (second cousins), and my second cousin Orlova, who later married my brother Ivan. The groom was attended by the Tsarevich, Grand Dukes Georgii Alexandrovich and Sergei Mikhailovich, and my brothers Ivan and Roman. After the ceremony we went in horse-drawn carriages to Vartemyagi,* where our fathers had arrived before us. The peasants there, and my husband's father, welcomed us with bread and salt.

My husband was ten years older than me, and was the only son of his father's first marriage, with Princess Olga Esperovna Beloselskaya-Belozerskaya. In 1877, while a member of the Corps of Pages, he passed the examination for the Artillery School, and in August joined the 22nd Artillery Brigade at the front, with the rank of ensign. When the war with Turkey ended he was transferred to the Fifth Horse Guards Battery, in which he served until 1891. He then became adjutant to Grand Duke Sergei Alexandrovich when he was made Governor-General of Moscow.

KHODYNKA

At 5.25 a.m. on 18 May 1896 I gave birth to my son Nikolai. Because of the early hour, my husband did not telephone the Kremlin to tell Father the news until 8 a.m. Father was then Minister of the Court. In return for my husband's news, Father told him what had happened at Khodynka Field.†

* The country estate of Count Paul Shuvalov, north of St Petersburg.
† A terrible accident occurred at Khodynka Field outside Moscow when a crowd estimated at 500,000 assembled to receive souvenirs on the day of the coronation. The crowd panicked, trampling or choking to death nearly 1,400 people. There was a fierce debate as to who was responsible.

My husband immediately telephoned for a troika, feeling sure that the Governor-General, Grand Duke Sergei, would go at once to the scene of the catastrophe. In the courtyard he found some officers of the Preobrazhenskii Regiment, waiting to be photographed with the Grand Duke. When my husband told them what had happened, they were all sure that the Grand Duke would not want to go on with the group photograph. My husband found the Minister of Justice sitting with the Grand Duke. When the Minister left he reported that a troika had been ordered, and gave his opinion that the Grand Duke should go to Khodynka Field immediately. The Grand Duke replied that he would have his photograph taken with the Preobrazhenskii Guards officers first, then go to see the Emperor in the Kremlin, and that my husband would go with him.

In the carriage the Grand Duke said, on the strength of Police Chief A. A. Vlasovskii's report, that nothing serious had happened. My husband, who had been given the details by Father, said that the catastrophe was very serious, and mentioned that officials of the Ministry of the Court had begged Vlasovskii the night before to send in police reinforcements, since people were assembling in their thousands. He further reported that N. N. Ber, who presided over the commission responsible for erecting the fair booths on Khodynka Field, had tried in vain to make an appointment with Vlasovskii. When Ber sought my husband's help he managed to speak to Vlasovskii on the telephone once, but when he called again, late at night, the receiver had been taken off the hook. (We learned later that a whole gypsy orchestra had been performing for Vlasovskii, and he did not want to be disturbed.)

At the Kremlin, when the Grand Duke had seen the Emperor and was ready to go home, my husband saw the other Grand Dukes, the Emperor's uncles, and realised that they had all visited the Emperor simultaneously. In the carriage Grand Duke Sergei told my husband "We won".

This turned out to mean that "we" had defeated Father, who had advised the Emperor that he and the Empress should not go to the

French ambassador's ball that evening, that he should order a national memorial service in the Cathedral of Christ the Saviour, and that he should make the round of the hospitals. Only the last suggestion was acted on.

The Grand Dukes had opposed Father's first two suggestions, arguing that what had occurred should not be exaggerated, and that accidents were always likely to happen when a crowd gathered. If the Emperor behaved as the Minister of the Court advised, they said, they would all resign. My husband supported Father's view, but the Grand Duke accepted Vlasovskii's report.

To illustrate Vlasovskii's reaction to the occurrence, two days later he happened to meet A. A. Kozlov, who had been Chief of Police for many years before him. Kozlov expressed his sympathy, but Vlasovskii said that accidents often happened in crowds, and that he did not accept that he was to blame. I do not remember the number of those killed at Khodynka, or the number given by Vlasovskii, but I do remember that when my parents came to see us that afternoon, Father mentioned the reported figure, my husband sat by the telephone, rang all the police stations and hospitals, and jotted down the number of dead in each morgue.

When the figures were added up the total was almost 100 times that reported. The hospitals also gave him the numbers of those injured. Father made a fair copy of all this, and took it to the Dowager Empress, who had asked for precise figures. She took it to the Emperor, but he preferred to believe Grand Duke Sergei.

Father had set up in the Ministry of the Court a press bureau for the reporters arriving from all over the world for the coronation. A few days later the Grand Duke asked my husband to call on Father and tell him that on his instructions the bureau was conducting propaganda for the Ministry and against himself, the Governor-General. My husband refused to go, saying that he fully shared Father's views on the event, and that, knowing Father, he was sure that the bureau under his direction was not conducting propaganda but merely stating facts. He said further that he would remain in the Grand Duke's service until the coronation, but would then resign, since his views and those of the Grand Duke were completely different.

N. V. Muraviev was ordered to determine whether the Ministry of the Court or the civil authorities were responsible for what had happened. He rather hastily – in a matter of days – concluded that the Ministry of the Court was to blame. Father informed the Emperor that he was not satisfied with the investigation, that he did not consider that either he himself or his subordinates should take the blame, since the Ministry of the Court had no police force of its own, and that he insisted on a senatorial enquiry. Once the coronation celebrations were over he would withdraw to his Tambov estate to await the conclusion of the enquiry, and if it found that the Minister of the Court was to blame he would resign. After the coronation the Emperor and the young Empress went to Grand Duke Sergei's "Ilinskoye" estate, and my husband could not join me and the children at Vartemyagi until they returned to Peterhof.

Grand Duchess Alexandra Iosifovna (wife of Grand Duke Konstantin Nikolaevich) sent for me. At the Marble Palace she greeted me with the words: "J'espère que vous êtes fière de votre mari: mon beau-père l'Empereur Nicolas [Nicholas I] aurait approuvé sa conduite, et aurait envoyé Serge en Sibérie en costume de lawn-tennis."

At about the same time Grand Duke Mikhail Nikolaevich invited me to lunch. After lunch he told his sons and his suite that he wanted to talk to me privately. He sat by the window of his study, which looked out on the Palace Embankment, and made me sit where passers-by could see me.

"I want Petersburg to know that you are here with me," he said. Everybody knew the window, and used to look in to see whether the Grand Duke was there. Ladies would bow, soldiers would salute, and civilians would doff their hats. The Grand Duke questioned me closely about the matters I have set out above.

Some six weeks later, Father sent a telegram from Novo-Tomnikovo to say that he would be spending some time at Peterhof and inviting us both to stay with him. We went there on the appointed day, and when we asked why he had come Father showed us a telegram from the Emperor, saying that the Empress would be travelling around Russia for the first time, then visiting foreign courts, and that he would like "You, dear Ilarion Ivanovich, to accompany us."

Did this mean that the Senatorial Enquiry had found the civil authorities to blame and cleared the Ministry of the Court completely? Or did it simply mean that the Emperor was generally well disposed towards Father? There was no way of knowing until the following day, when Father had an appointment to see the Emperor. Count Pahlen, a former Minister of the Court who had presided over the enquiry, was in Peterhof at the time.

Two of the Empress's ladies-in-waiting, with whom I was on the best of terms, Princess K. V. Baryatinskaya and Princess E. P. Vasilchikova, were living in the same house. When I offered to visit them and see what I could find out, Father consented. The two ladies and I decided that I should call on Count Pahlen. He was out at the time, but we got a footman to let us know as soon as he returned, and I ran out into the corridor to meet him. In answer to my question Count Pahlen said: "*Je n'ai pas le droit de tout vous dire, mais vous pouvez dire à votre père qu'il peut en toute tranquillité aller demain matin chez Sa Majesté.*"

Their Majesties set out on their tour of Russia. At the station in Moscow (they did not go into the city) they were met by the City Governor, A. G. Bulygin, not by the Governor-General, Grand Duke Sergei, and the Grand Duchess. They had heard the result of the Senatorial Enquiry, and on the eve of the royal couple's arrival left in a hurry to visit the Grand Duchess's brother, Prince Ernst Ludwig of Hesse, at Darmstadt.

We decided that it would not be right for my husband to leave the Grand Duke's service while he was out of favour. When the royal couple, returning from their European tour, joined the Grand Duke and Grand Duchess at Darmstadt, and from there arrived back in Russia by the same train, my husband wrote to the Grand Duke asking to be released from his duties, giving as his excuse his father's illness.

(He suffered a paralytic stroke in August 1895.) His resignation was accepted, and he was transferred to the Ministry of the Interior.

I should say that during our years in Moscow (1891–6), we had established a very close relationship with the Grand Duke and Grand Duchess. I had her permission to ring up and ask whether I could lunch with her on this or that day, and they used to visit us informally. But when my husband went to take leave of the Grand Duke, and asked to be received by the Grand Duchess, she refused to see him. From that day I did not ask permission to call on her. Especially as she had ignored my mother, pretending not to see her, at a great reception in the Winter Palace.

In the winter of 1896 I went for a walk in Moscow with my two eldest children. When we reached the Square before the Cathedral of Christ the Saviour I wanted to turn into the Boulevard, but my four-year-old daughter, however I tried to dissuade her, was determined to go on to the Square. I said at last that Pavlik and I would not go with her, whereupon she said that she would go alone.

"Go on then," I said.

My son was afraid that his sister would be run over, but I assured him that she would soon catch us up. This exchange was overheard by an old peasant wearing a sheepskin half-coat and a fur cap pulled well down over his eyes.

"See," I said to my daughter, "Grandpa's laughing at you as well, for wanting to go for a walk on the Square."

She very quickly caught up with us again, as I had foretold. Instead of scolding I simply told her that she should obey her elders. I should have forgotten this little incident completely but for what followed.

A few days later we were supposed to attend amateur theatricals at the Samarins' house, but I felt poorly and we decided to stay at home. That evening, after dinner, Mme Samarina telephoned and begged us to come, saying that Countess Sofia Andreevna Tolstaya and her daughter had asked to be invited to their show, because they had been commissioned by Count Tolstoy to seek an introduction to me. We had to dress up and go, without the slightest idea what it all meant.

When we had been introduced, Countess Tolstaya invited us to visit them at their Moscow home, telling me personally that "Lev Nikolaevich wants to meet you".

"Why?" I asked in surprise.

The answer was "He'll tell you himself."

[*After some delay, due to her husband's absence on duty in Petersburg, and after a second visit from Countess Tolstaya and her daughter, she attended one of the Tolstoys' Saturday soirées.*]

Countess Tolstaya met me at the door of the great drawing-room with the words: "Lev Nikolaevich isn't back from the bath-house yet. I reminded him that you would be coming, and he replied, 'All the more reason for me to get a good wash'!"

In one corner of the room someone was singing, accompanied on the piano, and at the other end stood a long table with tea and all sorts of sweets. My hostess sat me down by an occasional table laid for tea. Tolstoy appeared shortly afterwards, sat down by me, and was served with gruel and olive oil. Without preliminaries he told me that he was the "old peasant" in a sheepskin coat who had been amused by my conversation with my daughter, that he had liked my attempt to persuade her instead of ordering her, and the fact that I had not scolded her when she came back, or said that I would punish her, "as some unwise mothers do". He had decided to make my acquaintance, had followed us home, and had asked the yardman who lived there. The yardman had shouted at him, and told him not to loiter in other people's yards, but had ended by giving him my name.

I can't recall all that was said. I do remember that he was writing *Resurrection* at the time, and that he had been visiting a women's prison that very day. He made some unflattering remark about women, and I was up in arms immediately.

I desperately wanted to smoke and, after suffering in silence for some time, I said: "I know you're against smoking, but please allow me to."

"Ah, you smoke – at last I've found a fault in you – your only one."

I remember those words with pride. In my album he wrote: "Please don't smoke." My daughter insists to this day that it was only thanks to her that I came to know Count Lev Nikolaevich Tolstoy.

*   *   *

My husband was with the Ministry of the Interior from 1896 until early in 1898, when he was appointed City Governor of Odessa. We went there in March without the children and lived to begin with in a hotel. The Vorontsov Palace in Odessa, built by my mother's grandfather, Illustrious Prince M. S. Vorontsov, now belonged to my mother's brother, who had inherited his maternal grandfather's title by primogeniture. He was unwilling to lease the palace to us, but offered me the use of it, provided that, if he carried out major repairs, I would do the rest. The palace had long been uninhabited, the lintels and window frames were rotten, and the plumbing was in a state of disrepair. When the repairs were completed, and I had installed my furniture, I went to fetch my children from Vartemyagi to Odessa.

The palace stands on a cliff with a marvellous view of the sea. The garden used to run down to the shore, but part of it had been appropriated by the port. Tramps regularly spent the night in this garden. When we moved in, the police chased them away and put a man on duty there, but with my husband's consent I asked the chief of police to remove this officer, because I trusted the tramps. A few days later I received a letter thanking me and giving me their "tramps' word of honour" that nothing would ever go missing, that I could leave anything I liked out in the garden or on the terraces, and that I need not even shut the doors of the house for the night. And indeed, throughout our five years in Odessa nothing was ever lost, no one ever tried to get into the house, and when we left Odessa we received another letter from the tramps, with many signatures, thanking us for our kindness and regretting our departure.

In the opinion of those who knew it well Odessa became a "capital city" during my husband's governorship. He never drew his salary. He reorganised the police force on a contributory basis. He persuaded the factory owners to build a hospital in which workers were treated without charge. Contributions were levied according to the number of workers employed – to the best of my recollection at the rate of one bed to every fifty employees. There were also contributions from public funds and from private persons (ourselves included). A splendid hospital was built, with a whole department for the general public, as well as the named beds. The city streets were clean, and houses were numbered.

There was one pogrom: my husband rode through the city in person, pacifying the crowd. No shots were fired, no one was injured, and the pogrom was over quickly with not a single Jewish feather-bed ripped open. Rats from the ships brought plague to Odessa two years running in the spring, but timely measures prevented it from spreading any further. For this success my husband was promoted to the rank of major-general, and confirmed in his post.

The winter of 1901 was extremely severe, with heavy snowfalls. Antediluvian sledges appeared, looking incongruous amid the Odessan flora. On the morning of 24 December two young men came to tell my husband that five trains were snow-bound on the approaches to Odessa. The passengers were without food or heating, and most of them had no warm clothing, since they had been travelling to the south. As it happened there were in the Red Cross stores bales containing sheepskin coats, fur caps, felt boots, hoods and gauntlets, waiting to be loaded onto a vessel bound for the Far East.

The Dowager Empress was sending these things as a present to some unit of which she was colonel-in-chief. My husband was ex-officio chairman of the local branch of the Red Cross, and I was vice-chairman. We agreed that it would be right to undo these bales. This was done, and five supply trains (so to speak) of sledges, loaded with warm clothing, and each with a doctor and several volunteers on board, went to the relief of the passengers. Each of them was required to sign an undertaking to return the items loaned to them within 48 hours of arrival in Odessa. Only two recipients failed to do so.

My husband submitted a report to the headquarters of the Red Cross in Petersburg, promising to make up for the lost items. He was told in reply that he had exceeded his authority, but that a definitive response must await submission of a report to Her Majesty. We anxiously awaited the appointed day. I remember my husband emerging from his study with a telegram in his hand and a happy smile on his face. The telegram was from Her Majesty in person, thanking him and all his colleagues.

[Shortly afterwards Sandra went to see her sick mother in Petersburg. The Dowager Empress made an unexpected visit to thank her in person.]

"Je veux encore une fois en ta personne remercier ton mari pour ce qu'il a fait . . . "

I began saying that we were grateful to Her Majesty for her kindness, but she interrupted me: "Non, c'est moi qui vous remercie tous les deux; et si tout le monde agissait comme ton mari et toi, la Croix Rouge aurait été populaire."

She told me among other things that she had authorised payment for the items not returned by passengers.

We left Odessa in the spring of 1903. The reason for our departure was as follows. The Police Department and Grand Duke Sergei were at this time in favour of introducing into factories police agents who would organise lectures, entertainments, and libraries, while at the same time keeping an eye on left-wing elements and, if they thought it necessary, ordering their arrest. The initiator of this scheme was one Zubatov, an official in the Police Department, and it was accordingly known as the "Zubatovshchina".

My husband was notified by Pleve, the Minister of the Interior, that it was Odessa's turn to introduce these agents into the local mills and factories. My husband was indignant. He thought such a measure unworthy of the government. He went to Petersburg, submitted his opinion in writing, and when the Ministry insisted, resigned. To make matters worse, responsibility for the scheme was entrusted to a woman called Vilbushevich, who was, according to my husband's information, a double agent. On his departure, my husband sent in a report predicting that within six months there would be a workers' revolt. There had been nothing of the sort in the previous five years because the workers had seen my husband's concern for their well-being, and greatly respected him.

We left Odessa for our home at Vartemyagi. My husband was given a post in the Ministry of Internal Affairs, and the worthy General Arseniev was appointed City Governor of Odessa. A workers' revolt took place in late summer, as predicted, and I received a telegram from Pleve asking if he could come to lunch on a certain day. When I went to meet him, he said that he had come simply to tell me that I should be proud of my husband, that he had been right, and that now he, Pleve, would have to put up a fight against those who were introducing the Zubatov system.

On 4 September 1905 Grand Duke Sergei was assassinated in Moscow. The Emperor chose A. A. Kozlov as his successor, but he accepted only on condition that my husband went there with him. My husband said that there could be no thought of refusal at such a time, but asked to be appointed Moscow City Governor rather than Chief of Police. I was against it, and pleaded with him to refuse, but he said that no one had the right to do so in such troubled times, even if the appointment was, as I put it, "Promotion from priest to deacon."

[Their official residence was under repair. Prince N. D. Obolensky appealed on Sandra's behalf to the Emperor, who put the lower floor of the Petrovsky Palace * at the family's disposal.]

I then took the children from Vartemyagi to Moscow. Kozlov met me at the station telling me that my husband was very busy. I

* Built in 1775–82, the Petrovsky Palace housed the Moscow City Governor and his family.

learned later that he had been receiving threatening letters (the latest of which said that he would be killed together with his "whelps") and that the Governor-General had asked him not to go to meet me. I went to lunch with him every day, sometimes with one or other of the children, and he often visited us at the Petrovsky Palace in the afternoon or evening.

On 28 June I lunched with him as usual, and he said that he would come to dinner with me. He was expecting visitors, and I left without him when his personal assistant, N. N. Schneider, came to tell him "Everything is ready". These words I learned later, were supposed to mean that my husband's assassin, who had escaped from prison not long before this, was not among the visitors. As it turned out, he was, he had shaved off his beard and Schneider did not recognise him from his photograph.

Back at the Petrovsky Palace, Princess Orbeliani and I were just sitting down to tea when A. A. Kozlov came in and said that my husband had been wounded. When I left the room to put on my hat he told my guest that my husband had been killed. I went along hoping, believing that it was not all over, that my husband could be saved, and questioning Kozlov over and over again about the wound.

Even when I went into the house and saw him lying on a sofa in the hall I did not realise that he was dead. Nikita Belov, his valet, was standing by, and when I asked him whether my husband was unconscious or sleeping, he told me that he had passed away. I rose, went over to Kozlov, and said Belov had told me that my husband was "not alive", and asked whether it was true. Only when he confirmed it did I realise my loss.

About a year after my husband's death I received a letter from the "Revolutionary Executive Committee" in Geneva, saying that although my husband's political views and principles were completely different from theirs, they regarded his assassination as a political error, since he was a decent, honest, and kind man.

My father had one sister, two years older than himself. She was married to the son of Prince Field Marshal Paskevich. They had no children. She was very fond of her beloved brother's children, and we of her. She was very short (as was her mother, my grandmother). She always dressed simply, was very well read, and spoke excellent French. Throughout my childhood, and indeed until I was married, we children and our parents frequently walked over from No 10 English Embankment, to No 8, the home of Uncle and Aunt Paskevich.

I was born in Uncle's marvellous Rastrelli palace in Gomel. In my widowhood, with my father so far away (he was Viceroy of the Caucasus) I used to go to Auntie and pour out my feelings to her, and always went away comforted. I last saw her in autumn 1918 when I left Bolshevik Moscow in a Ukrainian hospital train, which stopped for a few hours at Gomel. The children and I took a hansom cab to the castle. Uncle had died in 1903, but Auntie was still living in a corner of the castle, though most of it was occupied by the German staff.

I exchanged letters with her from abroad. In one of hers she said how she longed to be with me. I appealed to all her relatives, on the Paskevich and the Vorontsov sides, to help me bring Auntie out of Russia. They all responded, and enough money was raised.

I went to Berlin. The old doorkeeper was still there at the Ministry of Foreign Affairs on the Wilhelmstrasse, and I asked him which of the former gentlemen was still in the ministry. He named one, I sent in my card, was received immediately and stated my business. I was told to come back next day. It had all been arranged. The Germans were still in Kiev, and the German consul would shortly be passing through Gomel in a sealed carriage. Auntie and her maid would be able to travel as far as Berlin without charge. But at the last minute she could not bring herself to leave, and humbly asked whether she should return the money. I of course replied that we all wanted her to keep it.

By then she had been evicted from the castle by the Bolsheviks, and was living with one of her Jewish former tenants. She was then almost blind – she suffered from amaurosis, and signed herself simply "I. P." She died on 1 April (Old Style) 1925, 90 years old, and completely blind. She had done a great deal of good. In Petersburg she always investigated personally those who sought her help. During the war, and in the years immediately before, she employed "*une visiteuse*" to make enquiries. In Gomel, besides helping individuals, she maintained an orphanage, an old people's home and a day clinic.

Aunt and Uncle had promised each other that whichever of them died first would "appear" to the other. He died first – and "appeared" to her. She was awakened one night by a bright light – an enormous dazzling patch of light, egg-shaped, she said, and Uncle's voice spoke from it: "*Irène, on est très heureux ici.*"

The estate was not very large when Uncle inherited it, though all the land on which Gomel stood was his. He presented this to the city council, bought land round about, and increased his holding to 100,000 *desyatins*,* most of it forest. Once a year Uncle would invite the best shots among his friends and relations to hunt in his forest.

After his death the local police inspector called on Auntie one day to say that the Governor of Mogilev province was coming to Gomel, and had telegraphed instructions to arrange a hunt in the Paskevich forest. My aunt refused outright, saying that only those she invited hunted there. The Governor called on her when he arrived. He evidently decided that this diminutive woman in a plain black dress would not dare to defy him.

He began by asking whether she lived in Gomel all the year round. She said that she spent part of the winter in Petersburg.

"I'm told that you go there quite late?"

"I go later than I used to now that my brother no longer lives there. We used to spend the whole winter there."

"So where does he live now?"

* *desyatin*: an old Russian land measure equivalent to 2.7 acres or 1.09 hectares

"In Tiflis."

"What does he do there?"

"He's in the government service."

"In what capacity?"

"If you must know – as Viceroy." When the Governor had pulled himself together there was not another word about hunting. "He was quite a different man."

When I went to stay with Auntie she would take me round all her charitable institutions, telling people as we entered: "I've brought our Gomel girl." But the fact that I was born in Gomel helped me to get my children (three daughters and two sons) and my Obolensky grandson out of Bolshevik Moscow: Gomel had been ceded to the Ukraine, and we managed to pass ourselves off as Ukrainians.

Auntie's maidservant informed us of her death, and her burial in the family vault. The Bolsheviks had at first refused permission for this, but gave way to pressure from the local population.

I last had the joy of meeting Empress Maria Feodorovna immediately before the (first) evacuation of the Crimea. I went to Alupka from Sevastopol, where I was staying with the children, and telephoned for permission to visit. There were no horses to be had, and I went along on foot. On the way I met A. V. Krivoshein. He was returning her son's account of Rasputin's murder to Princess Yusupova. Alexander Vasilievich was horrified by Yusupov's story, and could not understand how a mother could be proud of it or want others to read it.*

When I got to the Grand Duke Georgii Mikhailovich's residence, in which the Empress was staying, I saw Grand Duchess Xenia coming down the staircase with two second cousins of mine.

"Mama has chased us away." I was told. "She wants to talk to you tête à tête."

I went upstairs to her, curtseyed and kissed her hand. She kissed me, indicated that I should kiss her cheek, made me sit down, took a cigarette and gave me one.

* See p. xvi.

"*Toi qui viens de Moscou,*" she said, "*tu as peut-être des nouvelles à me donner sur mon fils. De Micha j'ai reçu dernièrement une lettre, de l'Empereur rien depuis longtemps.*"

This was after Moscow had heard the horrifying news that the imperial family had been murdered. I replied that I knew nothing definite, but to make my answer more reassuring repeated the words of a member of the Union of Russian People living in the same house as myself: "*C'est un rideau de fer qui s'est baissé, et avant qu'il ne se lève nous ne saurons jamais la verité.*"

The Empress wept. I wept with her and knelt to kiss her hand.

* * *

[From a letter to her daughter, Maria, 28 May 1957:]

Grandfather Andrei Pavlovich Shuvalov, when he was marshal of the nobility for the Petersburg *gubernia*,* petitioned the Emperor to liberate the peasants with individual allotments, and not, as was subsequently done, with collective landholdings.

The petition was signed by all the nobility of the Petersburg province, including Uncle Paskevich, who had been a childhood friend of Alexander II. The Emperor did not like this petition, and said: "Why did that fool Paskevich sign?"

When he heard of this remark, Uncle resigned his post as Adjutant-General, and left for Gomel with my aunt. When the memorial to his father was unveiled in Warsaw he and my aunt travelled there. Aunt had remained behind in the hotel when Uncle returned unexpectedly and said: "*Irène, faîtes vos paquets, nous rentrons à Homel.*" In the train he told her that Alexander II had greeted him with the words: "Why did you take offence, you fool?"

Uncle immediately left the scene of the ceremony. Your Grandfather Shuvalov's brother persuaded the Emperor to apologise, and was sent in pursuit, but when he reached the hotel Paskevich and his wife had already left.

* *gubernia*: a political area, larger than a *uyezd*.

For organising the petition mentioned above my Grandfather was offered the choice of living abroad or on his estate in Perm province. He chose to go abroad. It was a long time before he was allowed to live in Petersburg.

This affair also explains why Aunt Paskevich was never presented to Empress Maria Alexandrovna, nor to Empress Alexandra Feodorovna, nor to the Grand Duchesses, and why Uncle was never again at court.

You and I were at Gomel in 1918. The Germans were in the palace, but Auntie was living in her own room. After our departure, and when the Germans left, she was evicted from the castle and moved in with one of her former tenants, together with her faithful maidservant, Sasha. We corresponded. Auntie dictated her letters to Sasha, and simply initialled them, because she was almost blind. She died there, and was buried in the family vault under the church.

Sofka Demidov
(1870–1953)

The memoirs of Sofka, Sandra's younger sister and my great-aunt, open with accounts of her close relations with the imperial family, the assassination of Alexander II in 1881, and descriptions of walks and games with Alexander III, whom she held in deep affection and respect.

In 1893 she married Elim Demidov, who belonged to Russia's leading industrial family, whose fortune was made in the eighteenth century in the mines of the Urals, and whose members became even wealthier patrons of the arts in the nineteenth century.

The most colourful, if controversial, of the Demidovs was Anatole (1812–70), an entrepreneur and collector, who married Mathilde Bonaparte, the niece of Napoleon I. His nephew Paul, who had his Florentine title of Prince of San Donato recognised both by the Russian Emperor and the King of Italy, was Elim's father by his first marriage, while his daughter by his second marriage was Avrora, who married Prince Paul of Yugoslavia. After 1870 the Demidov family estate became Pratolino in the outskirts of Florence.

Elim, distinguished by a native intelligence and an independent mind, became a diplomat, serving successively in London (1895–1903), Madrid, Copenhagen, Vienna, and Athens (1912–14). War and revolution kept the Demidovs in Greece, where Elim died during the Second World War, and Sofka in 1953. Her memoirs contain vivid descriptions of the world of European diplomacy in the first half of this century.

[The following was written in a sanatorium near Lucerne in 1939. Sofka has been ill, on and off, since 1935. She feels weak and helpless, deplores her failing powers, and has little hope for the future. She thanks God that her husband, Elim, *is fit and strong. She intends to record her memories "as they come into my head, then if time permits, to arrange them in order". She warns the reader that even the clearest of her early memories she cannot always assign to a particular year. This extract begins with her account of her childhood on her father's estate at Berghof on the Baltic coast.]* For some reason I was kept on a strict diet, and allowed to eat practically nothing at all. We kept a vixen in a cage under the veranda, and fed her on bones from the table. I was so hungry on my diet that I used to creep into the vixen's cage and pick chicken bones with her. [*This went on until one day her governess came upon child and vixen "so absorbed" in their bone-picking that they had not noticed her approach.*]

At dinner one evening [*the children dined earlier than their parents*] I boasted to my older brother and my three sisters that I was afraid of nothing, and, although it was already dark [*autumn was setting in*], I would walk all the way to the sea, along a tree-lined avenue which was rather dark at the best of times. I was so carried away that I did not notice my father's presence until . . . I suddenly felt his hand on my shoulder.

"Very well", he said, "I will leave my handkerchief on the bench by the sea, and after supper, since you fear nothing, you can go and fetch it for me".

I can still remember how terrified I was. (I was only about 6 years old.) My father knew that I had only been boasting, and wanted to cure me of the habit.

After supper I went to fetch the handkerchief. I can still remember the terror I felt at every breath of wind and every rustle of leaves. But on I went, trying to master my fear, and keeping to the middle of the avenue. Sure enough, there was the handkerchief on the bench. I returned in triumph – resisting the temptation to run – and handed it to my father. Not till many years later did I learn that there were two or three menservants concealed in the bushes, with orders from my father to take me home at the first sign of panic.

* * *

[*Her father was "too much of a Russian in his soul" to feel at home in Berghof, and he sold the estate when they had spent only one summer there. In 1878 they moved to Novo-Tomnikovo, his estate in the province of Tambov.*] He loved the magnificent pinewoods and oak groves, loved the true Russian countryside. [*As well as his farm*] he had a string of racehorses. His stud was famous in Petersburg racing circles and won many prizes. [*Her father farmed, but his great passion was tree-planting.*] He liked to ride around in a two-horse, four-seater gig, with some of us children aboard. The others sat with our tutors and governesses in a carriage drawn by three horses, and Mama followed in a small pony-cart, because she was always terrified of big horses.

We would drive into the forest to view the newly planted saplings. On the same side of the River Tsna as our grounds there was an endless expanse of black-earth fields, sown with rye, wheat, oats, and barley. As far as the horizon nothing could be seen except this billowing sea of grain crops. On the opposite bank of the Tsna the soil was sandy, suitable for conifers, and there the forest of mature pines stretched for many miles into the distance.

It grieved my father to have to fell old trees, but he knew that left too long they could be disastrous to others. But the trees he felled were always replaced by a larger number of saplings.

We often cooked meals out in the forests. My father was head cook, and we children were his kitchen hands. He had learned to cook well on campaign as a young officer. He had fought in the Caucasus as soon as he was commissioned, then later in Turkestan under Skobelev, and finally in 1877 he had been Chief of Staff to Crown Prince Alexander Alexandrovich, the future Alexander III, in the so-called "Rushchuk Detachment". [. . .]

Once my brother Roman (who died of typhoid as a 19-year-old naval cadet) and I were playing the role of the fox. We led the field through the forest on the other side of the Tsna for a long time, then jumped into an open field, where the hunt caught sight of us. We urged on our horses and galloped into a little copse, beyond which there was a potato field, and beyond that again thick forest. We passed a peasant in a cart on the way. When our pursuers raced out of the copse they asked him whether he'd seen two people on horseback.

"Yes, just now" he said. "They've shot into the potatoes." This became one of our catchphrases. Back in Petersburg Sergei Mikhailovich and Alexander Mikhailovich told the story to the Heir and the Grand Duchess Xenia Alexandrovna. The result was that whenever the Tsarevich came to see us, or we were all together in my father's house on the English Embankment, this was called "shooting into the potatoes".

The house became the centre of "The Potato Club", the members of which were the Heir, his brother Georgii, his sister Xenia, Alexander Mikhailovich and Sergei Mikhailovich, my older brother, Vanya, Roman, we four sisters, and Olga Dolgorukaya. We ordered little golden potatoes from Fabergé and gave one to each member of the club. I still have mine.

Early childhood, for me, is connected with memories of Sunday outings to Gatchina, when Emperor Alexander III and Empress Maria Feodorovna were in residence. Then when the court moved back to Petersburg for the winter there would be skating, daily from three to five, at the Anichkov Palace, where a large lawn was flooded for the purpose. There was also an "ice-hill" for tobogganing, and we sometimes skated down it.

We used to play ice-hockey with Emperor Alexander III. He didn't wear skates, but stood on a patch of ice strewn with sand, and repelled the puck, or ball, with a hooked stick.

My father and the Emperor had been close friends from their early years. They had married at the same time, when the Emperor was still Tsarevich, and my father commanded the Emperor's Own Hussars at Tsarskoye Selo. I was born there, in the regimental commander's house in 1870.

In the winter of 1880–1 we went on a number of occasions to the Winter Palace to play with the children of Alexander II and Princess

Yurevskaya. The Tsarevich (the future Alexander III) would also be there with his wife and children. Princess Yurevskaya acted as hostess, surrounded by her three children. Alexander II was always very kind to us children.

I remember an occasion, one Christmas I think it was, when my prize in a raffle was a large number of exquisite china birds and animals, made in the Imperial Porcelain Factory. I was in ecstasies, I thought mine was the best prize of all – and so did one of the Emperor's sons, Gogo Yurevsky. He wanted to exchange prizes with me, I refused, we started quarrelling, and he even tried to take my prize from me by force.

In the heat of our quarrel we hadn't noticed the Emperor coming up behind us. Suddenly his hand took Gogo firmly by the ear, and I heard his voice saying that Gogo should be ashamed of himself, trying to take a toy away from a little girl, and telling him to stop it at once and apologise to me.

These elegant china birds and animals stood in a case holding souvenirs of my childhood at my husband's Petersburg home, until the Bolsheviks took over. I wonder what became of them? The whole house was wrecked and looted in the first days of Bolshevism.

I remember clearly Sunday 1 March 1881. Father had gone to the races, and we children were just going out for a walk when we saw Ramon, who had once been our butler, then gone to work for the Tsarevich, gallop up and ask for Papa. We learned from him that Alexander II had been seriously injured by a bomb. My father, who then commanded the Second Guards Corps, was informed at the race-course, and drove immediately to the palace. I remember what he told me later about that day.

* * *

Princess Yurevskaya disliked Papa, and the Emperor's entourage in general. She had already had several of them removed from Petersburg.

At the beginning of a court ball my father and mother were standing with a small group of young people near the door through which

Princess Yurevskaya entered. They were all chattering merrily, and just as the Princess entered there was a loud burst of laughter. It had nothing to do with her – they had not even noticed her – but after the ball she complained to the Emperor and insisted on my father's banishment from Petersburg.

A few days later he was ordered to leave for Turkestan, to take command of an army corps. This of course was meant as punishment. He already had seven children, my mother was expecting another in the spring, and he did not know what to do with us all. He was about to leave Petersburg when news of the attack on the Emperor reached him on 1 March. He rushed to the H.Q. of his corps, then to the Winter Palace.

When he saw blood stains on the stairs up which the Emperor had been carried, and the crowd in the ante-room outside the Emperor's quarters, he knew that there was little hope. The crowd seemed to make way for him more respectfully than usual, but my father detested this obsequiousness on the part of courtiers who had shunned him when he was out of favour. He stayed only a few minutes and returned to H.Q.

The Tsarevich was a close friend of his, and after the death of Alexander II, the order posting him to Turkestan was cancelled.

I remember Mama taking us children to the Winter Palace to pay our respects to the late Emperor's remains. His body looked so strange, so unnatural, doll-like. They had laid him in his coffin. There were several little wounds on his face made by fragments of the bomb. Princess Yurevskaya was standing by the coffin, sobbing loudly. We had evidently been allowed in before the general public.

After the funeral our parents moved to Gatchina with the imperial family. We children remained in Petersburg. Mama visited us frequently, but Father came less often, because he had been appointed commander of the imperial guard. He remained in this post for less than a year, before Alexander III appointed him Minister of the Court. He held this office throughout the reign of Alexander III, and the early years of Nicholas II's reign.

[The Shuvalov children, and several other children of aristocratic families, were regular guests at Gatchina on Sundays, travelling in a special carriage attached to the 9.30 train.]

Emperor Alexander III would be waiting, often in the grounds of the palace, with the Tsarevich and his brother Georgii and his sister Xenia, to go walking with us. (Later their younger brother Mikhail Alexandrovich would join the party.)

Soon after my older sister had reached her eighteenth birthday, and was to begin going out to balls and evening parties, we had all assembled to escort the Emperor, the Empress, and their guests in to dinner, and the Emperor approached her and said loudly: "Countess, I've known you since the day of your birth, and I've been used to calling you Sandra. Now that you're a grown-up lady I ask your consent to go on calling you by that name."

My sister was taken aback, but pulled herself together and said: "If you don't keep calling me Sandra, and also address me as 'you' [singular], I shall be offended."

"Right then", answered the Emperor. "I wouldn't want to offend you [singular] for anything, Sandra, so I'll go on calling you by your first name, and even 'you' [singular]." Next year, the ceremony was repeated for my benefit, and in subsequent years for my other sisters, Maya and Ira. (My older sister married Count P. P. Shuvalov, who was assassinated in 1905 when he was City Governor of Moscow. Another sister married Count V. V. Musin-Pushkin, and the fourth sister Count D. S. Sheremetev.)

Emperor Alexander III was for me the soul of honour. In our childish innocence we knew the value of his word. We used to show him the verses we wrote about each other, on condition that he showed them to no one else, and he always kept his word.

The Emperor's noble personality illuminated our childhood, and the Empress's kindness and merry laugh kept us cheerful. May their memory live for ever! If God had granted the Emperor longer life he would never have given way to Bolshevism. He would have governed with a firm hand. My father, who was his devoted friend and knew his innermost thoughts, told me that, in the notes he kept, Alexander III said how unfortunate it was that in the first years of his reign it had been necessary for him to keep the reins of government so tight, and that once order was restored he would gradually introduce more liberal policies.

He was pure Russian at heart, and loved his people, loved Russia. He found official receptions tiresome. The flattery of courtiers was distasteful to him. His honest, straightforward heart was sensitive to falsity. That, I believe, was why he loved the company of children. Their candour and artlessness were heart's ease to him.

The Empress never meddled in affairs of state. She devoted a great deal of effort to charitable activities. She was patroness of the Russian Red Cross. She was sociable, and loved dancing. I remember the so-called "English balls", to which people were invited not as of right, but at the discretion of the Emperor and Empress. The Emperor never danced and was often bored on these occasions. He would order the musicians to steal away one by one, until only the drummer was left. Only then would the Empress stop dancing.

Court balls were splendid occasions, especially the great ball in the Winter Palace to which some thousands of guests were entitled to attend by virtue of their military or civil rank. Since good dancers were needed the commanders of regiments were told to detail a certain number of young officers for this duty. Young ladies were invited according to their fathers' status. Ladies-in-waiting were entitled to attend.

In my time I have seen court balls in England, Spain, Denmark. I have seen Presidential receptions in France. But I can honestly say that ours were incomparably better. In England balls were magnificent, the etiquette was impeccable, the uniforms dazzling, the women were sumptuously dressed, there were diamonds every-where, and it was the same at the Austrian court, but when it was time to eat they all stood in a crowd at a buffet or, in Austria, trays were carried round with cups of "bouillon Maria Theresa", little dishes of ice-cream, and nothing else on them. At home nearly 3,000 people sat ten or twelve at a table, and a dinner of several courses was served.

The Emperor never sat down to supper, but, like a good host, circulated, with his entourage, pausing at almost every table to chat for a few minutes.

We nearly always had supper at the same table as the Heir. One or other of us often danced the mazurka with him. You were supposed to sup with your partner in the mazurka.

I got engaged at the Hermitage Ball in 1893. I danced the mazurka and had supper with the Tsarevich. I was supposed to dance the fourth quadrille, before the mazurka, with my future husband. He never liked dancing, and asked me to sit that one out.

We went into the winter garden, and he proposed to me there. Time went by, the quadrille had ended and the orchestra had played the opening chords of the mazurka without us realising it. The master of ceremonies suddenly hurried over to us and said: "Countess, everybody is waiting for you, we can't begin the mazurka without the Tsarevich, he's looking for you everywhere." I went with him at once.

My fiancé and I agreed that we would tell nobody about our engagement until I got home and told my parents. If the news got out, everybody would start congratulating us, and we wanted to avoid that. We didn't succeed. On our way back into the hall we met his sister, Avrora Karageorgevich,* who very much wanted us to wed. She had seen us sitting in the winter garden, and signalled to her brother – "Yes or no?" He signalled "Yes", and she was so overjoyed that she began telling everyone.

I too had to explain my delay to the Tsarevich, but I asked him to keep the secret until the following day. He, of course, agreed. I asked him also to keep the place next to mine at his table for my fiancé, and he of course did so.

* The daughter of Paul Demidov, from his second marriage; Elim's half-sister and the wife of Prince Paul of Yugoslavia.

From 1912 my husband, Elim Demidov, was Russian Ambassador in Greece. Previously he had served in London, Madrid, Copenhagen, and Vienna, as well as in the Ministry of Foreign Affairs in Petersburg and in Paris. His posting in Athens came to an end in 1914. But the War, then the revolutions of 1917, pinned us to Greece permanently, and we have lived here now for 21 years, instead of the expected two.

My father, because of his name, his wealth, and his position, had been in his time perhaps the most eligible bachelor in Petersburg society. My mother was ten years younger than him, and a great beauty. Moreover, her father and mother also possessed great wealth and historic names.

These recollections of wintering in the South of France, and of my grandmother Shuvalov, whom I loved very much, are my earliest memories of childhood. I dimly remember the villa that my parents rented, with its large, dark garden, and the orange grove at the bottom of it. I liked to wander by myself in those dim depths until I was forbidden to.

For some reason I was often made to observe a strict diet, and I used to pick up fallen oranges and wolf them down. Perhaps that is why a stop was put to my little walks. I don't know why I was kept hungry, but it was evidently good for me. My stomach has been able to digest absolutely everything ever since. My mother often said that "Vorontsov stomachs can digest stones". My favourite dish was cabbage soup with buckwheat gruel. Living abroad, we can only dream of sour cabbage soup, but we have buckwheat sent to us here in Athens from Yugoslavia. Elim and I are both very fond of buckwheat gruel.

My father's Petersburg house was at No 10, English Embankment. That was where we girls began our education. Our classrooms were on the lower floor, with windows looking out on the Embankment. When the Finland Regiment marched with their band past their Corps commander's home we would rush to the windows and some of the officers who knew us children would bow to us.

On Sundays children of our own age, mostly relatives or families of close friends of our parents, would often come to see us, among them our Balashov cousins. Pyotr Balashov, in boyhood and early adolescence, was in love with me, or imagined that he was. Later on he played a role in the State Duma, as leader of the Nationalist party. In Stolypin's time he was known as "*Lieder ohne Worte*", since he never made a single speech. He was none the less highly thought of in his party for his strength of character and straightforwardness. Even in childhood I was not in the least attracted to him, which greatly upset him, and even upset his mother (my mother's sister), who doted on him.

We moved to Gatchina after the assassination of Alexander II, in the following winter. My father's duties kept him most of the time at the Palace, where Alexander III and his family were generally in residence. My father was very fond of family life, and didn't want to be parted from us. He rented two adjacent villas, and a roofed wooden corridor was built between them. We children could run along it from our villa to the one in which mother and father lived, and they often walked over to see us.

Although his official duties kept him very busy my father would hurry over to see us several times a day. He kept a close eye on our education, and our manners, talked to our governesses and tutors, and entered into every detail of our young lives. I remember as if it were now his quick light step and the faint jingle of his spurs in the entrance hall.

I do not remember my father ever punishing us. If our behaviour did not please him he would gather us round him and discuss with us the misbehaviour of one or all of us, then make us promise not to repeat it.

Mother took no part in our education, her only concern was for our health. Her Russian was shaky when she got married, and although she learned to speak correctly she was never quite confident in that language. She always wrote to us children in French, and we replied in Russian. Later on, if she had to write a letter in Russian she would show one of us what she had written to make sure that there were no mistakes.

As a girl she had lived abroad with her parents for a long time, occasionally visiting Petersburg, or Odessa, where her maternal grandfather, Prince Mikhail Semyonovich Vorontsov, was Governor-General.

We studied in pairs: Vanya and Sandra, Maya and I, Ira and Roman. This was, of course, before my brothers entered the Corps of Pages, and Sandra sat for the governess's diploma set by the Third Boys' High School in Petersburg.

Our first summer at Tomnikovo was in 1878. I remember the train journey, which took 48 hours. Ours was a large party – eight children, governesses, tutors, nannies, maidservants, besides Papa and Mama, so that it was cheaper and more convenient to reserve a whole coach.

When we first went to Tomnikovo the house there was quite small and it was a tight squeeze for us. Father decided to build another house near the old one. A spacious kitchen was built at the same time, out in the yard.

The new house had three storeys. On the ground floor were the dining room, drawing room, billiards room, butler's pantry . . . A marble staircase led to the first floor. We children each had a room of our own on the second floor, which was reached by a narrow stone staircase at the side of the house. There were ten rooms altogether on our floor: Vava, of course, occupied one, and one of our maid-servants another.

Our family was on the best of terms with the peasants in the nearby village of Novo-Tomnikovo; and indeed with those of all the villages within the boundaries of the estate. My father always rose very early, in summer at 6 a.m., and after his coffee sat on a bench in front of the house to talk to peasants. They came not only from villages on the estate but from so-called "State lands", as much as 40 *versts* away, to tell him their troubles and seek his advice.

I remember one old woman who arrived on foot from a distant village and produced from under her headscarf a five rouble note, or rather the remains of a five rouble note. Weeping bitterly she explained that she had put it away in a safe place, but when she took it out a few days ago it looked as if mice had nibbled it.

"Show it to me," Father said. He looked at it, and said: "You see, grandma, the number's still there so they'll change it for a new one. I can easily see to it. Look, I'll give you a new one, and you give me yours." The old woman's gratitude knew no bounds. When we examined her note later we saw that there was only a hole where the number should have been. One of us asked Father why he had told her that it was there.

"Simply so that she would know that she could get another note at the bank, and so that she would think I was just changing it, not giving charity."

Some peasants would kneel and place their petitions on their heads. Nothing exasperated Father so much.

"What are you doing? Get up!" he would say. "It's only God you should kneel to. I won't receive your request till you get up."

From childhood on we knew almost every peasant in the village of Novo-Tomnikovo. We went to their weddings and christenings, and saw the foundation stones of churches and schools laid. There were three primary schools in Novo-Tomnikovo: the zemstvo school, the church school, and a school for girls built and maintained at my father's expense.

There was a zemstvo hospital in the village, paid for almost exclusively by Papa. I was one of the trustees of the hospital from an early age. There was another hospital twelve versts from Novo-Tomnikovo with a very skilful and devoted woman doctor, who had to be surgeon, pathologist, and gynaecologist rolled into one. The peasants in her village were terribly fond of her. Understandably, she wanted to go to Petersburg to improve her qualifications and take a further examination, but the peasants were reluctant to let her go.

In the end, she wrote to Petersburg and made all the arrangements without letting anyone know. But when the carriage arrived to pick her up early one morning, the peasants crowded round the hospital shouting: "We don't want you to go away and leave us!" The doctor tried to persuade them, promising to return in a few months, but in vain. They unharnessed the horses from the gig, and she had to stay. I don't know whether she succeeded in completing her studies after I married and moved with my husband to our London embassy. With her extensive clinical experience she had no need to improve her practical skills.

One day when I was about ten years old one of the ostlers from our stud came to see Father and said that he wanted to be christened.

"You mean you want to christen a child?" said Father.

"No, I want to be christened myself and christen my wife and children." It turned out that he was a Molokanin (members of that sect did not recognise our sacraments), was not christened, and had not married in church nor had his children christened.

"So you want to be christened, with your whole family?"

"Yes, and I want one of the little countesses to be godmother."

"Which one?"

"The one with the long plaits." (Myself.)

So I acted as godmother to a whole family of Molokane.

When revolution first flared up all over Russia in 1905, the peasants drove their cattle onto our meadows. The estate manager insisted on their removal, and the constable imposed a fine for damage to crops. The peasants defied them, and began threatening the estate manager. He took fright and sent a telegram to my brother in Petersburg. (My father had been appointed Viceroy in the Caucasus, and had transferred responsibility for the estate to Ilarion.) In his reply my brother instructed the manager to do nothing until he got there himself. The manager met him on his arrival and asked: "Where are your bodyguards?"

"Bodyguards?"

"I thought you'd come with bodyguards."

"I've come alone."

The steward told him that the peasants were very excited. As he left the station, Ilarion saw that every single carriage from the estate had been assembled on the forecourt.

"What's all this?" he asked.

"As I told you, I expected you to come with bodyguards. That's why the carriages are here."

When he got to the big house my brother called for a horse and rode out to the meadows into which the peasants had driven their cattle. The peasants had heard that the "young count" was coming and were out in force. When my brother asked why they were pasturing their cattle on our meadow they all began speaking loudly at once.

"Look", said Ilarion, "I insist that you remove your cattle from our meadows immediately, and then I promise to talk to you."

"What about the fine?"

"We can discuss that as well, but after you've removed all the cattle."

"We've always been good neighbours, and we've always found we can trust your word," they said, and they drove their cattle away, much to the bailiff's amazement for he had been afraid that they would do my brother some injury.

My brother then had an amicable discussion with them, cancelled the fine, enquired about their needs and returned to Petersburg. When he told me the story, my brother said that Father's cordial relations with the peasants were largely responsible, and that in any case the bailiff had been unduly alarmed, that he had shouted at the peasants too loudly, and that he need not have brought the constable into it.

In the autumn we sometimes went to the Kiev or the Podolsk *gubernia*, where my uncle and aunt, the Balashovs, had estates. The Balashovs spent the first half of the summer in Uncle's estate in the Podolsk region and the second in Aunt Kitty's estate, Meshnogory, in the Kiev province.

Aunt Kitty, my mother's sister, had inherited this estate from their grandmother, Princess Elizaveta Ksavierevna Vorontsova. It was a marvellous estate, with a spacious house standing on a hill, woods, and many thousand *desyatins* of fields and meadow. There was also a sugar refinery near the railway station. The estate had once belonged to Prince Potemkin, Catherine II's favourite. The refinery was built by my great-grandfather, and the railway station was called Vorontsovo-Ekaterinovka. Some 40 *versts* ride away was the Bobrinsky estate, the joint property of three brothers of whom Vladimir lived there almost the whole year round, managing their lands and their great sugar refinery.

We were friends with the fun-loving sons of Count Alexander Bobrinsky, although they were considerably older than us. We went hunting with them and, I have to confess, often had fights with them in the garden.

On the way back to Petersburg from Kiev province we visited the estate of our uncle Prince Paskevich. (He was married to my father's sister. They had no children.) She made magnificent embroideries, read a great deal, and presided over her own salon, in a house next to Father's on the English Embankment. I remember as a child seeing the writers [Dmitri] Grigorovich and [Alexei] Apukhtin there.

Uncle Paskevich was a great connoisseur of antiques, and the house was full of them. My mother told me that he had once been aide-de-camp to Emperor Nicholas I. One day the Emperor was angry because Uncle had not carried out his instructions precisely, and said, though not in his hearing, "That fool didn't understand my orders." Uncle was told about it, and immediately resigned, a very unusual thing for an aide-de-camp to do in those days. The Emperor was surprised, sent for him and asked him why he had resigned.

"Because", he replied, "fools should not be on Your Majesty's staff."

"I just lost my temper. I refuse to accept your resignation."

But Uncle insisted, and the Emperor could not dissuade him.

My father and Uncle Paskevich were on bad terms for years, and never met. The reason was that Uncle completely abandoned my Aunt, leaving her behind in their castle at Gomel while he pursued one lady after another, but mainly a certain Polish countess.

The Paskevichs once gave a dinner party, at which the countess was among the guests, wearing a pearl necklace which my Aunt recognised as her own. She pretended not to have noticed, thinking perhaps that she was mistaken, but after dinner found the case in which the pearls were kept was indeed empty. She returned to the dining room and still said nothing. In the long run, her patience was rewarded. In their later years together I never saw a more loving couple, or a more considerate husband, and it was difficult to believe that there had ever been a rift between them, and that she had lived alone for years either in the castle in Gomel, or in the Petersburg house, reading, embroidering, translating Russian writers into French, helping the poor, and doing all these things efficiently and effectively.

I was told by someone who visited Gomel in the 1920s that the local people took care of her, that she was housed in one room of the castle which had been her home, and that various people kept her supplied with food. She died in 1924 or 1925, completely blind. (She had always been very short-sighted.) This witness told me that she was always cheerful and uncomplaining. Her maidservant remained with her to the end. She was over ninety when she died. (She was older than Papa, who died aged 78 in 1916.) My sisters and I sent her parcels from abroad, addressed to her maidservant, who wrote to say that Irina Ivanovna was very grateful, was well, and wanted nothing.

My Aunt had money of her own, which she spent mainly on the poor. She received many requests, and a lady in Petersburg visited the addresses given by the writers on her behalf. On one occasion she visited the writer of a letter describing a tragic situation. A widow wrote that she could not pay for her husband's funeral, that her children were hungry, and that she had no money for her rent. My Aunt's representative went along, found a room bearing all the marks of poverty, with a coffin standing in the middle, children in tears, etc. My Aunt had given the lady a certain sum to help this family.

She, however, had seen a great deal of poverty in her time, suspected that all was not as it seemed, and left only half of what she had been given. But as she was leaving the building she changed her mind and went back up three flights of stairs. She reached the third floor, the door of the room was open, and she found the father of the family no longer in his coffin but sitting on a chair drinking coffee, surrounded by happy faces. They rudely chased the lady away. This sort of thing was nothing unusual in Petersburg.

Our menservants remained with us for decades on end. We were godparents to their children, and if the parents wished paid for their education, right up to university level.

The oldest servant in the house, whom I remember from early childhood, was my father's valet Grisha (Grigorii Nikolaevich to everyone else), a plump little man with waxed moustaches and an exceedingly dignified gait. He was always well-dressed, wore a beautifully cut jacket, and his little finger was adorned by a jasper, I think, set in a gold ring and with a monogram engraved upon it.

He often passed through the children's dining room on his way to the pantry for his morning coffee, and would always greet us with a solemn "Good morning, children." He was the nicest and kindest of men, utterly devoted to Father, and capable of forgetting his dignity and giving way to hearty laughter. He was very fond of saying "When the Count and I were young . . . ", which always introduced some story about the campaigns or journeys on which he had accompanied Father. He was an old bachelor, and very honest: he would sometimes bring Father petitions, saying: "I've been given this request and I couldn't refuse to pass it on to you, but I refused the money that was offered. What do I need money for?"

On one occasion we heard the jingle of spurs, and were surprised when the pantry man appeared wearing Father's boots.

"What's all this, Ivan? Why are you wearing the Count's boots?"

"Grigorii Nikolaevich gave them to me. They're too tight for the Count, and he told me to wear them in."

When we told Father he laughed a lot and called Grisha.

"Well, yes I did give Ivan your boots to wear in, you don't like tight ones."

Our house swarmed with menservants, all of whom except Grisha had served their time in the Hussars. One was Alexei, the "Lamp Man". In those days we had oil lamps with wicks, which had to be

Above: Countess Sandra Shuvalov and Sofka Demidov, Dimitri Obolensky's great-aunt, *c.*1880s.

Left: Countess Sandra Shuvalov, Dimitri Obolensky's grandmother, *c.*1880s.

From left, standing, c.1880s: The Tsarevich, the future Nicholas II; Xenia, the Tsarevich's sister; Countess Sandra Shuvalov. *In next row:* Sofka Demidov.

Count Paul Shuvalov, Dimitri Obolensky's grandfather and City Governor of Moscow, holding his daughter, Olga, c.1900.

Il'inskoe, 1896: Countess Sandra Shuvalov and Count Paul Shuvalov (*far left, standing*); King Ferdinand of Bulgaria (*fifth from left in white hat*) and his wife Queen Marie of Roumania, Queen Victoria's daughter (*second from left, seated*); Nicholas II, who had just come to the throne (*sixth from right, seated*), and his wife (*seated, holding baby*); Grand Duke Sergei, the Governor-General of Moscow and owner of Il'inskoe (*fourth from right, seated*). Count Paul Shuvalov and Grand Duke Sergei were both assassinated in 1905.

The State funeral in Moscow of Count Paul Shuvalov, City Governor, who was assassinated in June 1905 by a terrorist belonging to the Socialist Revolutionary Party.

The Vorontsov Palace at Alupka on the Crimean coast, from where Dimitri Obolensky "wisely fled at the age of one" in 1919. Once home to Winston Churchill during the Yalta Conference in 1945, it is now a museum of fine art.

Above: The Viceroy's wife, Countess Elizabeth Shuvalov.

Left: Count Ilarion Vorontsov-Dashkov, Dimitri Obolensky's maternal great-grandfather, Viceroy of the Caucasus (1905–15) and the owner of the palace at Alupka.

Prince Alexander Obolensky (1847–1917), Dimitri Obolensky's paternal grandfather.

Prince Dimitri Aleksandrovich Obolensky (1882–1964), Dimitri Obolensky's father.

H.I.M. the Empress Marie Feodorovna and the Grand Duke Nicholas on the quarter deck of
H.M.S. *Marlborough* in the bay of Yalta, just before the historic moment when the
Imperial Anthem was given in salute for the last time, 1919

General Peter Wrangel, the
Commander-in-Chief of the armed
forces of southern Russia, 1920.

Dimitri Obolensky with his mother,
Countess Maria Shuvalov.

Countess Maria Shuvalov, Dimitri Obolensky's mother, and Count André Tolstoy in Paris in the 1930s.

Count André Tolstoy working at the United Nations in New York, 1961.

The headmaster of the Russian school in Nice, Arkady Yakhontov (*right*), with his wife. The formidable man on the left is Mr Izergin, who was responsible for physical exercise, April 1929.

Dimitri Obolensky roller-skating in Nice, 1929.

Dimitri Obolensky in Nice with his mother and half-brother, Ivan Tolstoy, 1929.

Dimitri Obolensky's half-brother, Paul Tolstoy.

Dimitri Obolensky (left) and his contemporaries at the symposium at the Dumbarton Oaks Center for Byzantine Studies in Washington DC. Seated from left: Professor Roman Jakobson, who left Russia after the Revolution and was an expert in linguistics and medieval literary history, and Father Francis Dvornik, a Czech from Moravia and an expert in Byzantine studies.

wound up with a key. Ours was a big house, and a man was needed specially to look after the lamps. One day my father sat writing at his desk when someone came into the room. My father looked up and saw Alexei, completely drunk, holding one lamp under his arm and another in one hand, both upside down.

"Alexei, what are you doing? The oil from the lamp is running out on the carpet!"

"Surely you can see I'm drunk, Your Excellency . . ."

Father rose and gave a comic bow. "Forgive me", he said, "I hadn't noticed" – then went over to Alexei, righted the lamps, and sent him on his way.

My father was a true Russian – good, noble, chivalrous, considerate, utterly devoted to Russia. His example was a guiding light throughout my childhood and adolescence. Even after my marriage I often sought his advice at times of doubt and difficulty, and he always gave careful thought to my problems, discussed the details at length with me and gave excellent advice.

His efforts for the benefit of Russia were just as carefully thought out. He was greatly respected by all his colleagues and close associates. I remember reading an article in a left-wing newspaper after the Revolution from which I quote almost verbatim: "If Nicholas II had had a few more collaborators as enlightened as Count Vorontsov-Dashkov [*Sofka's father*] there would have been no revolution in Russia."

In the Caucasus he was much loved by the whole population. When he made his official entry into Tiflis, on his appointment as Viceroy, his train stopped on the outskirts of the Caucasian capital. Father then mounted a white horse, and rode into Tiflis surrounded by his retinue and all the senior army officers. Once there, he went first to the Russian cathedral, dismounted, was greeted by the clergy, kissed the Cross, entered the cathedral, left after a few minutes, went to the Georgian cathedral, where the same ceremony was repeated, from there to the Armenian cathedral, and finally to the mosque and the synagogue.

There was general amazement. Father's intention was to show all the ethnic groups in the Caucasus that as far as he was concerned they all enjoyed equal rights as subjects of Great Russia. His predecessor, Prince Golitsyn, had not been Viceroy but Governor-General of the territory, and his policy was in my view completely wrong. He tried to create strife between the ethnic groups in the Caucasus, thinking that this would reinforce Russia's authority, and treated the Russians much better than the "other breeds" as he called them, thinking that by these means he would Russify the region. Whereas the thought behind all of my father's words and actions was that they were all Russian subjects, with equal rights.

He was appointed Viceroy in 1905, when revolution was flaring up all over the Caucasus, and bombs were thrown in the streets of Tiflis. A delegation of loyal Caucasian subjects visiting Petersburg at the time was asked by the Emperor who could restore order in the Caucasus. They replied with one voice: "Only Count Vorontsov-Dashkov." The Emperor sent for Father and asked whether he would be willing to go to the Caucasus as Governor-General.

"Not as Governor-General, Your Majesty," Father replied, "but I would as Your Majesty's Viceroy. I wouldn't like Your Majesty to think that I want that title out of mere vanity. No, it's for purely practical reasons – as Viceroy I shall have more extensive powers, and I don't want to be always attached to the end of a wire, having to consult the Ministry of the Interior on every little detail."

The Emperor thought for a while, and finally said: "I agree with you, Count, I've always thought that was the most effective arrangement."

* * *

[*Undated material, after 1918:*]
I should like to dedicate these pages to the memory of the villainously murdered Emperor Nikolai Alexandrovich. Much has been written about him, and no doubt much more will be, but as a friend of his childhood and adolescence I shall try to tell all that I know about his early life, his character and his upbringing. I have no wish to assess his merits as "Autocrat of All the Russians", only to show the purity

and nobility of his nature. I was a frequent, sometimes a daily, witness of the future Emperor's circumstances and his development from my early childhood until I married at 23.

We, his childhood playmates at the Gatchina and Anichkov Palaces, were very fond of "Nikolai Alexandrovich" as we called him [*i.e. not* "*Your Imperial Highness*"]. Thoughts of any advantage we might derive from our intimacy with him never entered our infant heads. We loved him as a playmate and as a merry, good-natured intelligent youngster.

The future Emperor was two years older than me, the same age as my brother, Vanya. My earliest memories of him date from 1881, when he, his brother Georgii and his sister Xenia, used to play with us at his grandfather's, Emperor Alexander II, Petersburg residence, the Winter Palace. The Emperor had recently married Princess Yurevskaya. Their liaison went back many years, and they had three children. Alexander II wanted to bring his grandchildren (Nikolai, Georgii and Xenia) and Princess Yurevskaya's children together. He had arranged three or four children's parties for this purpose before his assassination in March 1881.

I was ten-and-a-half years old at the time, and I remember how merrily we raced about the state rooms of the Winter Palace, and slid down the waxed, wooden helter-skelter erected in one of them. I can still see Nikolai Alexandrovich laughing and joking with the others, and launching himself down the "wooden hill".

I am not sure when exactly our excursions to Gatchina began, but I think it was in autumn 1881. A horde of us – my brother Vanya, we four sisters, three Sheremetevs, three Baryatinskys, Kira Naryshkin, and friends visiting from Moscow – would descend on Gatchina. We played games on the palace lawns, watched over by Nastya (Anastasia Grigorievna), the Grand Duchess Xenia Alexandrovna's nanny. (She never had a real governess. Nastya spent her whole life with Xenia Alexandrovna, went into exile with her, and died at an advanced age.)

Nikolai Alexandrovich's upbringing was supervised by Adjutant General Danilovich, who drew up a study programme for him in consultation with his parents. There were also two tutors, one

English and one French. Mr Heath, the Englishman, was very popular with us. He invented all sorts of games, ball games and others, for us. We sometimes pretended not to understand the rules of a game, and he would pretend to be angry. When we were naughty, Nikolai Alexandrovich was often the ringleader, and his brother Georgii was never far behind. But Nikolai would always be the first to beg Mr Heath not to be angry, to take the blame for our naughtiness and to promise that we would play according to the rules from then on.

The French tutor was also very nice but, like most Frenchmen in those days, did not know many games, so we preferred Mr Heath. Nikolai Alexandrovich, who was by nature affectionate, became very fond of this honourable, upright and good-natured man, the first male person to have charge of him after he left the nursery. Mr Heath, I believe, understood the shy and irresolute character of his charge, and had a proper respect for his intellect and his spiritual qualities. The French tutor was of the same mind.

As for General Danilovich, he was not, I fear, a good choice. Whatever the Emperor's reasons for appointing him, he most certainly could not inculcate in his charge qualities which he did not possess himself. I remember him advancing slowly along the galleries of the Gatchina Palace, I remember his appearances beside the rink at the Anichkov Palace, muffled up, in a fur-lined military greatcoat, and wearing a padded service cap. His voice was low and toneless, he was terrified of catching cold. I believe that as supervisor of the future Emperor's upbringing he was acutely aware of his responsibility to Russia as a whole but, soft and uncertain of himself, he was incapable of deciding on any programme of character development. His white side-whiskers were always exquisitely trimmed, his grey-white hair neatly combed.

When people criticised the choice of Danilovich as tutor to the Tsarevich, the answer was always the same: he was a very cultured man, the author of this and that book on military matters, and what was more incapable of intrigue, honest and decent. Danilovich was undoubtedly an honest and honourable man, but looking back it seems incontestable to me that such a weak character could not reinforce the character of his charge, could not give him that which he did not himself possess. As far as the general education of the Tsarevich was concerned, Danilovich was, I believe, qualified to supervise it.

Nikolai Alexandrovich undoubtedly possessed what is called "charm". He inherited it from his mother – but also inherited her weak and vacillating character.

When my husband was First Secretary of our Mission in Copenhagen, I had the opportunity to get to know the Danish royal family. They were all splendid people, goodhearted and friendly, but not one of them was remarkable for strength of character, and I realised that Nikolai Alexandrovich had inherited his weakness from his Danish forebears.

Nikolai had a quick and clear mind. His tutors and later on his ministers (so Sazonov told me) all commented on his ready grasp. As a boy he always prepared his lessons systematically. He had always been shy, but when he got used to someone was candid, cheerful, and witty.

Emperor Alexander III kept a close eye on his heir's progress, and often spoke to Danilovich about it. The general assured the Emperor in all sincerity that the Tsarevich was doing well in all subjects. But did he, I wonder, mention the shyness and weakness of character of which I have spoken? I think not, though this defect in the future autocrat was what above all required attention.

I have heard it said that his parents let Nikolai Alexandrovich see that they loved him less than their other children, and that his awareness of a certain coldness on their part accounted for his reserve and his diffidence. The explanation of the royal couple's coldness towards their firstborn was supposed to be that theirs had not been a love-match. Empress Maria Feodorovna (then Princess Dagmar of Denmark) had been betrothed first to the future Emperor Alexander III's older brother, Nikolai, whom she loved dearly. Nikolai died in the South of France of tuberculosis. On his deathbed he placed Princess Dagmar's hand in that of his brother and told them to marry.

The future Emperor Alexander III had himself been in love with one of his mother's ladies-in-waiting, Princess Meshcherskaya. He had sought permission to marry her from his father, offering to renounce all right to the throne for himself and all his descendants. Princess Meshcherskaya was beautiful, clever, modest, a universal favourite in Petersburg society, and she returned Alexander Alexandrovich's love. Alexander II refused to allow their marriage, and thereafter they very rarely saw each other. When they did happen to meet they did not speak.

The future Alexander III and Princess Dagmar married, then, not for love but out of duty, and their first-born son represented a duty to Russia duly performed. But (the story goes) as time went by they came to appreciate each other, and so to love their other children more than their eldest son.

I reject this story out of hand. I never noticed any difference in the royal couple's treatment of their firstborn and their other children. Alexander III, who had an aversion to great receptions, and the flattery and obsequiousness that went with them, was sincerely sorry for his heir on such occasions. Once, at the Anichkov Palace, the Tsarevich's sister, Xenia Alexandrovna, and we four girls were called upstairs to the Empress's smaller drawing room, which looked out on the Nevskii Prospect. The Emperor and Empress often drank tea there, with a snack of some sort – cold cuts, caviare, meat patties – before going to the theatre.

The Empress was very fond of that cosy little room. She kept her books and photographs and souvenirs there, and in one corner was a table just large enough for a samovar, two place settings and plates with biscuits. There were no footmen in attendance. The Empress brewed tea for the Emperor and herself. The five of us entered and each took a chair. The Emperor was wearing a double-breasted jacket, the Empress a "tea-gown". The conversation was in Russian. After a while the Emperor rose to leave, saying that he had documents to read. The Empress then said to him: "Sasha, have you given Niki permission to go to the circus this evening?"

"Yes, it's Saturday, and he has no lessons tomorrow, so he can get up later."

"I quite agree," said the Empress, "but won't you let Georgie [sic] go to the circus with Niki?"

"No, Georgie's still too little."

"But Georgie so much wants to go, he begged me to ask you."

The Emperor, upright in the middle of that small room, said: "Georgie will have plenty of time to amuse himself, he'll just be a Grand Duke. But we must look after Niki and help him to enjoy life. His lot will be quite different, he will have to bear a great responsibility, so we must help him to enjoy himself as much as possible while he's young."

I found it strange at the time that his father seemed to feel sorry for Nikolai Alexandrovich. Did he mean it wasn't nice being an Emperor?

Of course, all the Emperor's children were shy with their parents. But whose children weren't in those days? Looking back, I can see that even we were a little bit afraid of Mama, and none of our contemporaries – the Dolgorukys, the Balashovs, the Sheremetevs, the Baryatinskys, the Naryshkins and so on – were quite at ease with their parents. Our upbringing was strict. We were not allowed to talk at table, unless one of the "old people", as we called our parents, asked one of us a question, in which case we were required to answer in one short sentence.

I remember that on one occasion, when I was almost 20, I got into conversation with a guest at the family dinner table, became rather heated, and raised my voice slightly. Suddenly, from the other end of the table, I heard Mama's voice: "Please stop talking, just remember that at table with grown-ups children are supposed to listen, not to air their views."

I stopped talking at once, but felt offended. *Children?* I thought. *I'm not a child, my sister is married already and expecting a child.*

In my time, children were generally brought up strictly, but when I come to think of it, the Emperor's children were brought up less strictly than we were.

* * *

We had fun skating and sliding down the specially constructed "ice-hills". Emperor Alexander III was there every day too. Once, when the ice was covered with snow, the Emperor sent for brooms and shovels and we got busy clearing the rink under his command. It was tiring work and we started grumbling.

"Are we Finnish peasant girls or something? At least they get paid for their work, and we have to do all this for nothing."

It was a joke, of course – and we did this when the Emperor was near enough to hear us.

"Tired are you, and want to be paid?"

"Of course we do."

"Very well, here are your wages."

He took several gold coins from his purse and distributed them among us. I still have my golden five-rouble piece with Alexander III's head. Many photographs were taken on the rink, and one of them, yellow with age, still stands on my escritoire in Athens.

Alexander III was very fond of teasing and playing practical jokes. One fine day we got back from the rink and began changing into the dresses we had brought with us. Only one thing was missing – our shoes had vanished. We questioned Xenia Alexandrovna's maid, Vera, and Nastya, but they both said they knew nothing. We were completely at a loss, standing there fully dressed, but without shoes. Then we heard the Emperor calling to us from Xenia Alexandrovna's drawing room, where tea was always served. Xenia Alexandrovna's shoes would not fit us, so she gave us a pair of slippers each, and we went into the drawing room. The Tsarevich and some of his friends were already there – and what should we see but five pairs of freshly polished shoes arranged like a garland on the tea table. The Emperor, passing through Xenia Alexandrovna's bedroom, and seeing five pairs of shoes in a row, had not been able to resist carrying them off and decorating the tea table with them. He had strictly forbidden Vera and Nastya to say anything to us, and ordered the footmen not to disturb his table decoration. He was delighted that his prank had succeeded, and we all laughed heartily. [. . .]

We were married in Petersburg on 18 April 1893 (Old Style). My husband's grandmother, Avrora Karlovna Karamzin, had come from Helsingfors to her favourite grandson's wedding, and we went back to Finland with her.

My husband's mother had died the day after he was born, and his grief-stricken father had entrusted the child to his mother. Her first husband – my husband's grandfather – was Pavel Nikolaevich Demidov. After his death, she had married Andrei Karamzin (the son of the famous Russian historian). She was widowed for a second time when he was killed in the Crimean War.

It was impossible not to love Grandma Karamzin, and I became very attached to her. When my husband was seven his father had married again, and was persuaded by his new wife to send the child to school in England (near Dover). Grandma Karamzin often visited him there, and when his father sent him to a pension in Switzerland she took up residence in a hotel nearby.

*   *   *

In summer 1915 I was on my way home from Greece to St Petersburg. Railway travel was of course difficult in wartime and, as it turned out, I had to stay in Odessa for a few days. I sent a telegram to my husband in Greece. He replied *"puisque tu restes à Odessa je te prie aller voir belle-mère"* [his stepmother]. I confess that the idea gave me no pleasure at all, but since my husband thought it necessary, and I had nothing much to do in Odessa, I decided to try.

I telephoned to say that I was staying in Odessa, and should like to see her. I was told that the message would be given to the Princess. There was no response, so I telephoned again the same day. I received the same reply – followed by silence. After a third attempt next day, with the same result, I decided to call on her without further ado. I took a cab to her house, which was surrounded by a large garden and a high wall. The gate was high and solid. I rang, a little window opened, and an eye and part of a bearded face appeared.

"Does Princess Demidova live here?"

"So they say."

"What do you mean, so they say?"

"Well, I've been employed here five years and never seen her," was the strange reply, "but what do you want?"

"I want to see her."

The eye stared at me in surprise.

"And who may you be?"

The eye seemed to look at me unbelievingly when I gave my name. After a long silence, the eye had still not disappeared from the window.

"Look," I said, "go and tell whoever it may be that I'm here."

The window closed. I stood at the gate for a while, then went to sit in the cab. At last the gate opened and a little man in a frock coat (obviously hastily donned) burbled: "The Princess greatly regrets that she cannot receive you. She slept badly. You must have seen a manservant run past just now – she's sent for the doctor. Yes, the Princess is terribly sorry, but she's ill, she can't possibly receive you."

I managed not to laugh in this self-important little fellow's face, and said, as calmly as I could: "What a pity. Please tell the Princess from me that I too am sorry, and hope that she will soon recover."

"Yes, yes, she's ill, she was taken ill suddenly," the man in the frock coat kept saying. Once back in the hotel, I laughed heartily – and was overjoyed that my husband's stepmother had refused to see me.

My husband, of course, received a long telegram from her, telling him how devastated she was that she had not been able to see me.

*   *   *

From Finland, we went on to Pratolino via St Petersburg. Pratolino was my father-in-law [Paul Demidov]'s estate near Florence, which he left to his second wife, together with a very fine collection of pictures, including all his family portraits, and a lot of old silver. My husband's stepmother made a present of this estate to her daughter Maria.

After Pratolino we went to Switzerland, to Vevey, then to England, and finally to Paris, where we stayed at the Hotel Bristol, Place

Vendôme. Grandma Karamzin joined us there, and stayed in the same hotel.

On our arrival my husband wrote a note to Princess Mathilde Bonaparte,* his great-aunt, to say that he would like to present me to her. He then left the hotel, and I went upstairs to sit with Grandma Avrora. No more than half an hour had passed when I was told that Princess Mathilde had arrived and was waiting in our room.

Grandma was unwilling to go with me, and I hurried down alone, suffering torments of shyness. She greeted me with the words: "*Ma chère nièce. Elim vient de m'écrire que vous êtes à Paris, et, comme je sortais à ce moment je suis venue, voulant au plus vite faire la connaissance de ma nouvelle nièce.*" I apologised for making her wait, explaining that the hotel staff had not immediately realised that I was upstairs with Grandma Karamzin. On hearing that she too was in the hotel, Princess Mathilde immediately expressed a wish to see her. Grandma agreed, and we went up to her sitting room immediately.

The two sisters-in-law (they had been married to the Demidov brothers, Pavel and Anatole) had not seen each other for a long time. They embraced, sat down together on a sofa and began reminiscing.

Princess Mathilde invited us to her home on several occasions during our stay in Paris. She questioned us closely about the whole family, and about what was happening in Russia.

"*Car vous savez que je tiens à la Russie,*" she told me one day. "*Du reste, comme vous savez, je suis payée pour cela.*" Princess Mathilde and Anatole Demidov had never divorced, but had lived apart. As his widow she received a very large income from the Demidov factories, something like 200,000 roubles, which the family paid punctually.

One day, when I arrived to dine with her, she called my attention to the magnificent emeralds she was wearing and said: "*Ceci après ma mort sera à vous.*" I did not understand why she said this, and on our return to the hotel asked my husband what it meant. He explained that the emeralds belonged to the Demidov family, and that she had

---

* The niece of Napoleon I and the wife of Anatole Demidov.

many other jewels, all of which, according to her marriage contract with Anatole, should revert to the Demidovs after the Princess's death. She died, if I remember rightly, in 1908.

Her nephew and heir, Prince Louis Napoleon Bonaparte, in reply to my husband's enquiry about the jewels, said that they "had not been in her possession on the day of her death". This was more than strange. In her will the only jewels mentioned were those which belonged to her personally. Her heir claimed that she had sold the Demidov jewels before she died. I do not believe that she was capable of selling what did not belong to her. I wanted my husband to sue, but my husband did not want to drag his aunt's name through the courts. Besides, it would have been a costly business, and money was short because the family's Urals factories were going through a crisis.

In any case, when the Princess's jewels were put up for sale in Paris not so much as one little brooch or ring from the Demidov collection was among them. This confirmed my view that someone had sequestered them after the Princess's death.

In the autumn we returned to Petersburg. My husband's extended leave was over, and he started going to the Ministry of Foreign Affairs regularly. The senior official in the Ministry at the time was Prince Valerian Obolensky, a narrow bureaucrat. He took a dislike to my husband, but Elim was too independent to worry about that. No careerist, he always carried out his duties punctiliously. He wrote well, in Russian, English, and French. His despatches were admired in retrospect not only for the clarity of their analysis and the soundness of the advice given, but as veritable works of literature.

Izvolsky – under whom my husband served as First Secretary in Copenhagen, then as personal aide in the Ministry of Foreign Affairs, and finally as counsellor in our Paris embassy – once said to him in my presence: "I envy your talent as a writer, you not only express your thoughts clearly and effectively, but what I envy is your literary style. Your despatches read so very easily, like a good story."

Obolensky disliked my husband simply because he wanted to choose his subordinates for himself, not to have them wished upon him. My husband was impervious to his pin-pricks, and this irritated him even more. Elim had been forced upon him by no less a personage than Emperor Alexander III. On one occasion (before there was any talk of our betrothal), the Emperor remarked to the then Minister of Foreign Affairs, Giers: "I hear that Demidov has joined the Ministry. What department is he in?"

"The Administrative Department," said Giers.

"There you are, then!" the Emperor exclaimed. "You're always complaining that no one of good family goes into the Ministry, they all prefer the army, and when somebody does you hide him in the background. Transfer him to chancery."

"But Your Majesty, there are no vacancies in chancery."

"So he'll be a supernumerary."

My husband was transferred next day, to Obolensky's great chagrin.

There was a small bedroom in the department for a duty officer, who would be awakened if an encoded telegram arrived. My husband, on duty once, went to bed, but before he could fall asleep bugs began biting him. He did not realise what was happening until he lit the lamp and saw them. He rang for a ministry messenger, and showed him the bugs. Next day, he went to Obolensky and asked not to be put on night duty until the bugs were exterminated. The room was put in order, and all his colleagues were very grateful, but Obolensky became even more hostile.

One day he sent for my husband and asked him (you were still asked in those days) whether he would consent to be posted as third secretary to Washington. My husband realised that Obolensky merely wanted to ease him out of the chancery, and said that he had no desire to go to America because his business affairs in the Urals did not permit it. He would, however, happily go to London as an attaché [*a supernumerary member of the embassy staff*]. Obolensky made no objection, but told my husband to approach Baron Stahl, our Ambassador in London, himself. Stahl was in Petersburg at the time, and readily consented. This was how we came to be in London, where we spent eight very happy years.

Baron Stahl was a subtle and clever diplomat, from whom a great deal could be learned. He was like a kindly father to my husband throughout those eight years, and openly admired his abilities. I remember him calling on me one morning and saying: "I'm here because I know your husband is in chancery, and I want to make you my ally." [Stahl told her that he had refused to accept any nominee other than Demidov as Second Secretary, and asked her to "be his ally" in persuading her husband to remain in the diplomatic service, where such able people were "very precious", rather than leaving to look after his properties. He asked her not to tell her husband about their conversation: she did tell him, and he was "very moved".]

[A clique of jealous rivals spread unpleasant rumours about Elim, who considered it beneath his dignity to deny them. In 1905 he was appointed First Secretary in Vienna, where Prince Lev Urusov was Ambassador. Ambassadors were no longer consulted about appointments to junior diplomatic posts. Elim's ill-wishers filled the Ambassador's ears with stories of his "unpunctuality, laziness and excessive obduracy".] Urusov telegraphed the Ministry asking them to appoint someone else, because, although he did not know my husband personally, he was aware of his reputation. The Minister replied that the appointment stood, and that the Ambassador would see for himself that what some people said about my husband was untrue. My husband was serving in Copenhagen at the time under A. P. Izvolsky. We went straight from there to Vienna, without first requesting leave, as was usual on transfer to another post.

The Ambassador received my husband very coldly, which surprised him, since Urusov, as an orphaned child, had been looked after by Grandma Karamzin. One day, an acquaintance of my husband's arrived from Petersburg with the diplomatic mail, and we invited him to a meal. He asked how my husband was getting on with the Ambassador, and Elim replied that Urusov had given him a chilly reception to begin with, but after six months seemed rather more forthcoming.

Our guest saw that Elim had no inkling of Urusov's objection to his appointment – and told us all about it. My husband wanted to go to Urusov immediately and hand in his resignation, but our guest and I, with some difficulty, dissuaded him. A little while later, after one of their morning meetings, Urusov handed my husband a letter addressed by him to the Ministry and told him to read it.

The Ambassador had written that he had been "profoundly mistaken about Demidov", that the letters he had received at the time of my husband's appointment were utter nonsense, that he regretted his reluctance to accept Elim, and that he had never had such a punctual, efficient and intelligent First Secretary. (Urusov had previously served as ambassador in Rome and Paris, and as minister in Roumania.)

"You probably know that I was against your posting here," he said.

"Yes, Mr Ambassador, but I learned that only quite recently. Had I known right away I should not have accepted the appointment."

"I'm glad that you didn't know, and as you see I regret my telegrams and my personal letter to the Minister." After this, relations between my husband and the Ambassador were excellent.

Urusov now had complete confidence in Elim. Before leaving for Carlsbad to take a cure (while the counsellor, Sverbeev, was on leave in Russia) he gave my husband several blank sheets of paper, bearing his signature. My husband addressed messages to the Austrian Ministry of Foreign Affairs on such sheets, and also signed himself "Urusov" in reply to coded telegrams from Petersburg. (Urusov would obviously not have gone to Carlsbad if important political discussions had been in progress.)

On one occasion, someone spoke of Urusov as my husband's "chief", when both of them were present. My husband turned to Urusov and said: "Forgive me, Ambassador, but I do not regard you as my chief, I regard you as *primus inter pares*. I am always ready to carry out your instructions . . . but I shall give you my opinion on the matter in hand first." Urusov agreed completely, but was somewhat surprised. In his young days people trembled before their "chiefs", and no one dared express an opinion of his own.

It was quite different with Shevich, our Ambassador in Madrid, a pompous and peevish person. My husband was posted to Madrid from London. Five previous first secretaries had found it too much for them, and agitated for a transfer. My husband was appointed to Madrid in the hope – so they told him in the Ministry – that he would be able to conciliate Shevich.

We regretted having to leave London, where we had been very comfortable, but Spain of course had its attractions.

When the train drew into the station at Madrid we saw a tall, stout old man with a monocle, obviously on the lookout for someone. He came up to us and introduced himself as Shevich, Russian Ambassador to Spain. We were somewhat surprised – such politeness after all we had heard about him! We could share his carriage, and he would take us to the hotel in which we had reserved rooms.

He came into the hotel with us, made himself comfortable and launched into what was in effect a monologue lasting about an hour, painting Madrid society and life in Madrid in the darkest colours. According to him the Spanish were haughty, uncouth, and hostile to foreigners – no foreigner ever penetrated a Spanish home. He snubbed them in return.

I remember one example of his behaviour towards them, as described by himself. At perhaps the only dinner to which the Duchess of X invited him he was sitting, as Ambassador, on his hostess's right. "N'est ce pas, Monsieur l'Ambassadeur," she asked him "que nous sommes très hospitaliers à Madrid – les étrangers sont très bien accueillis?"

Shevich replied: "Je ne sais pas, Madame, car je ne suis pas ici que depuis six ans, et je n'ai pas eu le temps de le remarquer."

"That's how I deal with them!" he said.

After his departure, my husband remarked that if only a quarter of what he had said was true – "what a wasps' nest we have landed in!"

I replied that we must judge for ourselves, and that Shevich struck me as terribly jaundiced. In fact, we found Madrid society remarkably hospitable, friendly, and easy-going. The Duchess of Alba was very kind to me right from the start. I had not previously made her acquaintance, but her son, whom we had met in London, came to see me and said that his mother would have been happy to come herself, but that she had a heavy cold and was forbidden by the doctors to leave the house, and begged us to dine with her on a certain date.

When Shevich heard that we had been invited by the greatest lady in Spain he said to me (he always spoke French): "*Vous allez voir, l'on vous mettra au bout de la table, toute étrangère que vous êtes.*"

I replied: "*Si mes voisins seront agréables, cela ne me fait rien . . .*"

Next day he called on me to enquire where I had been seated – "*c'est tout au bout de la table, n'est-ce pas?*"

"*Non*", I replied, "*mais à la droite du maître de maison.*"

"*Pas possible.*"

"*Pourtant, c'est un fait.*"

* * *

We moved from the hotel to a spacious house, surrounded by a garden, on the Boulevard Castellano, but we remained in Spain for less than a year. Russia had few dealings, either diplomatic or commercial, with Spain in those days. A coded telegram from Petersburg was quite an event. There was nothing to do in chancery, but Shevich insisted that the whole diplomatic staff – the First Secretary (my husband), Second Secretary and Attaché – should be present every day. All three were required to attend twice daily, from 10 a.m. to noon, and from 3 to 5 p.m.

On their way to the chancery they had to look in on him. He would be sitting in his office, watch in hand. On one occasion he remarked that my husband was four minutes late. Looking at his own watch Elim saw that Shevich had set his own watch five minutes fast. All in all, life there was intolerable. Even I was the victim of Shevich's fault-finding. He would instruct me what dress I should wear for this or that occasion, and whether diamonds, pearls, or other jewellery would be appropriate.

On Wednesdays the whole embassy staff was commanded to lunch with the Ambassador. These lunches were torture for me. Shevich was at his most irritable and sarcastic on these occasions. I had steeled myself to attend, not wanting to make my husband's position more difficult still, but after one particularly ugly scene I told Elim that nothing on earth would ever compel me to lunch with Shevich again. As the only lady present, apart from his wife and daughter, I was sitting next to him. The attaché Kolemin had failed to appear. Shevich asked whether I had seen him that day. I had not.

"A quoi attribuez vous ce manque d'égard?" he asked, when lunch was half over.

"Je ne sais pas, mais je crois assez probable que Kolemin a peut-être simplement pris un jour de la semaine pour l'autre, il croit peut-être que c'est mardi. Dans tous les cas, à moins d'un accident, il vous aurait prévenu de l'impossibilité de venir à déjeuner."

Lunch was almost over when Kolemin flew into the dining room.

"Monsieur l'Ambassadeur, je vous prie de m'excuser, je ne sais vraiment comment vous dire mon désolement, je pensais qu'aujourd'hui c'est mardi."

Shevich showered him with vulgar abuse, then said ironically to me: "Et vous dîtes que vous n'avez pas vu Kolemin depuis quatre ou cinq jours."

I flared up, and said: "Monsieur l'Ambassadeur, je n'admets que qui que ce fût doute de la véracité de ma parole."

After which I avoided conversation with him. We went from the dining room to Shevich's study. In the course of conversation, my husband expressed an opinion on some unimportant matter, and Shevich suddenly shouted at the top of his voice: "C'est moi ici l'Ambassadeur, et c'est moi seul qui peut exprimer son avis!"

Knowing my husband's character, I was afraid that there would be a scene, and immediately rose to leave. Shevich was still shouting as we left. Mikhail Konstantinovich Zograf, our guest at the time and a great friend of my father's, had been present at the lunch, and remained behind when we left. As soon as we got home my husband telegraphed Petersburg, applying for leave and asking to be transferred to another post afterwards. Zograf returned with an offer from Shevich to express regret after a fashion, if Elim would take the initiative in seeking a reconciliation. "I am the Ambassador, you see, and cannot possibly apologise to a Secretary."

"What you fail to understand," said Zograf (who had been on intimate terms with Shevich since their youth) "is that Ambassadors, too, are just human beings."

The Ministry granted Elim's request for leave, and before he left Madrid telegraphed to inform him of his (temporary) posting as First Secretary to Copenhagen. The Ministry understood exactly what had happened.

I remained in Madrid for a while after my husband's departure to close the house and put the furniture in store. I called on Mme Shevich and her daughter Vera to say goodbye, but did not see him. On the day of my departure, my driver was surprised when I told him to circle the station and not to drive on to the concourse until the station clock showed that the train was due to depart in three minutes' time. (I knew that my maid and manservant were on the station with the tickets and sleeper reservations and I was carrying only one small bag.) I did this because I had seen Shevich's carriage in the station precinct. It all went according to plan. Quite a number of people had come to see me off. I jumped out of the car and ran to my compartment, surrounded by acquaintances, and, to my joy, the engine's whistle blew and the train began to move just as Shevich came hurrying towards me, so that I could not hear what he said, and we did not make our goodbyes.

In Petersburg, the Minister of Foreign Affairs had asked Elim about Shevich's standing in Spain. Everyone knew, my husband said, that he had left Spain because Shevich was difficult to get on with, but he did not intend to gossip, and enquiries about Shevich's standing should not be addressed to him.

When Shevich was asked to retire in 1905, I was told that he blamed my husband and me, but the reason was quite different. When the Baltic fleet was on its way to the Far East, Admiral Rozhdestvensky put in at one of the Spanish ports and requested Shevich by telegraph to come and see him. Shevich replied that it was not for the Ambassador to come to the Admiral, but for the Admiral to call on the Ambassador in Madrid. He had finally gone too far, and was removed from his post.

After Madrid, my husband served as First Secretary in Copenhagen, under A. P. Izvolsky, for about a year. Izvolsky was well-disposed towards him. They sometimes differed to begin with on political matters, but reached agreement after lengthy consideration. It was on the whole an agreeable partnership – unlike my husband's experience with Shevich, who only knew how to give orders, and made any exchange of views impossible.

Mme Izvolskaya was very kind and considerate. Shortly after my arrival I was taken ill with acute appendicitis. She came to see me several times on the day she was told of it, and sat with me for a long time.

Since my husband had been told that his posting to Copenhagen was temporary, and that a First Secretaryship would shortly fall vacant in Vienna, we had not transferred our effects from Madrid or looked for an apartment, but moved into a hotel.

While we were there, King Edward VII and Queen Alexandra paid a state visit to King Christian (Queen Alexandra's father). The whole diplomatic corps turned out to meet them at the station, and ambassadors and ministers were lined up in order of seniority, with embassy secretaries behind them. Apart from the diplomats there was also, of course, a large Danish welcoming party, with the King and the whole royal family at its head. As the King and Queen of England passed along the line of diplomats Edward VII suddenly caught sight of my husband, half hidden by Izvolsky, reached out a hand to him through a gap in the ranks of the envoys, drew him forward and said: "What are you doing here?"

"Well Sir, I am First Secretary of the Russian Legation here."

"I thought you left London a year ago for Madrid?"

"Yes, Your Majesty, so I did, but I have lately been transferred from Madrid to Copenhagen."

"Where is your wife?"

"She is in bed, having had a strong attack of appendicitis."

"Oh, I am sorry, may I come to see her?"

"Certainly, Sir, she will be delighted, she has been in bed for over three weeks, and she is very pleased to see anybody who is kind enough to come and see her." *

After a little further conversation, the King resumed his hand-shaking with the diplomats.

Izvolsky told me later in the day that there had been a certain amount of grumbling among his colleagues about the King's casual treatment of them and the special attention he had shown the Russian First Secretary. They had even tried to make Izvolsky resentful.

"He merely shook your hand and said a few polite words, whereas he conversed with your First Secretary longer than with anyone else."

His colleagues were surprised when Izvolsky said that he found that quite normal, since the King and he had not previously met, whereas the King and my husband had often met in London.

Two days later the King telephoned to ask whether he could take tea with me. I, of course, said yes. He chatted merrily, drinking tea at my bedside. I drank none, since I was still on a strict diet. He suddenly asked me whether I would do him a great favour.

I laughed, and said: "It depends what it is you want."

"Your motor car," he said. "If you could just let me have it for the rest of my stay here. You're bedridden and can't use it, and I shall be here only for ten days. The Danish court carriages move so slowly, and I know that you have a closed coupé."

I was of course glad to oblige.

He paid me frequent visits, and during one of them he and my husband began discussing foreign policy. The King mentioned the desirability of an Anglo-Russian rapprochement.

"You," meaning Russia, he said, "are politically close to France, and so are we, so our two countries should draw closer together."

My husband seized the opportunity to ask the King whether he knew Izvolsky, and whether he had spoken to him about it.

"No," said the King. "What can you tell me about your Minister?"

* Conversation in English in the original.

"That he is a very intelligent man, a subtle diplomat, and our future Minister of Foreign Affairs."

The King looked thoughtful.

"I strongly advise you", said my husband, "to talk to my Minister, tell him what you have just told me. You will see for yourself that he is a very intelligent man, and, I repeat, it is a 99 per cent certainty that he will be at the head of our Ministry of Foreign Affairs in the near future."

Two days later, the British Minister's wife, Lady Goshen, called on me.

"Just imagine," she said, "the King was to dine with us this evening, and the only other guests were to be important members of the English colony. But as usual the guest list was submitted to the King before invitations were sent out. He approved it, but this morning sent his adjutant to say that he would like your Minister and Mme Izvolskaya also to be invited. I have nothing against inviting the Izvolskys. As you know, we are on friendly terms, but this means that the placement has to be completely rearranged at the last minute, and the character of the dinner changes completely. We meant it to be an occasion solely for the English colony, we have invited none of Izvolsky's fellow envoys, and by inviting the Izvolskys my husband and I have incurred a few sour remarks. Don't you find it strange?"

Remembering my husband's conversation with the King, I mumbled something vague.

When Elim got home from Chancery on the following morning, he told me that after dinner at the British Legation the King had asked Izvolsky to sit beside him on a sofa, and had begun by mentioning his recent conversation with my husband on the desirability of a rapprochement between Russia and England. The King spent the whole evening on the sofa beside Izvolsky, and rose only to say goodbye to the British minister, Lady Goshen, and their guests.

The King had asked Izvolsky to keep their conversation between themselves. A. P. remarked that he was bound to report the gist of it to the Ministry of Foreign Affairs in Petersburg. The King said: "Yes, of course, but can you let me have a copy of what you write?"

Izvolsky wrote out a rough draft of their conversation, and asked Elim to write it out in French – since the King and he had spoken in that language.

My husband set about writing the report in his own room at home, and had nearly finished when I was informed that King Edward had called to say that he was coming to tea with me. I was no longer confined to my bed, but had not yet started going out. I received the King in our drawing room. This was a day or so before he was due to depart. After a little while my husband came into the drawing room to show the King his draft, and they began talking about policy again.

"Don't forget," the King said, "that I very much want more friendly relations between England and Russia, but I am obliged above all to go along with the views of my ministers, with public opinion, and also, of course, the Press."

Nevertheless, in this conversation with Izvolsky, the King laid the foundation for the Anglo-Russian Agreement.

We left Copenhagen for Vienna in spring 1905, before Izvolsky was appointed Minister of Foreign Affairs. After three and a half years as First Secretary in Vienna, my husband was recalled by Izvolsky to serve as his personal aide in the Ministry. Elim had requested a transfer to Petersburg because his factories in the Urals required urgent attention.

*   *   *

Throughout our eight years in London, King Edward VII and Queen Alexandra (Empress Maria Feodorovna's sister) had treated us with great kindness and generosity. England differed from other European countries in that newly arrived diplomats were not supposed to initiate social contacts. A new Embassy Secretary, with no contacts, was of course quite lost in a big city like London. An Ambassador or Minister made acquaintances immediately, but a new Secretary's arrival could pass unnoticed. My husband had English acquaintances from his schooldays, but had left Eton at the age of 15, and had not visited

England since. He was, moreover, a stay-at-home by nature, and so made no great effort to look up schoolfriends on arrival.

We arrived in England at the height of the London season in 1895. We were invited to Embassy dinners, and also to a "drawing room" – as Queen Victoria's official receptions were called. The whole diplomatic corps, and all London society, paraded before her and the rest of the royal family, the women curtseying and the men bowing low. We were also invited to court balls. But this was the limit of our penetration into London society in that first year.

Since Ambassador Stahl was the doyen of the diplomatic corps, we, that is to say the Russian embassy, presented ourselves before the Queen first. Almost all of us ladies wore traditional Russian costume (a tall head-dress and a long, sleeveless gown), which always created a sensation among English ladies and others with no national costume of their own for women. A head-dress with three ostrich feathers (the Prince of Wales's insignia) and, of course, a long train, were *de rigueur*.

Our social life was more or less limited to these few official occasions during our first year in London. I don't remember clearly whether it was in our first or second year that we were invited to dine at Marlborough House, then the residence of the Duke and Duchess of Edinburgh. She, of course, was a Russian Grand Duchess, sister of Alexander III. They knew my father-in-law and my own parents, and had met Elim when he was at Eton.

Staying with them at the time was their daughter, Princess Marie,* wife of Crown Prince Ferdinand of Roumania. It is difficult to imagine a more strikingly beautiful young woman than Princess Marie. She was fair-haired, shapely, with clear eyes and regular features. She died last autumn, as dowager queen of Roumania.

Our circle of acquaintance gradually widened. I had many relatives in England, because my great-grandfather, Count Vorontsov, had been Russian Ambassador in the reign of George III, and had given his daughter in marriage to the Earl of Pembroke. They had a son and

---

* Princess Marie of Edinburgh (Queen Marie of Roumania), Queen Victoria's grand-daughter.

five daughters. The daughters all married into aristocratic English families, and most of them had numerous children. Their descendants, although only distant relatives of mine, considered it their duty to be polite, and invited me to lunch or dinner. The Earl of Pembroke himself invited us to the famous grouse and pheasant shoots at his Wilton estate.

My husband was a good shot, an accomplishment greatly prized in England at that time, and we at once found ourselves invited to house parties elsewhere. We were guests of the Duke of Devonshire at Chatsworth, of the Earl of Ilchester, Mr Willy James, Lord Wimbledon and many others. I made friends with Mrs Willy James, and they regularly invited us, spring, summer, autumn, and winter to live on their estate of West Dean Park. There was a beautiful house with all conveniences, marvellous grounds and gardens. There was even a golf course, and it was there that I began to play that game.

The elderly Duchess of Devonshire was very kind. She invited us to hunts, we celebrated Christmas at their seat four years running, and we were often invited in summer to a smaller house of theirs outside London, where we could shake off the dust of the capital in the green countryside.

The Duchess was German by birth, and a great beauty in her early years. She had previously been married to the Duke of Manchester, but she and the Marquess of Hartington (the future Duke of Devonshire) were lovers for many years. The affair was broken off, and for some years after they seldom met until (as the Duke himself told me) the day when he was caught in a rainstorm almost outside the Duchess of Manchester's home. (She was a widow by then.) He had no umbrella, and it occurred to him that he could call on his former lover. It was 5 o'clock, and the Duchess was taking tea. She showed neither surprise nor pleasure when he appeared, but looked him straight in the eye, and said: "Do you still take two lumps of sugar in your tea?"* He became a frequent visitor, and eventually married her.

* In English in the original.

When we were in London, Hartington was an influential cabinet minister. One of his colleagues was Joe Chamberlain. On one occasion when we were Christmas guests at Chatsworth I found myself seated next to Chamberlain at dinner. I remember part of his conversation. He expounded his theory that every ambassador or minister ought to use his own language in his dealings with the Foreign Office of the country to which he was accredited. The Foreign Office personnel would also use their own language. Confidential interpreters would be on hand, whatever the language used.

"You Russians are marvellous linguists – you, for instance, could be taken for an English woman by any of us, you have no accent at all, but with rare exceptions we English know absolutely no languages except our own. It would be helpful to us, our young people would start learning foreign languages, and you Russians would be seen to be superior to us – at present, of course, French is the recognised diplomatic language in all chanceries."

King Edward VII and Queen Alexandra were always very kind to us. When we first came to London, Queen Victoria was still on the throne, and they were Prince and Princess of Wales. The Princess seldom went out, but the Prince often appeared at small dinner parties given in his honour. My husband and I were frequently invited "to meet H. R. H. the Prince of Wales", and after his accession, "H. M. the King". When he accepted an invitation, his hosts submitted their guest list to him in advance. He could approve it or strike out names and add others if he wished. Right at the beginning of our time in England we were invited to a soirée at Marlborough House. It was an evening of music and conversation. Most of those present were members of the royal family, including the Prince and Princess of Wales. It was there that I first met King George I of Greece,* the brother of our Empress and of the Princess of Wales. We had a long

---

* From a later memoir: When we arrived in Athens in August 1912 my husband presented his credentials to Crown Prince Constantine, who was acting as regent. We then left Athens for a time, and returned at the outbreak of the so-called "Balkan War". My husband had arrived a month before me. The day after my arrival King George left for Salonika, in the

conversation in the drawing room, and he introduced me to several other guests.

At those small dinner parties, the Prince of Wales liked to play a few rubbers of bridge, and my husband, who was considered a good player, was often one of the foursome.

After his accession, someone, I couldn't discover who, passed on some unflattering gossip about us, and the King told some of our friends to break off relations with us, giving no reason except that "they are not nice people". Some of our real friends stood up for us, and asked the King what stories he had been told, and by whom, but they were left none the wiser.

* * *

Sophie Torby was a great friend of mine, and a very clever, kind, jolly, hospitable woman. We made friends at once, and remained friends until the day she died. Her mother was Russian, the daughter of our great poet A. S. Pushkin, and her father was the Duke of Nassau.

Countess Torby told me that the King had said that she ought not to continue her friendship with us. She said that she knew us too well to let idle gossip end our relationship, and asked the King what had been said, and by whom, to turn him against us. The King declined to answer. She and I discussed at length who could have said what, and what we should do about it.

"In your place," she said, "I should seek an audience with the King and find out for myself."

"What grounds have I for requesting an audience, when neither I nor my husband feel that we are guilty of doing anything to offend him? If we did so it would, in my view, mean that we did feel guilty."

"What else can you do then? I'll think about it, and maybe find some way."

wake of the Greek army, which shortly afterwards took Salonika under Crown Prince Constantine's command. The King then entered the city – and was assassinated, so that I was not to see King George in Greece, and after England met him only once, briefly, in Russia, when he was the guest of Empress Maria Feodorovna.

A few days later we received an unexpected invitation from the Duke of Manchester "to meet the King". My husband and I thought it over carefully. We had no wish to risk a public scene with the King. We knew, however, that according to the rules of etiquette the guest list would have been submitted to the King, and that the same etiquette made it impossible to refuse the invitation except in case of illness or absence.

The result of our deliberations was that, since the invitation was addressed to me, I should write to the Duke regretfully declining, with a few polite words, but without giving reasons. The King, we felt sure, would notice our absence and the breach of protocol that it entailed. If any enquiry was made, I told my husband, it was obvious how we should reply: that knowing that meeting us could give the King no pleasure, we felt obliged, if only temporarily, not to appear where he would find himself in an intimate gathering of people he liked. There followed another invitation to dine and meet the King, which we also declined. Our would-be hostess, meeting me after our refusal, told me that she had shown the King her guest list and that he had sanctioned it.

"How can I explain your absence to him? He knows that you are in London, and probably also knows that you are out and about, so that it is not illness that prevents you accepting the invitation."

Without going into detail, I replied that I knew that our presence could not give the King pleasure, and that we would not wish to cause him the slightest discomfort.

Towards the end of the summer season we went on leave to Russia. We visited my parents in Tambov province, then went to Ryazan province where my husband's uncle had an estate. After spending the rest of the summer there we went on to Paris, by-passing Petersburg, I think. After ten days there my husband's leave was coming to the end, but he sent a telegram to the Ambassador in London, and requested an extension for a few days. Baron Stahl agreed, but said that he had been trying to track us down for some time, because an invitation from the King and Queen to go and stay with them at Sandringham for a few days' shooting was waiting for us in the Embassy.

The King's birthday fell on one of the days in question. My husband, half jokingly asked me, since I was the one who had favoured the tactic of absenting ourselves from the King's horizon, whether we should go. I, of course, replied at once that we should accept this invitation, since the King was evidently now better disposed towards us, and it was more than kind of him to show it so clearly. In fact, diplomats were rarely invited to Sandringham, the King's private estate.

Back from Paris, we almost immediately received an invitation from the Duchess of Manchester to dinner "to meet His Majesty the King". We, of course, accepted, and arrived a few minutes before the appointed time. All the other guests were present when the King arrived. He paused briefly in the doorway, saw us all standing in a semi-circle at the other end of the not very large room, quickly made for my husband, clapped him on the shoulder, and said how sorry he was that some misunderstanding had arisen between us and himself.

I remember him saying: "I was wrong", and that he would be very glad to see us at Sandringham. "Wherever have you been all this time?" he asked.*

"Your Embassy did not know where you were, only that you were in Russia . . . you were probably on some secret mission somewhere on Russia's Asian frontier . . ."

All this was said so kindly, and amiably, and the last part of it laughingly . . . My husband and I could scarcely believe our ears. Our respect for the King increased after he had so humanly acknowledged his error, and been first to seek a reconciliation.

King Edward VII was generally a good judge of people, but perhaps sometimes too ready to take offence.

* * *

We companions of Emperor Nicholas II's youth were cold-shouldered, except for Dimitri Sheremetev, whom he took with him on all his

---

* In English in the original.

excursions around Russia. This was of course explained by the influence of Empress Alexandra Feodorovna. She snubbed all of us because she was afraid that we might influence the Emperor.

Alexandra Feodorovna was a strange person. Her family life with the Emperor was irreproachable. But, realising the weakness of his character, she surrounded him with her own people, who would not dare to express an independent opinion. I was received by her only once. I arrived in Petersburg on one occasion, I forget from where, and Mama said "You've come just at the right time", and told me that I must accompany her to the Assembly of Nobles, to a concert to be given in the presence of the Emperor and Empress. I did my utmost to cry off, pleading fatigue after the journey. I very much wanted not to go to that concert. But Mama insisted.

We drove up to the small porch by which the imperial family and their retinues were to enter. Mama was then a senior lady-in-waiting to Empress Maria Feodorovna. She went to the Emperor's box, while I, with a number of other ladies, remained in the long through-gallery of the Assembly of Nobles. After a while the Emperor and Empress Alexandra Feodorovna with their suite entered on their way to their box. The other ladies and I stood lined up along the walls of the gallery. The Empress, as usual, walked by, bowing, but looking neither to right nor to left, but straight ahead. The Emperor, however, did look around, and bowed very politely. He suddenly caught sight of me, left the procession, came over and said: "You here! I'm sorry I didn't know."

"I got here only today," I replied.

"Are you here for long?"

I told him my plans.

"Right, we shall be meeting often."

At that moment the Empress, still marching ahead, looked round, saw the Emperor talking to me, came back, gave me her hand without a word of greeting, and said: "Niki, come on" – and off he went behind her. I stayed in Petersburg for three weeks or so, but of course was not invited to the Palace.

Count André Tolstoy
(1891–1963)

Count André Tolstoy, my stepfather, spent his childhood partly in the Hermitage Museum in St Petersburg, of which his father was the last pre-revolutionary Director, and partly on his parents' estate in Kagarlyk in the Ukraine.

Hopes of an academic career in natural science were dashed by war and revolution. He enlisted in 1915 as a cavalry officer in the elite Chevalier Guards regiment, fought the Germans and, after 1917, the Bolsheviks. In 1920 he served in the Crimea as aide-de-camp to General Wrangel, the Commander-in-Chief of the armed forces of southern Russia.

The extracts from his diary cover, in the main, the crucial months from 25 May to 14 November 1920, until the final evacuation of the whole army from Sevastopol. They shed light on the details of the fighting in this "last stand" of the White armies, and on the author's official and personal contacts with the British and American allies of the Whites, and contain some shrewd observations on Wrangel's character and behaviour.

In 1922, in Cannes on the French Riviera, André married my mother. They lived first in Nice, later in Paris, where they spent the war under German occupation, and then moved to New York, where he died in 1963.

25 MAY 1920: DZHANKOI

The offensive is developing successfully. Wrangel nervously paces the platform. So much sleep and so little action obviously does not suit his active nature. He feels frustrated, not being able to take part personally in the fighting in progress beyond the Isthmus.

Slashchev's landing was carried out successfully, but no news of his subsequent operations has been received. He is supposed to provide a covering force south of Melitopol, and cut off the advance of the Reds to the north. So far 14 cannon have been captured by General Kutepov's corps. Here in Dzhankoi there are two stationary trains, facing each other, one of them ours, with the Commander-in-Chief and Shatilov on board, the other housing the operations section and a whole collection of high-flying generals whose function is still not quite clear to me.

Ulagai, Yuzefovich, Pavlov, and our former divisional commander, a Don Cossack whose name escapes me for the moment [Bochayevsky]. The whole lot of them assemble for lunch and dinner, and discuss "battles in which they smote together". Ulagai's appearance is remarkable: a pure Asiatic, with a yellowy-brown complexion, vaguely Kalmyk but handsome features, and a narrow nose. He is very young-looking, without a single grey hair, and has a slight cast in his eye.

Georgievich, the general for special assignments, who is by way of being my chief, is an utter nonentity, and obviously an inveterate "staff rat". Wrangel's adjutants are both Cossacks. One of them, Pokrovsky, a Kuban Cossack, is a professional at his job as adjutant, and worships the Commander-in-Chief.

Wrangel seems very well disposed to me, and sometimes calls me in for a chat. Apparently he can't stand being alone. He is sociable by nature, and needs a lightning conductor for his vehement gestures and staggering remarks. His eyes are his most striking feature: they are light-coloured, whitish in fact, and when he feels the slightest emotion, or sometimes for no reason at all, they open wide and seem at first sight to express excitement. In reality their expression does not, in my opinion, change in accordance with his feelings. They are rather like beads. They might lead you to suppose that the man has no soul, and that he is entirely a creature of reflexes.

In the presence of some very powerful people I feel overawed. Strange as it may seem, Wrangel does not intimidate me in the least. He is extremely tactful and well-bred in his demeanour. He sometimes shouts at people who have acted wrongly, but is never rude and offensive. He sometimes gives you the feeling that he would like to get blind drunk, and "go full speed ahead", as he used to say in time gone by. According to Drizen, he always shows great interest and asks questions when he is told of some jollification.

Shatilov (decorated with George Crosses, Fourth and Third Class), makes an enchanting impression. He is Number One here, and perhaps the only person with some influence on the Commander-in-Chief. A very courteous and pleasant man, but. . . "General Staff". He is reputed to be very clever and talented. Very young-looking for a lieutenant-general. On operational matters most orders come directly from Wrangel. Shatilov only gives advice. Where civil administration and certain appointments are concerned, I think it possible that he has great influence. However, since Krivoshein's * arrival the burden of civil administration falls mainly on him.

The train has arrived at Novo-Alexeevka – a place familiar to me from last year, when we were advancing and retreating in spring 1919. Wrangel has inspected the footsoldiers of the Kuban units, and what is left of Kornilov's troops, some 500 men in all. They make a good impression, but there are so few of them. We are playing our last card.

Wrangel proposes to make his stand along the line of the Dniepr, turning the enemy's flank from Alexandrovsk to Melitopol or, more likely, to take position in groups. The Melitopol group will obviously, just in case, be facing Makhno,† who recently declared his support for Wrangel. The explanation for this is a crafty calculation, which unfortunately it is too dangerous to write about. Slashchev, who has landed with his 12,000-strong corps on the peninsula south of Melitopol, has probably already cut off the Bolsheviks' retreat.

I don't know what sort of impression the troops we saw made on Wrangel. They were strictly speaking mere remnants of former greatness. If he succeeds in creating a great Russian army from them he will be a bigger man than Napoleon! He undoubtedly has all the makings of a great man, but it is still hard to believe.

* Minister of Agriculture, 1906–15.
† Ukranian anarchist leader who led a peasant force hostile to the Reds and the Whites.

I have just seen the line units that were recently in battle. I envied them their tired faces and red eyes, their muddy boots and rain-soaked shirts, and the reverent awe with which they met Wrangel. Not so very long ago I viewed with contempt all those neatly turned-out, clean-shaven adjutants, and suddenly I find myself one of them. I feel bored, disgusted, aching to return to the regiment. It may, at this very moment, be manning some outpost, with blood relatives of mine unable to sleep, and anxiously straining their ears in the darkness.

Tomorrow they will move on, along the old familiar road, north-wards towards the Dniepr, with the same halting places, the same punishing skirmishes, the same warm sleepless nights ahead of them. The last card has been dealt. We have staked everything on it.

For the present I have absolutely nothing to do. Not knowing Wrangel as intimately as Drizen does, I cannot very well take the initiative and run along to his saloon, although my coupé, with its double bed, is located between his sleeping compartment and his saloon.

Since I shall probably be doing this job for at least two months I hope to settle into it quickly and make sure exactly which discussions I am allowed to be present at, and when I am expected to make myself scarce, retire into the background. What I shall miss terribly is exercise and the open-air outdoor life.

A remarkable man here is Lieutenant-General Babiev, commander of one of the Kuban regiments. He has been wounded fourteen times, his right hand is paralysed, and he wants to have it amputated and replace it with a hook, so that he can take hold of his sabre. Meanwhile he goes into battle holding the reins between his teeth and shooting from a revolver with his left, his one and only hand.

26 MAY 1920 : DZHANKOI

The news from the front is excellent. We have taken another two field pieces and 1,800 prisoners, trapped on the banks of the Sivash by Morozov's cavalry as they were retreating eastwards from Perekop. Slashchev has still not got through to the railway line. There will probably be news from him this evening. Here everyone's morale is high.

Wrangel has had the brilliant idea of letting all the prisoners make their way home and announcing this in proclamations dropped from aeroplanes behind Bolshevik lines. From what I have heard the English are trying to put pressure on us in our peace talks with the Reds, vetoing the passage of some freight through Constantinople. The visit to the front planned for today did not take place.

Wrangel is waiting for Slashchev's tactics to take shape, and for positive results on the right flank. What I still can't quite make out is whether Wrangel fully realises all the consequences of what he says and does. His enormous advantage is his ability to take lightning decisions and the boldness of his conceptions. The impression he gives is of instant decisiveness. Shatilov, in my view, acts as a brake on him, moderates his ardour, and at times soberly explains the possible consequences. It would be interesting to know whether he always keeps the Commander-in-Chief fully informed, or keeps some of it back, as Romanovsky used to with Denikin. He undoubtedly plays first violin.

Yesterday I had a lengthy *tête-à-tête* with Wrangel. I got him talking about the main actors in the early stages of the Revolution, and the more prominent generals of that period. I find his judgements unsatisfactory. I cannot help fancying that I hear the jingle of spurs in them. He evidently judges people superficially, without ever considering their reasons for acting in this or that way. Talking to him is extremely enjoyable. He is a brilliant, lively conversationalist, with expressive gestures, and a fund of mimicry. All this is extraordinarily interesting.

I sometimes wonder why I always feel impelled to look into other people's souls, and extract all that they have to offer so that I can clearly delineate for myself their personalities. I am probably one of those people who can be called "students of life". Wrangel is planning a trip to Melitopol as soon as his communications with Slashchev are in order, and then, for one day, back to Sevastopol, ready for a tour of the front by motor car once he takes up position on the Dniepr again. This will be interesting.

It is amusing to find that Wrangel blushes easily. Especially when he can be suspected of weakness, physical or mental. Pavlov (Lieutenant-General) is a remarkably modest and likeable man. Every such *tête-à-tête*, of course, raises my stock in this stagnant staff atmosphere. It's *War and Peace* – there's no more to be said.

27 MAY 1920 : DZHANKOI

In some sector or other the natives – a Circassian riff-raff of some sort – have cleared out. Revishin has been relieved of his command of that brigade, and replaced by Colonel Shinkarenko, who until now has been travelling with us and, like Ulagai and Pavlov, was part of our stock of "spare staff officers". Things apparently continue to go well.

According to a renegade officer taken prisoner, the Bolsheviks are being given a lot of trouble in the Alexandrovsk and Verkhnii Tokmak area by Makhno's forces, who are hanging Jews in large numbers. I walked round with Wrangel this morning, but only as one of his "suite". The Don Cossack ataman Bochayevsky is back. The one and only way in which I feel I can be useful is by reporting promptly all abuses and complaints urgently requiring investigation.

Yesterday, for instance, we had to prosecute the commander of a Don Cossack unit for illegal requisitioning of horses. At present, of course, all this is on such a minimal scale that the Commander-in-Chief is very approachable. If it could be done on a larger scale, that would be ideal.

Wrangel, of course, has absolutely no intellectual depth. Anyone who mentions anything at all out of the ordinary to him he regards as a hopeless madman. Konovalov (the Quartermaster-General) flew out this morning to join Slashchev and has not yet returned. Wrangel is worried about him – he seems to value him highly. Konovalov returned in the evening. He had spoken to Slashchev personally. Melitopol is expected to be taken by nightfall. In the course of his landing Slashchev took 1,800 prisoners, 20 machine guns, etc. Wrangel proposes to go to Melitopol tomorrow evening, and then back to Sevastopol for two days.

After dinner I went for a drive, and a walk round the grounds of a small estate, with Wrangel and his adjutant. Afterwards drank tea with him. He reminisced in very lively fashion about his regimental service before and in the early days of the war. Most people, according to him, are "Homeric blockheads". Including M. V. Rodzyanko,* who recently wrote him what seems to have been a really stupid letter, full of gratuitous advice.

28 MAY 1920

Shatilov got back from Sevastopol this morning. I don't know what news he brought. He will apparently be staying here with the operations section of the staff when we go to Sevastopol.

Slashchev has occupied Melitopol. I doubt whether we can get through to it today, since our centre has not yet advanced far enough north. The Dniepr crossings are expected to be in our hands by evening. Particularly important, of course, is the bridge in the village of Kakhovka.

I have remembered an amusing story about Babiev. Last year, in the Caucasus, he got very drunk in some Kuban Cossack village, gave orders for a cannon to be lugged into his room and discharged a live shell at his own reflection in a mirror. The house was, of course, wrecked, and burnt down to its foundations.

I have just heard the impressions of the Englishmen who have arrived from the Perekop sector. They say that the morale of the troops is astonishing. They observed the engagement at Chaplinka. They saw our regiment among others. It has evidently seen little action so far, and has had only one soldier wounded. The mixed units,

* President of the Duma, 1911–17.

on the other hand, have suffered heavy casualties. About two-thirds of Markov's force are said to have been knocked out.

Wrangel has been extremely busy since Shatilov's return. Consultations of some sort are in progress – in all probability on foreign relations. Wrangel seems to have begun hating the English. I wonder how he feels about the Germans? At table, conversation is almost exclusively about his Caucasian campaigns, and whenever he forgets something an obliging chorus helps his memory. He is, I find, biased in favour of his own units (meaning those with whom he began the campaign), which, however, is understandable. All the people who came to the fore in the Kuban campaigns. His favourite is undoubtedly Colonel Shinkarenko, who at 28 is about to be promoted to general. In capturing Melitopol, Slashchev has cut off three Red armoured trains. Our victories continue. If we succeed in capturing the quartermaster's stores in Kakhovka and preventing the enemy's supply wagons from crossing the river, his *débâcle* will be complete.

Grain prices in Sevastopol fell by 50 per cent on the first day of the offensive.

Our trip to Melitopol will probably take place tomorrow. General Georgievich (aide-de-camp) has more influence than I thought. A revolting character, makes me sick to look at him. But too soft to do much harm.

Today I was present at Shatilov's evening report. He undoubtedly carries enormous weight in operational matters. He reports fully and comprehensively with incredible speed. Wrangel took his advice today on two points. Shatilov expresses his opinion very tersely and positively. I wonder whether his advice is invariably accepted? The resistance of the Reds in the Perekop sector is getting stiffer: they have thrown in a fresh division from across the Dniepr. Slashchev reports stubborn fighting on the approaches to Melitopol too. I don't want to be a pessimist but there seems to be a bit of a hitch: we have run out of reserves. And before they reach the Dniepr line they may lose half of what is not a very big army to begin with. I spent the evening with Wrangel.

Good news from the flanks this morning. The advance continues, but with fighting. Pisarev has made a mess of things again. His combined corps consists mainly of Cossacks. Yet again a number of them abandoned their battery and ran away in the night.

Wrangel spoke to the corps commander on the direct line and shouted so loud that it could be heard out on the platform. Wrangel shares his strategic plans with me in the evening. He apparently needs an audience so that he can think aloud. He doesn't want any special response – you just have to show "unbounded interest" and give occasional respectful sighs of admiration. You can capture his interest only with adventure yarns or anecdotes from the battlefield.

The heat is tropical. Wrangel makes no attempt to conceal his anxiety when things are not going as well as he could wish. He just can't keep still today, he's so worried for the Cossacks. The news from Slashchev isn't bad: he is advancing towards Serolazy in the rear of the group attacking Pisarev. Kutepov, who seemed hard-pressed yesterday has made a stand and thrown the Reds back. Wrangel, who has dashed to the aerodrome several times a day to meet pilots as they fly in, seems no longer anxious about the outcome of the operation.

Yesterday I took a walk with Flag Captain Androsov, whom I may not have mentioned before. He is my neighbour at table. I liked him from the start for his outspokenness at table. He earns a plus mark. I was struck, and a little alarmed, by the similarity between his and my observations of Wrangel's entourage.

The central theme of our discussions was, of course, Shatilov. Androsov has been with Wrangel two months, yet his conclusions are remarkably similar to mine. I deduced from his conversation that he had been considerably closer to Wrangel to begin with, but had apparently been squeezed out by the General Staff clique. He mentioned, among other things, having heard it said on various occasions that Shatilov is now what Romanovsky was in earlier circumstances. He gave me much illuminating information, and confirmed many of my suspicions.

30 MAY 1920: DZHANKOI

Good news from the front. Our troops have taken Aleshka. Kutepov's forces are ten *versts* from Kakhovka. Slashchev is also advancing, north-westward. The assault on the Kakhovka bridgehead has begun.

[Wrangel] is, of course, no ruler. He is a military man, a cavalry general, pure and simple. He has not the slightest desire to educate himself in the arts of government. But he is terribly enthusiastic about military planning. He talks about his plans for the future remarkably readily, openly, and sometimes quite unguardedly with many others present. He is quite naive at times, like a child.

As soon as Kakhovka was taken, we left for Sevastopol. Kutepov has come out on the Dniepr, i.e. is occupying a line from Aleshka to Kakhovka and beyond. Wrangel appears to be very tired. He talked to Yuzefovich and Ulagai throughout the journey. I too sat with him a lot. He talked mainly about technical military plans for the future. People often approach him for permission to change names, or take additional ones. People in a hurry to take advantage of his "caliphate for an hour", so that they can do their little deals.

31 MAY 1920 : SEVASTOPOL

Our arrival here caused such a commotion that my head was simply spinning. Wrangel has been receiving dignitaries all day long without a break. The topic of the day is a monarchist plot involving that block-head Romeo, who, however, has managed to escape abroad by sea.

Many prominent regular officers were arrested just before Wrangel's arrival. The ringleader was a dreadful scoundrel, and a Jew into the bargain. The amateurishness of this conspiracy is astounding. I do not, however, know the details. The most important person here, of course, is Krivoshein. God willing, he will finally take over the whole civilian administration. This is made easier by Shatilov's continued absence at the front. Relations with the foreigners have greatly deteriorated since Wrangel launched his offensive in spite of their categorical veto.

The English now apparently intend not merely not to help but in every way possible to hinder and delay our shipments in Constantinople. I am able to write very little while we are here. I shall try to catch up later, on the train. Life is very uncomfortable at present, since Drizen's room is occupied by Baroness Wrangel, and I have to live like a pig. I hope that next time she will no longer be here.

1 JUNE 1920: SEVASTOPOL

Just a few more words before finishing the dispatchable part of my short journal. The *Benbow* returned today, quite unexpectedly. Carpendale is very enthusiastic because of Wrangel, doing all he can sending desperate letters and telegrams to de Robec. Milne's chief-of-staff is expected to arrive with most important news. When he arrives, we shall probably go to the front again that evening.

I went to the *Benbow* on an errand for Wrangel, and was very warmly welcomed by old friends. Alesia Wrangel loads me with little commissions of her own, which I consider pretty tactless, although she is very nice. At present Wrangel is holding grandiose meetings of some sort, the content of which is unknown to me.

News from the front is good: six more cannon and a number of prisoners taken. A new medal has been authorised: the Order of Saint Nicholas the Miracle-Worker, awarded for exceptional bravery in battle. Only one officer has so far received it.

3 JUNE 1920: DZHANKOI

We left Sevastopol at 5 today and arrived here at 10 p.m. The same hustle and bustle went on throughout the last two days: an incredible commotion. I personally had enough to do receiving an enormous quantity of petitions, complaints, proposals, and reports.

The current sensation – the monarchist conspiracy among the sailors, in which Leikhtenbergsky was also implicated, ending with a summons to appear before Wrangel, and a tremendous telling-off, after which they were dismissed looking like scalded cats. They were all amnestied except for the actual ringleader, Loginski, undoubtedly a Bolshevik provocateur, and the matter was not brought to trial.

I personally feel that I helped to bring about two good things. First, I persuaded Wrangel not to send to the British authorities some ill-chosen excerpts from the Bolshevik newspapers, although Trubetskoy, head of the administration of foreign affairs, was insisting on it. Secondly, I saved the writer Anatole Kamenski from expulsion from the Crimea: he was the producer of a pornographic play by Arthur Schnitzler, *Khorovod*,* banned by the censor. This last achievement cost me a great effort. In my opinion we have too few talented people left to be banishing them from Russia for such trivial reasons.

A new land law has been promulgated, but is unlikely to be the last. Its preamble is a brilliant explanatory note finalised by Krivoshein. Some, of course, will be satisfied, others dissatisfied, as always. The morale of the high command is at present tremendous. Operations at the front are reaching their conclusion with the complete defeat of the enemy, who is already running as fast as his legs will carry him.

The whole Dniepr line, from the estuary to Alexandrovsk, will be occupied within a couple of days. This means enormous reserves of grain and of foodstuffs generally. Prices have plunged in all the towns except Sevastopol itself. Robberies, except for horse rustling by the cavalry, have ceased completely and, if we believe our information, the population gives us a very good welcome. The stocks of shells and cartridges taken by us are also large. Our card is not yet beaten! We have got through the first stage!

---

* *Reigen* (1900), translated into English as *Hands Around* but perhaps best known as *La Ronde*, the title of a 1950 film directed by Max Ophuls.

Morale on the staff is further raised by the arrival of General Drashchenko, our military representative in Batum. The information brought by him is as follows. The Terek province and almost all the mountain peoples have risen against the Reds. The Batum district, which now calls itself Adzharistan, humbly petitions Wrangel to appoint their ruler when the British occupation ends. Georgia offers us a military alliance. Azerbaijan, like Batum, pays homage. The rebellion in the Yekaterinoslav province is spreading.

With regard to our allies, there too things are not as bad as it seemed. We have received a telegram from Struve,* who is now in Paris. He reports a statement by Lloyd George in the House of Commons, that in view of Wrangel's offensive, Britain considers itself free of all obligations to him, and is terminating all aid. But another telegram from the same source, received one day later, says that a ship has sailed from England, bound for the Crimea, with a cargo of rifles and ammunition. Planes and shells (originating from France) are on their way via Serbia and Bulgaria. The main thing now is to obtain petrol.

The Poles are taking a hiding in spite of their numerical superiority. They will undoubtedly be smashed in the end. Our tour of the front begins tomorrow.

4 JUNE 1920

We left Dzhankoi at 4.30. No special news from the front. Managed to get 90 saddles from the English and send them to Barbovich.

Wrangel read me an order he had written for the troops and asked my opinion. The order was worded excellently. He is unquestionably talented.

Had a quite interesting conversation with a very sensible Englishman in charge of troop movements. Like all of them, he is in raptures over our women, and especially their spiritual beauty. We shall be in

* P. B. Struve: Liberal politician (an ex-Marxist) and Wrangel's Minister of Foreign Affairs.

Melitopol by evening, and spend the whole of tomorrow there. We shall go on from there to Pisareva, and then to Sevastopol for two days.

MELITOPOL

We arrived in the evening. Met by Slashchev in his clownish fur-trimmed uniform. He was, as always, under the influence of a heavy dose of cocaine, and giggled incessantly. After a quick conference with him, Wrangel inspected the guard of honour and thanked them in a brief speech. There was an enormous crowd on the platform. We then dashed to the cars with cinematographic haste and sped to the cathedral square for a service, and an address from Bishop Antonii. An enormous crowd, about 3,000 people, packed the square.

When the service was over, Wrangel mounted the dais and made an absolutely stupendous speech. He really is a staggeringly accomplished orator! This was one of the most powerful speeches I have ever heard. His theme was "what are we fighting for?". There was dead silence. He mentioned the Jews, and even the "master" whom the Russian people would choose for itself. He ended by calling for "three cheers for our poor mutilated motherland". The cheering was colossal, the crush incredible. Many people were throwing flowers. Women wept, and old men crossed themselves. He must have made an enormous impression with his bearing and his gestures.

After this we left with the same cinematographic haste. It is now late night and we are bound for Dzhankoy, from which we shall set out tomorrow morning in Kutepov's direction. I sat for much of the journey *tête-à-tête* with Wrangel, and we talked quite frankly. He seems very well disposed to me, and, strange as it may seem, is interested in my opinion. He complained of a shortage of able people. He will try to get Boyle (the Canadian) sent from Bucharest and perhaps Misha Tereshchenko,* though not of course in the role of minister. (The last named is unlikely to accept a secondary post.)

* Minister of Finance, then Minister of Foreign Affairs in the Provisional Government, 1917.

We arrived this morning. Shatilov left for Sevastopol at 2.

I saw V. Pashkov en route. He is getting ready to go abroad to settle family business. My friend Littledale, newly arrived from Genichesk, gave me a lot of interesting information about Bolshevik atrocities and Jewish highhandedness there. I quickly reported this to Wrangel and to my great joy immediate measures were taken. In addition, I have primed Colonel Ilinskii, who is on his way there to take command of the garrison. We leave for Yushun tonight, and after inspecting Kutepov's corps, go on to my brother regiments on the Dniepr.

6 JUNE 1920

We left by car at 8 for Chaplinka, H.Q. of Kutepov's First Corps. Heat, terrible dust, and wind.

We lunched at H.Q., then went with Kutepov to inspect the Kornilov division. Marvellous troops, staggering morale. They gave us no end of food and drink. There has been absolutely no looting by Kutepov's corps. From what the officers say the civilian population, who were initially distrustful, are astounded.

We went on to Markov's division and a repetition of our experience with Kornilov's. I was struck by one of Markov's regimental commanders: 23 years old, a colonel, with a George Cross and one arm, and an extraordinarily attractive appearance. At table one of Kornilov's officers produced a splendid gold watch and chain, and laughingly declared that he had done well out of the capture of Kakhovka. When I later informed Wrangel of this in private conversation he was incredibly indignant. There really is no looting except among the Don Cossack corps, where superhuman efforts to suppress it are being made.

We shared a car with Kutepov throughout the inspection. He was very nice to me, and recalled Novorossiisk and our previous meetings. Vanik says that Kutepov always singles him out too and treats him with special attention and courtesy.

Wrangel's conversations with Kutepov are extraordinarily comic.

Kutepov apparently worships him. They discussed the liquidation of the Jews, etc. In general these two understand each other perfectly.

We reached Kakhovka before sunset, and found it directly at the disposal of our squadron, which is quartered moreover in the same houses as last year. They sent us horses when we were a *verst* away from the outskirts of the *shtetl*,* so that dust raised by the cars would not attract artillery fire from across the Dniepr.

As I rode along the street to my billet I recognised a group of comrades including both Vanik and Roman Pushkin. Mishka Bezobrazov, who is the new commander's adjutant, had ridden out to meet us beforehand. I rode up to greet them and learned the programme for the evening: first, inspection of the troops, i.e. the combined Guards Regiment; then a dinner for the senior officers with Danilov (brigade commander); followed by a glass of wine with all the officers in somebody's assembly room. We all got thoroughly drunk. I sat between Vanik and Roman Pushkin.

The officers of our unit of course swarmed round me like flies. Happily, I had brought parcels and letters for several of them. Wrangel himself drank a fair amount, and called me over several times to ask me to take him home in time before he got too drunk. Inevitably, a lot of speeches were made. All the officers were very pleased with his speeches. He is undoubtedly a talented orator.

Resnyansky's appointment has created a great feeling of unity among all the officers, including those of the second Guards Division, who now form a single regiment with ourselves. Danilov was very nice to me and invited me to spend the night at his place. The regimental inspection went well. Our own troops (Cuirassier Division) are still all on foot. The Commander-in-Chief went home at 2 a.m., and I made my way to Vanik's quarters, to join a gathering of our closest friends. We had, of course, much of interest to tell each other. I sat with them until 5 a.m., after which I lay on a sofa in Danilov's quarters for two hours.

* *shtetl*: a small Jewish town or village.

Happily, my present function has not affected people's behaviour towards me in the least. One person particularly pleased to see me was Bezobrazov. Kossikovsky tried at first to interrogate me, and avoided meeting my eye, which enraged me. But after a few unsuccessful attempts I gave up trying to converse with him. Danilov, our host at dinner, asked me to sit next to him and, naturally, the ice melted. There was a good deal of talk about Wrangel, who has caused much dissatisfaction among the officers by appointing Resnyansky and incurred the hatred of the Cuirassiers themselves, who consider that he was rude to Danilov on the telephone. We parted, all in all, on good terms, and I didn't see him again. He behaved quite stupidly at the feast, trying to supervise the drinking and minor festive observances, which irritated Vanik unspeakably. But, by and large, the celebrations went very well, and Wrangel was cheered heartily. He seemed to be very pleased with the look of our soldiers, and with the evening's proceedings.

7 JUNE 1920

We left for Bolshiye Mayaki at 9 a.m. to inspect Second Brigade, which forms part of Barbovich's division. Another inspection, and another lavish and interminable lunch. Yerofeyev, a poet and singer belonging to the Akhtir Regiment, sang while we lunched. Charming and moving songs full of ancient Akhtir lore.

Between the inspection and lunch, Wrangel went for a wash and took advantage of that moment to call me in and question me about the regiment and about the local mood. He evidently thinks that Resnyansky's appointment was a great mistake. Wrangel has promised Danilov to get rid of Resnyansky quickly – which made him indescribably happy.

When we got back to the train at Yushun I again spent the whole evening talking to him. I suggested to him that he should take along a large sum of money to meet the needs of petitioners encountered on his tours. He seized on this eagerly, realising how it could increase his popularity. We have received a telegram to say that Percy, the head of the British mission, is leaving on 12 June, and would like to see Wrangel before he goes. Wrangel plans to be in Sevastopol on the evening of the 11th. We were all terribly tired after our travels and slept a very long time. The Kornilov regiments were presented with banners and ribbons for their efforts, which seemed to make them immensely happy.

8 JUNE 1920: DZHANKOI

We got here early in the morning. This was a busy day for me, since a whole pile of correspondence and papers of all kinds were waiting for the Commander-in-Chief. He too was busy all morning and for much of the afternoon. After tea I went for a walk with him, and we spent some time together after dinner.

Our conversation was again about the internal life of the regiment, and our common concerns. Wrangel is a very tiring person in large doses. He keeps jumping up and running to the map. His head is at work in one direction all the time, he is terribly absorbed in his task. There is never a minute in which he is not chewing over some plan, or impatiently awaiting somebody's arrival.

There was a very interesting communication from a Guards officer who had just escaped from imprisonment by the Bolsheviks. Officers whom they manage to get as far as divisional headquarters are not then harmed, and are offered a choice between concentration camp with forced labour, or service in the Bolshevik forces after a three-month course in which they are given a "communist look". He had escaped from the other side of the Dniepr, which he swam across with great difficulty. He also said that the local people are very favourably disposed to us, and give food to prisoners in villages along the way.

In the evening I had a very interesting conversation with Georgievich and the Commander-in-Chief. As soon as the conversation developed into an assessment of persons around us, that "nonentity's" face assumed a cunning and absent-minded look. He asserted that it is extremely dangerous for Wrangel to pay attention to trivial matters which those around him mention, and as an example mentioned Androsov, whom he regards as a fool. Georgievich is, it seems, shortly leaving this place. Let's hope that he is not replaced by someone worse. Shatilov is due tomorrow, and we shall then pay a visit to Shatilov in Melitopol where more car rides await us.

It is assumed that the Reds cannot go over to the offensive in less than a month's time, because they are too preoccupied on the Polish front. If this is true, there is some chance that our card will win! I am very much afraid that plotters may succeed in bumping Wrangel off. A second planned attack on our train has been discovered!

9 JUNE 1920

Shatilov arrived this morning, but brought no special news. Another arrival was Miklashevsky, who is trundled round in the role of "special assignments general", and evidently given only casual work to do.

At teatime I witnessed an unusually warm dispute between Shatilov and Wrangel. I could see, however, that Wrangel does not always give in to him but sticks to his guns in important matters. He, of course, is the one who sparks it off. It was all about the impossibility for the government of immediately redeeming with banknotes promissory notes issued in return for requisitioned horses. Wrangel shouted that this meant cheating the civilian population, that he would withdraw the army back into the Crimea, but whatever happened refused to become known as someone who defrauded civilians, that he would deprive his staff of their pay, and so on. Shatilov tried to show him that in this respect there was no difference between paper money and the gold reserve.

Wrangel is introducing what I regard as a very harmful measure: giving Stogov, commander of the Sevastopol garrison, full powers to expel anyone he wishes from the city. This enables Stogov to clip Krivoshein's wings drastically, and in general, if he is ill-disposed towards him, to make things very unpleasant for Krivoshein and even cause bad blood between him and Wrangel. At the first clash between them Krivoshein will refuse any compromise and will quit his post to take up a very lucrative position in the Paris banks. [Boris] Chicherin and Levka Gagarin passed through, on their way to Sevastopol, then to our regiment, as a consequence of the withdrawal of the British mission.

We left for Melitopol at 5 p.m. I spent half the journey reading all sorts of trash, even sinking as low as Arsène Lupin,* and after dinner in the evening sat talking *tête-à-tête* with Wrangel about bygone carousals and balls in Petersburg. From the animation and interest with which he talks about these things it is evident that he would dearly love right now to go on a spree. He complained that he has no private life at all.

We are supposed to be in Sevastopol at 11 p.m. We shall spend the time till then inspecting Slashchev. We reached Melitopol at 12 midnight.

10 JUNE 1920

We left around 9 a.m. Slashchev met us on the station at Fyodorovka.

We reached Bolshoy Tokmak at 1 p.m., where the usual ceremonial was observed, comprising a religious service, "organised civilians", and inspection of the troops.

News arrived that the enemy has gone over to the attack throughout this sector. We could hear the bombardment. I wonder whether this is the beginning of a major offensive or merely a local probing operation?

From Tokmak, where we saw one brigade of 34th Division, we proceeded on horseback to Molochnoye, where we inspected a second brigade, commanded by General Tuneberg, former commander of the Novorossiisk garrison. He has very few effectives, but they are fighting fit.

In the German settlements the pastors had organised receptions

---

* A reference to the French gentleman thief created by Maurice Leblanc (1864–1941).

wherever we went. We dined with Tuneberg, and young German ladies waited at table. Once again, I spent the whole evening *tête-à-tête* with Wrangel. He seems to find my company agreeable but, apart from that, he cannot bear being alone, he has to have someone to talk to. He takes a very optimistic view of the Red offensive in the Tokmak region, as of everything else, and thinks that it will be halted as soon as we have completed our regrouping. I have a definite impression that Shatilov takes a serious view of this matter.

We arrived at Melitopol around midnight. The Reds have changed our plans for us and instead of further tours of inspection we are returning directly to Sevastopol for a few days, with some prospect of a day in Yalta, which would suit me very well. Our arrival in Sevastopol is timed for midday tomorrow.

11 JUNE 1920: SEVASTOPOL

We arrived around 2 p.m. On the journey I sat with Wrangel and Miklashevsky. The same old subjects of conversation. As usual the senior officers were on the station to receive us and report.

In our quarters I found a whole heap of requests, which I pored over for several hours. In the afternoon I went looking for the Pashkovs and had tea with them. Alka is definitely returning to his regiment, and Vasilka seems to have arranged his departure and will probably travel via Malta.

We have already received several collective resolutions from the peasant assemblies of large villages expressing their gratitude for the new land law and their total support for our army. I find this quite significant.

12 JUNE 1920

Very busy this morning. A kaleidoscope of familiar faces in the Commander-in-Chief's reception room. I am more and more overwhelmed by the flood of petitions and petitioners. Any number of unfortunate widows of men killed in the Volunteer Army, in receipt of no relief. Their position is disastrous, and I am absolutely powerless to help. For one thing because the government is short of bank notes, and for another because of the hold-ups to which these papers are subjected by military bureaucrats.

An order promulgated today appoints Krivoshein assistant to the Commander-in-Chief for Civil Affairs. They've finally tied him down! I regard this order as a matter of enormous importance. This combination is unlikely to impress the Western democracies favourably!

Makhrov (Chief of Staff) is being sent to represent us in Poland, and Shatilov officially takes over from him. After dinner I drove to Balaclava with the Wrangels and Krivoshein. I had never suspected that there was such a charming spot only eight *versts* away! I have never seen any seaside place to equal its singularity and its theatrical picturesqueness.

13 JUNE 1920

Went to the baths till 11 a.m., then was terribly busy all day till dinner time.

There was an official farewell lunch for the British, who are leaving only six people here, under the Chief of Staff, Percy. Wrangel made another excellent speech, indeed the speech of a diplomat, brilliantly translated by Zvyagintsov. Percy's speech in reply, though of course not so good, was warm and sincere. After they left I stayed on with Piper, discussing his closest assistants (!!!). Krivoshein joined us, then, after his departure, we went down to the ladies, and put ourselves at the disposal of Mme Shatilova, who is not very young, but not very repulsive. I held my own for an hour, then went to my own house, where I have managed to make myself quite comfortable, and to bed.

The news is that Novorossiisk has been occupied by rebel Kuban Cossacks under the command of Colonel Rostikov. If the whole Kuban has risen it changes the game completely, and our chances are multiplied. Petrol and coal have arrived in great quantities.

14 JUNE 1920

This morning the usual kaleidoscopic comings and goings in the reception room. No special news from the front.

A submarine with General Artifeksov on board has sailed for Novorossiisk to check the rumour that the place has been taken by rebel Cossacks. In the afternoon saw the Pashkovs, and went with them to bathe in the sea from a boat. Water 23°C.

In the evening tried to get drunk at Dmitri Ivanovich's girlfriend's place. Failed to get drunk, and the lady makes a nuisance of herself.

15 JUNE 1920

Usual sort of morning. The petitioners inevitably include ladies who come along mainly for "little chats" with the adjutants. Sometimes there are very dramatic scenes.

Saw the Pashkovs again this afternoon. The American Admiral McCoy and his flag captain, Köhler, were invited for after dinner. Krivoshein and Mme Shatilova (a vulgar blonde of Balzacian years, with a quite pretty physiognomy) also joined us. The Admiral speaks French with incredible physical difficulty, and is a laborious and silent thinker. His flag captain, on the other hand, is a remarkably lively, intelligent and rather uncouth polyglot. Really more German than anything else.

They invited Wrangel to take a day trip to Yalta, returning the same evening. Departure time 9 a.m.

16 JUNE 1920

We left, not without a few oaths, because Wrangel's launch arrived late at the quay. This is the first time I have been aboard an American naval vessel.

On this torpedo boat, I am bound to say, everything, not excluding the food, was considerably worse than it is with the British. We wasted 1½ hours *en route* because of a breakdown in the boilers, after which we sailed to Yalta at 29 knots. We had warned them specially by telephone that we wanted no receptions or guards of honour or formal reports. We were met only by Kutuzov and Kolotinski.

Our departure was timed for 8 p.m. We went on foot to the "Rossia" Hotel, to take tea with Kutuzov. Then we drove to Mamandra, where the Americans were welcomed with wine. After which we shook off the foreigners at the quayside and visited Maria Vladimirovna Baryatinskaya's place.

Nothing in her house has been touched. Everything is where it should be: all her souvenirs, albums with ancient yellowed photographs. The garden is well-groomed, the blinds down in every room. The uprush of memories, and the sight of all those familiar faces in portraits and photographs quite took my breath away.

In an album I found Tolstoy's mother, and saw a photograph of Nelly Baryatinskaya for the first time. From there we went back to the "Rossia", where a light lunch with Zykov had been arranged.

Drizen, who is beginning to sound rather hysterical, was also present. He thinks of returning early in July. He informed me that Wrangel had told him how pleased he was with me, and that he would like to keep me on when Drizen goes back, and had asked him to find out what I meant to do. I had, however, foreseen this and taken steps to settle the matter in advance.

Yalta's "care-free charm" is appealing – but this only annoyed my hard-working superiors. Naked bodies littering the beaches, bands playing anywhere and everywhere. We left at 8 p.m. and took 2¼ hours to get back to Sevastopol. At 12 midnight we left for the front.

17 JUNE 1920: MELITOPOL

We got here at about 2 p.m. We were in such a hurry to get here because a breakthrough by Zhloba's Red Cavalry had caused something of a panic yesterday. The breakthrough seems to have been contained successfully.

The attitude of the Jews here is undisguisedly hostile, and police officers have been fired on from the bushes in the evening. The Russian population on the other hand is not only in its majority well-disposed to us, but in a mood for pogroms.

Of the corps commanders, Kutepov is here, in reserve, with his "iron fist" extended from the Dnieprovski *uyezd*.*

On the other side of the Dniepr, the Reds are also showing signs of activity and apparently preparing to make a move.

The provision of mounts for the Army is going pretty well. From what Gendrikov says I conclude that the civil administration in the newly conquered territory is still not on a firm footing. (Gendrikov is the head of civil administration attached to the Don corps.) Our squadron is here outside Melitopol to fetch horses for the division, and while they are about it to find mounts for themselves. Vanik has stayed behind in command of the other squadrons of the regiment on the Dniepr, while Kossikovsky has come here with Roman Pushkin and the younger officers. I saw Roman today, and shall probably see Kossikovsky tomorrow.

Our planes have started flying again all out, so that we have much more information about the enemy. From remarks by Wrangel today I conclude that the remains (large consignments) of the equipment already dispatched by the British are being sent on, and that in addition prospects are looking good with France and the Slav countries.

One interesting event today was a messenger from Makhno, wearing brand new Ukrainian national costume. Makhno promises to help us in every possible way. Wrangel has promised me that I will be present when he meets the famous bandit. It's the middle ages again, no two ways about it!

A visit to the Don Cossacks is scheduled for tomorrow. Shatilov will probably soon go to Sevastopol. I wonder how things will develop at the front. This is the second stage of our gamble!

---

* *uyzed*: an administrative division, part of a *gubernia* (province).

Kossikovsky turned up late at night. He has been rounding up horses with feverish energy. He appeared at my place around midnight and sat talking till 2 a.m., after which, it turns out, he drove to Gendrikov's. He told me when Drizen returns to come back and relieve Roman Pushkin, who is apparently suffering from severe nervous strain. He was received by Piper this morning, but it seems that none of his projects were successful. He was naïve enough to offer himself as temporary regimental commander, until the new commander arrives – just as long as "Riesling" is removed. After that he was supposed to try and persuade Wrangel not to break up our reserve units. And, finally, to inform him that I am needed in the regiment. I don't know whether he got round to the last item on his agenda, but on the first two he certainly had no success. He left in a terribly bad temper, hardly pausing to say goodbye to me.

Zhloba's offensive has apparently been checked, but they are trying to cross the Dniepr to confront our division, though so far not in great force. The Corps has moved in, and the enemy, it seems, must suffer a cruel defeat on this front. It would, of course, be of major importance if we could destroy the famous Zhloba's cavalry.

There was no particularly interesting news from the front today. Zhloba is behaving very cautiously. Today Wrangel and Shatilov were urgently discussing diabolic plans of some sort against the enemy. He is seemingly in for a surprise. Once again I have very little to do and, mostly, I sleep.

The Pushkin brothers got here in the evening. Roman says that Kossikovsky was incredibly upset after his talk with Wrangel. Mainly because Wrangel is unwilling to appoint him regimental commander *ad interim*, on the grounds that, when the question arose, not one of the senior officers mentioned him even once. He spoke of it with tears in his eyes.

After dinner I strolled with Wrangel and Gendrikov, whom I definitely do not like. The conversation was mainly about bygone regimental carousals and jollifications. I recently found myself talking to Wrangel about art. He is interested in painting. He doesn't know much about it, but the rudiments of good taste and sound judgement seem to be there. He boasts ungovernably!

Georgievich feels that I do not value my post, and have absolutely no fear of my superiors – which is what he finds attractive in me. I even got the impression today that he was trying to use me in his intrigue to get Androsov, whom he hates, removed. Androsov is decent and firm, but stupid and tactless.

19 JUNE 1920

Konovalov, Quartermaster-General, woke Wrangel early this morning with an urgent report. It seems that the situation may become critical by evening, or may end in the most terrible defeat for the Reds. They are pushing in from the north and about to fall into a trap. If this operation succeeds our worries will be over for some time ahead, and we shall have won the second round.

According to a telegram received yesterday, the marksman Kapnist [Nikita Rostislavovich] was killed by a gang of Greens,* between Sudak and Theodosia.

It appears that Zhloba, trying to advance too far, has been repulsed by Kutepov and the Don Cossacks, and has taken flight back to where he came from. Two Latvian regiments are reported to have crossed the river near Kakhovka.

Our unit, fortunately, is at present supposed to be in reserve, but in all probability has also gone into battle. With what result we shall hear tonight.

After lunch I went with Georgievich and the adjutants to bathe in the River Molochnaya. The Kakhovka incident is over. Barbovich led his troops into the attack himself and threw the enemy back into the Dniepr. They intend to pitch into Zhloba in the night. The master was in a bad mood this evening.

* Peasant supporters of Makhno (see p. 137).

This morning I was temporarily transformed into an inspector of charitable institutions. I "found myself" visiting orphanages, which are in a dreadful state, with a view to their possible evacuation from the Crimea.

Yusupov (the younger) is making all his villas available for charitable purposes, to Baroness Wrangel, who has also taken an active hand in the matter.

Zhloba is completely surrounded. I hope that he will not be able to break out, and that this will be the end of him. We shall probably go to see the Don units tomorrow, as soon as the operation is completed.

Zhloba's corps is utterly destroyed. We have captured, at the present count, about 30 cannon (i.e. all of his artillery), 70 machine guns, a huge number of horsemen with their horses, together with baggage trains and H.Q. staff. According to information, not as yet fully confirmed, he himself has been taken. If he is delivered here alive the interrogation will be an intriguing one.

Wrangel is as happy as a little boy. From the military point of view it is an astounding operation. Although everybody urged him to strike earlier, and not to let Zhloba advance so far, he stood firm and, as a result, swallowed him whole. Zhloba's cavalry corps, after Budenny's, is the most dangerous Bolshevik force.

In the northern direction, on the approaches to Alexandrovsk, Slashchev is hard pressed. The enemy has not yet been completely eliminated at the Kakhovka crossings.

The battles with Zhloba were seen as a rout without precedent. Of his 6–7,000-strong corps, about one and a half thousand men got away. Our official count includes about 1,500 cavalrymen taken prisoner, 40 cannon, 200 machine guns, an enormous number of supply wagons, shells, and cartridges, the staff of Second Division, its chief included, an incredible number of saddlers, etc. This has been a tremendous boost to morale at our H.Q.

Gendrikov came along in the evening, with the same old jokes and reminiscences. Kossikovsky, who apparently intends to resign in the autumn, turned up late at night.

21 JUNE 1920

The heat for some days has been fierce. The temperature on the train is so high that you are continually drenched in sweat.

The Reds are bringing up reinforcements to the Dniepr crossings. Towards evening it becomes clear that the Reds have been mopped up all along the Dniepr and that the crossings are in our hands. The pressure on Slashchev has also come to an end, and this group will evidently not be pinned down.

Some shells exploded in Sevastopol without causing much damage. The petrol was saved, and no more than 80 shells went off. Barbovich, it appears, has taken another 200 prisoners and 10 machine guns.

Had a long talk with Georgievich, who is not so stupid as he looks, but is undoubtedly an intriguer. He abused Drizen, calling him stupid and tactless, and there I partly agree with him. Drizen is not stupid, just unimaginative, but he is most certainly tactless. But he knows his business.

Kossikovsky returned in the evening, asking for news. His mobilisation is going well, and he expects to bring Barbovich 500 horses. The Chief of Staff of Zhloba's Second Division, captured in battle, is being sent here. He will probably be hanged after interrogation. Zhloba himself, it seems, jumped out of his car and escaped on horseback. His Corps Chief of Staff was captured and shot himself.

22 JUNE 1920

Staggering news arrived by telegraph – detailed description of battle with Zhloba. A truly astounding and inspired operation.

At 5 p.m. we went to meet Kutepov and Slashchev. A regrouping, and the withdrawal of the cavalry to the rear is planned, for redeployment and reinforcement.

Some of Zhloba's officers – divisional chief of staff, chief of staff of one of his brigades, chief of his intelligence department – were brought in for interrogation. Two of them were regular officers, one had gone through the shortened General Staff course. Wrangel detested them and refused to talk to them. They don't seem to have given any particularly interesting information. They said that the Bolsheviks' plans on that front rested entirely on Zhloba. His defeat was completely unexpected. They were required to attack us that very morning. The conclusion drawn from the information gathered is that, after the liquidation of the northern group, which will probably be completed within the next 24 hours, we shall have two quiet weeks to redeploy. So we shall have taken the first trick!

Wrangel's plan for the next few days is to leave for Sevastopol after inspecting the Don Corps, and to devote all his energy exclusively to the business of supply, which is still going slowly.

Slashchev's style of dress is quite fantastic: a single-breasted coat of coarse grey linen, fastening at the side, and with a gathered waist. The cuffs are of deer hide, the front is braided, it has a stand-up fur collar, and lapels of the same material. A white tunic underneath this gives us a glimpse of a Vladimir. He wears general's shoulder-boards, edged with volunteer's cord, suspended from a white belt we see a "sword"(!) comprising a ruby-studded hilt, a brass crossbar and a scabbard big enough for a broadsword. Add to all this a round fur hat of the sort worn by police constables and a badge inscribed *For Defence of the Crimea*, awarded to him and his troops. This costume obviously makes Kutepov want to vomit.

Wrangel looked very handsome in the Kornilov-type uniform recently presented to him: all in black with a station commandant's peaked cap. Slashchev chatted with me very amiably, giggling madly. His complexion is corpse-like – probably from cocaine. We returned to Melitopol for supper. Tverskoy (head of the Civilian Administration) arrived in the course of the evening. Wrangel pressed him hard to do something about the misconceived "explanations" attached to the agrarian law by Glinka (Minister of Agriculture).

Unfortunately I have no time to describe a number of feats of unprecedented bravery on the part of regimental commanders in First Corps, especially Manstein, the one-armed and one-legged commanding officer of the First Drozdovsky Regiment.

23 JUNE 1920

Left at 9 a.m. by car for the Don Corps. Almost the whole corps is now horsed, and it constitutes a most imposing body of cavalry.

Wrangel was as happy as a child, and praised the Don Cossack officers extravagantly: the sight of those fine horses, and the excellent condition of the troops, made him forget that the horses and buggies were all stolen. So much for all the thunderous telegrams he had sent to General Abramov (commander of the Don Corps).

Here he displayed the thoughtlessness that was part of his character. We came upon one of the brigades just as a battle was about to begin. His arrival was, of course, bound to raise the spirits of the troops who rode past him. Those Cossack faces were radiant. He also talked to the German settlers. The day was uncommonly sultry.

We travelled more than 180 *versts*, driving through the sites of the battles with Zhloba. We got back late in the evening. The newspapers have published Glinka's "explanation" of the agrarian law – which greatly vexed and alarmed Wrangel. Glinka writes that leasehold agreements with landowners concluded for the current year remain in force, which means that in many places the law is rendered inoperative. I can't imagine how they will get out of this awkward situation.

Among the mass of congratulatory telegrams was a dispatch from de Robec: pretty significant! Kutepov has liquidated the remnants of the Red forces attacking from the north. The operation can be considered complete, and now a start will be made on regrouping. Georgievich is leaving us to take up the post of Chief of Staff in

Ulagai's corps. With his departure, and until his replacement arrives, I shall have twice as much work to do.

24 JUNE 1920

I like the fact that Wrangel is very much afraid to take too high a tone in the answers to telegrams which I draft for him.

I don't know whether it's the magnetic influence of Wrangel that I am experiencing, but I feel more energetic than ever before. My memory has improved three times over in the past month. I sometimes feel quite positively that I am being of some use. I think that this tension, this state of being eternally "*éveillé*", would be exhausting over a long period.

26 JUNE 1920

Batum has been finally evacuated by the British and ourselves. Although the Georgians expressed a wish for us to stay the British would not allow us to do so.

In reply to the British announcement (about a week ago) that Russian refugees would be returned to Russia, and that there would be no further provision for their maintenance, permission was requested to declare (or recognise) the independence of White Crimea. No official reply has so far been received, but Red radio bulletins have hinted at some statement on the subject by Lloyd George.

The Baroness has begun poking her nose into policy rather too often. So far this only irritates Wrangel, but Krivoshein lends an ear to her twitterings – only, I think, because he has a weakness for the female sex.

27 JUNE 1920

This evening I attended a charity concert with Wrangel and the Baroness. I had to sit importantly in the front row, without showing my unspeakable embarrassment. I hate attracting attention, and although I am bound to say that I have almost completely got over my shyness – it can still sometimes affect me quite seriously.

28 JUNE 1920

Found myself this morning attending a "solemn service", conducted by Bishop Veniamin, with panegyrics and prayers for Wrangel. Excellent choir at the cathedral, the place was crowded. The official part of his birthday celebrations ended there.

In the afternoon, while all sorts of ministers and retired blotting pads signed the greetings book, the birthday boy and his spouse sought the arms of Morpheus. There was a glass of champagne at dinner, but no guests.

After dinner, Wrangel joined those celebrating the "campaign on the ice", and stayed so long that his guests had all assembled ("for a cup of tea") before he returned.

30 JUNE 1920

Sat answering congratulatory telegrams all morning. Obviously showed a certain inventiveness, since I earned praise from the Highest. If it pleases the Lord that I should ever make a speech, I will use the language of these telegrams! I have evidently caught his style, and his diplomatic line with regard to certain organisations.

1 JULY 1920

When the "Sovereign Lady's" guests left, I sat for some time in the intimate company of Napoleon and Josephine. I told them about the news brought by Woodward. He had told me very confidentially that great changes for the better in Britain's relations with us were on the way. He claims that Lloyd George is on the way out. It will be interesting to see how much truth there is in this.

2 JULY 1920

Something very interesting has turned up from America: the million-aire Whittimore, who has travelled to Batum on a destroyer, and from there to Tiflis, and bought up all the school manuals in Russian and brought them to Sevastopol.

He says that, as a cultured man, he cannot reconcile himself to the thought that a whole generation in Russia might be left without education. He is therefore offering our schools in the Crimea an unlimited supply of linen, books, and money. In addition, he offers to maintain the schools evacuated to the islands at his own expense. He asks only that we should pay the teachers' stipends.

I interpreted his conversation with Krivoshein, who was so moved that he burst into tears – something I would never have expected.

4 JULY 1920

One thing I regret is that I have not succeeded in getting to know Shatilov more closely. I have come to the conclusion that his work is invariably positive, and that he is the ideal complement to Wrangel.

5 JULY 1920

I had a long and very interesting talk with Whittimore, who knows some of my relatives from Novorossiisk. A very interesting man, well-rounded, has seen a great deal of the world, goodhearted. I am, however, not altogether sure about his morals.

7 JULY 1920

I feel that the American Whittimore, with whom I had such a long talk the other day, has a tremendous understanding of the situation. He is possibly an occultist, or anyway something like that. Of course, I haven't completely fathomed him as yet – which is what makes him interesting. Strangely enough I seem to have made an impression on him. As he left he said: "We will keep in touch, shall we not?"* I hope it will be "not in too close a touch". It seemed to me rather suspicious that he is looking for a secretary to go to America with him and enter a university there (?!!!).

11 JULY 1920

I cannot suppress recollections of the past – however painful the memory is. The courtyard flooded with sunlight, a circular lawn, the grass rather scorched, yellow charabancs with coachmen in canvas coats, old Ivan with a handkerchief over his bald patch . . .

12 JULY 1920

Three admirals have arrived in Yalta simultaneously: the commander of the American Mediterranean Squadron, Hope and McCully.

The Bolsheviks do not disguise the fact that what makes Wrangel dangerous to them is above all not his Army but his agrarian law and his attempt to solve the "worker question".

14 JULY 1920

The first contingents of Budenny's army transferred from the Polish front have just appeared on our front.

15 JULY 1920

Staggering news from Krivoshein: the Entente is said to be about to recognise us as the all-Russian government, probably on account of the Polish débâcle.

---

* In English in the original.

There is, of course, a trace of falsity in W. [*Wrangel*]. With our officers he speaks in the tone of the old Guards regiments, and as to people of the same social level. With others he speaks differently. Moreover, it is not particularly safe to rely on promises he makes without witnesses. This is perhaps the one fault in him that could damage the cause. There is, though, in my opinion one other: he is a poor judge of people, especially those close to him. Though he seems to make no mistakes in his choice of military leaders.

17 JULY 1920

He [*Wrangel*] told me that he intended to settle the question of my return to the regiment. I consider further delay tantamount to finally quitting the regiment, and so have decided to declare categorically my desire to return, when Drizen gets back.

18 JULY 1920

It would be interesting to know whether he [*Wrangel*] has sized up the situation correctly: politically, he is playing what is more or less the S. R.* game, varied at times with the most reactionary militarism. I do not doubt that if fate grants more leeway in future he will, of course, abandon his "flirtation with the people", and take everything in hand.

The most surprising thing is that Krivoshein, the old bureaucrat, immediately understood Wrangel's line and adopted it without hesitation.

W. told me (in reply to my rather blunt questions about his state of mind in the past) that for a long time he had no faith in our final success (he undoubtedly has now) but that after his second inspection of the troops at the front he had realised that the Crimea was no longer in danger.

* A reference to the Socialist Revolutionary Party.

We have received an official telegram from the French government, offering to recognise our government if we assume a measure of responsibility for the old debts proportionate to the territory regained. Wrangel replied that since for us it could only be a question of recovering our whole territory, or of complete disaster he was willing to promise that in the event of our winning back all our territory he would assume complete responsibility for all debts.

21 JULY 1920

W. said at lunch that he had been given a letter from a certain (completely trustworthy) officer describing the assassination of the imperial family. This officer, who lived opposite the Emperor's house, supplied the following information.

The Heir died two weeks before the execution: someone threw a grenade into the courtyard, which injured him only slightly, but caused a fatal haemorrhage. The Emperor and his whole family were shot inside the house. He personally had seen their bodies – except for that of Tatyana – carried out that evening and burned.

All this coincides with the information obtained by General Dietrich's investigation, and contained in his report. Mikhail Alexandrovich also is supposed to have perished. Bezobrazov, however, insists that he is alive, somewhere between Shanghai and some other Chinese city, en route for Europe.

22 JULY 1920

As for the allies – the French, of course, have pride of place. He said that he hoped other nations would shortly follow their example and recognise an all-Russian government on our "little territory with great tasks to perform".

Walsh was terribly piqued by this speech. The head of the British mission thought that he should have mentioned the help given by the British in the past. Woodward redoubled his importunities, obviously having received instructions concerning the latest complications with the British in Constantinople; firstly, because of the radio, and secondly because of a ship carrying saddles detained by the British.

23 JULY 1920

Yet another Englishman is hoping to get a stranglehold on me – the "Lord Journalist", a snob friend of Woodward's, more like an Armenian or a Jew than an English "Honorable" [sic]. He speaks excellent French, but is a dreadful gas-bag.

24 JULY 1920

At 3.15 an interesting interview with the English newspaperman Hay, at which I was present. In my opinion W. gave a remarkably good and clever account of his policy. The other man was delighted. It's a pity that the publication he writes for is one of secondary importance. To listen to him, England's lords are all either in his pocket or related to him. He is at pains to emphasise that he is not primarily a journalist, but by nature a pure-blooded aristocrat. I find that the first article he has sent to England is so extravagantly eulogistic that he has left nothing in reserve for the future.

26 JULY 1920

Supper with Woodward and others.

Woodward took me aside to another table and announced that a destroyer would be arriving tomorrow with extremely important news. He hinted that he thought a complete change of policy in our favour was imminent, that the warships had even been given instructions to be prepared for military action, that the assembled British authorities request W. not to go away until this news arrives, and so on.

I, of course, reported all this to W. that same evening. It greatly excited him. After supper went out into the garden and continued drinking wine. Finished up in Woodward's apartment, and got pretty squiffy.

27 JULY 1920

The destroyer *Swallow* has arrived. We all await delivery of the important missives with great impatience. Towards evening it emerged that they are waiting for a radio message from London, and that if the Bolsheviks have rejected the British proposals the fleet will commence military action immediately.

Krivoshein "graciously jests" that if the information given by me turns out to be false I shall answer with my head, and if the contrary is the case I shall be given a bottle of wine.

At the front things are going only moderately well (they have become terribly slack lately). The Bolsheviks who have crossed the Dniepr have been defeated in some places but continue to advance in others. We shall very probably drive to the front tomorrow but, I think, without any foreigners.

Late in the afternoon I saw Woodward, who is going around looking self-satisfied and important. In London the decision is to be taken tomorrow morning, but he asserts that it will mean success (for us).

Lukomsky came to supper. They discussed the possibility of closing the Crimea to blackmarketeers from Batum, who have flooded the towns and brought about terrible price rises. Had supper for the second time with the two English lady doctors and Woodward. One of the ladies – to whom he is, I think, not indifferent – is quite attractive. The other is an old hag with a mouthful of piano keys. When we said goodbye to them it was on the tip of my (malicious) tongue to ask: "Which of the two do you find attractive?"

Late in the evening still nothing from the British.

This morning still no news from the British. The papers now full of the negotiations [*with a Bolshevik mission*] in progress in London. At breakfast had to translate British radio message to the effect that the attempt to reach agreement has dragged on for several more hours. However, all necessary measures have been taken in case of failure (which for us means success). The British fleet has entered the Baltic, and 400 French and 200 British officers have left for Poland.

Our departure is set for 4 p.m. Zvyagintsov looked in, but brought no news. Woodward, too, has received no information – or else is concealing it: he may have heard something in Feodosia. We took along Rugovich to Dzhankoi, on his way to join his regiment. An échelon of our reserves was standing in Dzhankoi, bound for the station at Rykovo. Saw Gleb Gagarin, Boris Chicherin, Shebeko, Sandro and the little Pushkin. We gave Shebeko a lift as far as Grammatikovo, where our field hospital is, with Dr Zakharov.

No further losses in the regiment. It has performed brilliantly, as always, and is now on the move in the direction of Kakhovka: to mop up from the rear the Reds filing across the Dniepr. It's a pity they aren't being allowed a rest.

We took the little Pushkin to Feodosia to see his father, who will go on to Dzhankoi with us to meet Roman, and then travel with him to Constantinople.

31 JULY 1920

Telegram from France arrived before supper: Millerand informs us that France officially recognises us as the all-Russian government – which was the subject of a question in the British parliament. Lloyd George found himself in a most foolish position.

I got a very interesting issue of *Temps* from Struve today – full of our affairs, and the complications that have arisen between Britain and France in connection with Millerand's recognition of us. The effect produced in the British papers is staggering: the majority of them do not even find the reported declaration of the French government plausible.

9 AUGUST 1920 [SEVASTOPOL]

Slashchev has been dismissed after the incredible losses he has sustained on the Dniepr. He is losing his mind completely as a result of using cocaine. He turned up with his wife. He was thanked in a special order and (at his own request) given the appellation Slashchev-Krymski [*meaning "of the Crimea"*].

10 AUGUST 1920 [IN TRANSIT]

We left at 6 a.m., taking with us another American correspondent – on the important *Chicago Tribune*. He is, of course, in my charge, since he does not speak a word of any language. I had a long conversation with him in the evening. He is a typical young American of about my age. I succeeded in reducing him to a state of unqualified enthusiasm.

The atmosphere of G.H.Q., with its intense concentration on a single problem, undoubtedly has a powerful effect on all foreigners. The remarkable hypnotic influence produced by Wrangel's personality also of course plays a great part. The American says that he feels W.'s magnetism from the other end of the table, and cannot take his eyes off him.

11 AUGUST 1920 [KERCH]

Wrangel only has to appear for victory to follow. From a conversation by direct line with Krivoshein we learn that the Poles are continuing to rout the Reds. They have taken 15,000 prisoners, Lomzha and Brest-Litovsk, and cut off almost the whole of their army in the North, which threatens them with a major defeat.

12 AUGUST 1920 [KERCH]

I am getting the impression that our forces in Northern Tauria* are becoming exhausted by heavy fighting and enormous losses.

13 AUGUST 1920 [KERCH]

I am now a dab hand at giving a literary form to his [Wrangel's] resounding phrases, which always make a great impression on the British and the Americans.

14 AUGUST 1920 [KERCH]

It is certain that another critical moment in our epic struggle is imminent. The pressure on our front will most probably now be relaxed by the Reds, who as a result of their terrible defeat on the Polish front will begin to transfer troops to the West.

15 AUGUST 1920 [KERCH]

This is Wrangel's first serious failure: he mistakenly calculated that Cossack support would be considerably stronger.

* The area between the Crimea and the lower Dnieper.

16 AUGUST 1920 [KERCH]

I don't understand the American position. On the one hand they approve of France's recognition of Wrangel, while on the other they repeatedly advise Poland not to advance beyond the frontiers established by the Versailles Treaty.

17 AUGUST 1920 [MELITOPOL]

. . . the Bolshevik forces are roughly three times as great as ours . . . A crowd one-and-a-half thousand strong awaited Wrangel's appearance outside H.Q., and roared at the tops of their voices when he emerged for lunch and dinner.

His appearance of course plays a great part – all in black, in the uniform of Kornilov's army, which increases his already imposing stature. As for the women – they are simply in convulsions at the very sight of him.

18 AUGUST 1920 [MELITOPOL]

The British radio talks about a speedy conclusion of peace between Poland and Soviet Russia.

28 AUGUST–2 SEPTEMBER 1920 [MELITOPOL]

This turns out to be a very interesting moment in our international relations. Messages have been sent to America, France, Roumania, and others, the precise content of which is unknown to me, but their object is to ascertain whether we shall be given aid. We left Sevastopol in great force on 30 August. Our caravan was made up of a huge number of coaches. Unfortunately, I had to take charge of the lot.

In addition to Krivoshein and his secretary Kotlyarevsky, our fellow passengers included the heads of all the foreign missions, seven foreign correspondents – two Americans, two French (*Matin*,

Petit Journal), two Italians, and one Englishman (*The Times*). This whole menagerie travelled with us in eight cars, headed by Zvyagintsev.

Dinner with the Kornilov veterans was certainly moving. The officers sang at table, and the Commander-in-Chief and Krivoshein both made marvellous speeches. I saw tears falling from the French correspondent's moustache . . . Even Wrangel let fall a slow tear, to my extreme surprise.

I am bound to say that my menial occupation is beginning to pall: what vexes me most is that I am subordinate to a single individual, not an organisation.

11 SEPTEMBER 1920

Drizen and I are thinking of changing our occupation, which is degenerating into something of a sinecure. I think it very likely that one of us will be appointed to a post abroad, or some sort of diplomatic role with the foreigners here.

15 SEPTEMBER 1920

I am, as ever, besieged by correspondents of all nationalities. In (junior) foreign circles my "good will" is in great demand.

26 SEPTEMBER 1920

We left Sevastopol on the 26th, towards evening.

Drizen was given the task of escorting a new party of correspondents, whom we are transporting to the front: an Englishman, a Frenchman, two Russians and an Italian.

The most remarkable of them is the Frenchman (*Temps*) who spent about ten years in Russia, right up to 1916. A remarkably brilliant and clever man. I had several interesting conversations with him, particularly on the Jewish and Polish questions, which he has made his special subject. He is such a good talker that he has even made an impression on Wrangel and Shatilov. "*La Pologne est mûre pour son quatrième partage*" is one of his sayings. It appears that when he was leaving Warsaw he made this remark to some Polish politician who asked him for his general impressions.

The Englishman, too, is interesting. After 15 years in Russia he spent three months in the Butyrka prison as a hostage. He has arrived here now as Reuters representative.

Before leaving Sevastopol, I received a very friendly letter from Gould, asking permission to write once a week to inform me of the situation in Constantinople. He apparently wants to make sure that de Robec's communications will not all go through W., with whom they are probably dissatisfied, or to prevent this assuming a semi-official character.

27 SEPTEMBER 1920

It looks, alas, as though the Poles are going to make peace. If it comes to that our position will change appreciably for the worse.

The moment of decision will confront us once again: either complete and decisive victory or withdrawal into the Crimea beyond the isthmuses. I am in any case doubtful whether it would be possible for us to hold the Dniepr Line if the Reds come down upon us in full force.

The spate of telegrams from the peasants, wishing us well and thanking us, is not abating.

The idea of introducing help from the troops in getting in the harvest belongs entirely to the Commander-in-Chief. It came to him in my presence. This measure had an enormous influence on the attitude of the peasants to the regime and its troops. It would do no harm to show these telegrams to the correspondents, as they pass through on the return journey to Sevastopol.

28 SEPTEMBER 1920

Just now got hold of Tolstoy's *Khadzhi-Murat*,* which I then passed on to Vorontsov – let him read about his great-grandfather. It will be interesting to see what impression it makes on him, in comparison with what happened in his day.

30 SEPTEMBER 1920

I have collected for the *Temps* correspondent a great deal of material in the form of greetings telegrams, and thank-you telegrams from peasants, cantonal *zemstvos*, village meetings, *zemstvo* assemblies etc. – most of them in response to the land redistribution.

4 OCTOBER 1920

The Bolsheviks have obviously said to hell with the Polish front, and are now turning their main forces against us. Their broadcasts are full of hysterical appeals and insane vilification of us.

11 OCTOBER 1920

In the distant future, as far as I am concerned, I foresee the collapse of all my hopes.

There is no doubt that if I stay with him [Wrangel] I shall never be able even in the future to quit the service. My dreams of studying, of pursuing higher interests, of living in freedom, are of course destined not to come true – and anyway there will probably be too little money for it. I already feel my interests waning, and a sort of moral indolence towards learning and self-improvement: a feeling quite unknown to me before the Revolution.

---

* A 1912 novella translated as *Hadji Murad*.

Received a telegram from Feodosia to say that our friend Colonel Boyle has arrived at last. I am expecting him by the first train from Feodosia tomorrow. I cannot wait to see him. In excruciating boredom of this place he will be a great resource for me.

The situation at the front is obviously in accordance with the overall plan for the time being. The decisive engagement has not yet begun. The main body of the Reds has been let through in the direction of Perekop and Sivash.

20 OCTOBER 1920

This morning Wrangel informed me that the evacuation of Tauria by our forces was inevitable: all our troops will probably have been withdrawn beyond the isthmuses by tomorrow evening.

It's sad, having to say goodbye to rosy dreams . . . No doubt the Reds have overwhelmed us with their great superiority in numbers . . . but it is also true that the victor has a bloody nose.

The bitter pill of failure was somewhat sweetened today by the news that enormous stocks of clothing, equipment, and shells have arrived from France. There is enough clothing to fit out the whole army at one go.

21 OCTOBER 1920

The evacuation is concluded. Most units got through overnight. If we carry it through successfully we can consider the Crimea out of danger.

We shall be leaving Tauria littered with the corpses of the Reds. No prisoners were taken, of course, during our counter-attacks. The morale of our troops is splendid.

27 OCTOBER 1920 [IN TRANSIT]

We left suddenly and just in time. As far as I can judge, things are taking a catastrophic turn. From what Kutepov tells us it has become clear that the troops are losing heart. This is the most unexpected, and the worst, thing that could happen.

I know that preparations of some sort are being made for evacuation, but evacuation to where? Outer space?

Once again we are living through a difficult – and panicky – time. Panic, however, has still not penetrated far behind the lines. In Simferopol all is quiet.

28 OCTOBER 1920 [SEVASTOPOL]

Commotion in the "spheres". Slowly but surely panic is seeping into the upper strata. Krivoshein, who is notorious for his cowardice, is already overcome by fear.

Evacuation of the wounded is to begin tomorrow. All the top brass are very pessimistic.

Boyle, who got back today after inspecting the collieries, said that, although he was in a hurry to return to Roumania, he would, in view of the situation which had arisen, stay with us to the end.

29 OCTOBER 1920

Our frontline forces are hanging on in the last line of trenches, and suffering enormous losses. There is panic, but a sort of subdued panic, in the city. Whereas the commotion in the "palace" is fantastic.

We learned this afternoon that after repeated desperate counter-attacks our forces had succeeded in regaining control of the last line of trenches.

Admiral Nore arrived this morning, but had nothing to offer except words of sympathy. They say that the *Benbow* is being sent in a hurry, but no one knows when it will arrive.

Woodward looks in once an hour, more or less, to hear the news and "put his mission in the picture". He is directing large numbers of people to the *Centaur*, which is to leave by night carrying women, children, and useless generals like Miklashevsky, Pavlov, etc.

I paid a visit to the Commander-in-Chief's cutter. It was anchored quite a long way beyond Chersonese. People in frock coats, wearing armbands, and the band playing on deck, made a strange contrast with the mood of those on shore. Drizen and I are unclear so far when and with whom we shall go. The Commander-in-Chief does not want to keep us with him to the last minute. He wants only Artifeksov and Pokrovsky beside him. In spite of ardent protests on my side he wants us to leave with the operations personnel, which we consider utterly pointless since we can be of most use in conversations with foreigners. The matter is still not settled.

The latest news from the front is that Yushun has been occupied by the enemy, i.e. that we have abandoned the last line of our fortifications in that area. Slashchev left for the front last night. It is not clear whether this was of his own accord, or on orders from Wrangel. Because of this, absurd rumours that we have won some sort of victory are going round the town.

It is to be expected that our final retreat will begin tomorrow, and that nightmarish panic will break out in the city the day after. The humiliating business of loading our belongings under cover of darkness has begun.

Dimitri Obolensky

TIME OF TROUBLE (1918–23)

On 3 September 1958 a Greek cruise ship, chartered by the London-based Society for Hellenic Travel, docked in the early afternoon in the Crimean port of Yalta. After sailing a week earlier from Venice, with the aim of circumnavigating the Black Sea, SS *Hermes* was on its way from Odessa to Sochi.

During its 24-hour stop in Yalta, the 200 or so passengers, most of them British, were taken on several excursions, one of them along the Crimean coast.

On board were some notable figures, drawn by the rare, possibly at that time unique, opportunity of sailing in Soviet Black Sea waters and landing on the coasts of Russia and Ukraine in places usually inaccessible to foreigners. Among these passengers were Rose Macauley, Diana Cooper, Juliet Duff, and Stewart Perowne. The cruise lecturers were Robin Burn of Glasgow University, and Geoffrey Lewis and myself, both from Oxford.

The south Crimean coast is narrow, fertile, and studded with natural harbours. Its picturesque scenery is reminiscent of the French and Italian Riviera. To the north the coast is dominated by several parallel mountain ranges, partly wooded, the highest of which rises to 1,500 metres, and which act as a beneficent screen against the bitter north winds. Climate and geography thus ensured that the southerners who, from time immemorial, settled on this coast – Greeks, Romans, Byzantines, and later Italians – became trading and cultural intermediaries between the Mediterranean world and the steppes of Eurasia. In the nineteenth century, after the Crimea had been reconquered from

Ottoman suzerainty by Catherine the Great, the coast was adorned with palaces, villas and summer-houses belonging to members of Russia's aristocracy.

We visited one of them, the Vorontsov Palace at Alupka. It stands, 17 miles west of Yalta, beneath the grey, craggy mountain peak of Ai-Petri, whose name recalls the Greek colonists who, in the sixth century BC and later, settled on this coastal fringe. The Palace (home to Winston Churchill and the British delegation during the Yalta Conference in 1945 and now a museum of fine art) was built between 1828 and 1848 by Edward Blore, architect to King William IV and to Queen Victoria, and one of the builders of Buckingham Palace, for Count (later Prince) Michael Vorontsov, my great-great-great-grandfather.

His early youth was spent in England, where his father, Count Simon Vorontsov, was Russian ambassador. In 1823 Michael was appointed Governor-General of "New Russia", the name given to the recently acquired Ukrainian lands north of the Black Sea. He had fought Napoleon, was wounded at the Battle of Borodino and, after Waterloo, commanded the Russian occupation forces in France.

Michael's English connections were reinforced by the marriage of his sister Catherine to the eleventh Earl of Pembroke. He thus became the uncle of Sidney Herbert, Secretary of State for War and close collaborator of Florence Nightingale. Catherine lies buried in the parish church near Wilton House, the Pembroke family estate.

One of the wealthiest men in Russia, Michael proved an outstanding soldier and a gifted administrator. In 1845 he was appointed Viceroy of the Caucasus by Nicholas I. His only major military disaster was his defeat in the same year by the Chechen forces of the imam Shamil. The outbreak of the Crimean War was a severe blow to this confirmed anglophile. He died in November 1856, soon after the war ended.

His palace at Alupka by the sea, a curious Tudor-Gothic-Moorish edifice built in local grey-green granite, with 150 rooms, became Michael Vorontsov's favourite home. "Carved white lions guarded the entrance to the house, and beyond the courtyard lay a fine park with sub-tropical plants and cypresses." Sir Winston Churchill, the author of these words,* became so enamoured of these lions that – it is said – he asked Stalin's permission to take one of them back to England. Stalin refused. The last male owner of the house was my great-grandfather, Count Ilarion Vorontsov-Dashkov, Viceroy of the Caucasus from 1905 to 1915. He died in Alupka in 1916.

We spent several hours in Alupka. In the rooms open to the public, family portraits adorned the walls, interspersed with statistics bearing disapproving notices of Michael Vorontsov's wealth. I fought back any outward sign of emotion as I reflected that in October 1918, as a baby, I had stayed in the house while my family prepared to embark for the safety of the West to escape the Bolsheviks. Rose Macaulay got wind of this and, in an article she wrote for *The Queen*, referred to me and the Alupka house "from which he wisely fled at the age of one".

In one of the rooms I noticed a little old lady dressed in black, standing in a corner and looking as though she belonged to the museum. Acting on a hunch, I went up to her and asked in Russian: "Have you lived here long?"

"Yes," she replied, "all my life."

I couldn't resist asking the next question: "Did you by any chance know the former owners?"

At this she looked worried, and I felt that between us a curtain had fallen. In an attempt to put her at her ease, I began name-dropping, and mentioned various members of the family who, I reckoned, had stayed in the palace in the days before the Revolution. The effect was instantaneous. Clearly now trusting me, she smiled and said: "Of course I remember them, and the Count's death in 1916." She recalled the date accurately, nearly a half-century later.

"There was the assembled family," she added, "and so many priests ... And one thing I remember, as though it were yesterday: they brought his horse along, and it followed the funeral procession, and – do you know? – the horse was weeping."

* *History of the Second World War, Volume Six: Triumph and Tragedy* (1954)

At this she began to resemble the horse, and so very nearly did I.

For several moments we stood together in silence. Then she said: "How long ago this was . . . How many years, difficult years, we have lived through since . . . But I will say this: the former masters, they were kinder than the present ones."

Who she was I never knew. I felt I shouldn't ask: she might start worrying. My grandmother, who was still alive in Paris and knew the house well, felt sure she was one of the servants. This is quite possible, given the accuracy of the unknown lady's memories of my great-grandfather's death. But there is no real evidence.

Needless to say, I have no memories of my first stay in the Crimea. It marked a pause in the first long journey of my life, which began soon after my birth in Petrograd on 1 April 1918, and was to end a year later in Malta. A month or so after my birth (in my grandfather's house at 45, Sergievskaya Street) we moved to Tsarskoye Selo, and by early August found ourselves in Moscow, staying in my grandmother's flat.

During the next few weeks my parents came to a momentous decision. It was to leave Russia. Bolshevik power, now fairly well established in the two capitals, Petrograd and Moscow, was making life increasingly uncomfortable and dangerous for prominent families of the Tsarist regime. But in the country at large Bolshevik control was still shaky and in some places non-existent. In the south and south-east, in the Don and Kuban territories, an anti-Soviet army had been forming under the command of the "White" generals Kornilov and, after his death on 13 April, Denikin. In the west and south-west, the situation must have seemed to the Soviets even worse.

On 3 March 1918 the Bolshevik government was forced to sign with the Germans the Treaty of Brest-Litovsk, by which the western regions of the former Russian empire – Ukraine, Poland, Finland, Lithuania, Latvia, and Estonia – were surrendered by Russia.

Almost immediately the Germans occupied Kiev, the Ukrainian capital, and began to extend their power over much of Ukraine. Such was the complex and perilous situation that faced my family during the summer of 1918 in Moscow. It must have seemed more menacing still when the news came that the former Emperor and his family had been murdered by the Bolsheviks on 16 July.

The best route of escape pointed south-west, to Kiev. The railway from Moscow was still open. To placate the local landlords and the well-to-do classes, the Germans had appointed as their puppet the Russian General Paul Skoropadsky, who assumed for the occasion the faintly ludicrous seventeenth-century Cossack title of *hetman*.*

My grandmother, who proved the soul of efficiency in the oncoming operation, was able to obtain false Ukrainian papers for my parents and myself on the somewhat bogus grounds of having been born in the town of Gomel, which was now part of "independent" Ukraine. We were strictly forbidden to bring out any valuables: their discovery by the Bolshevik authorities, she surmised, no doubt correctly, might well mean instant death.

And so, on 1 October, we boarded a Ukrainian hospital train, bound for Kiev. The journey, in a fourth-class carriage, crammed full and filthy, was, in my mother's words, a nightmare. It lasted ten days. After the first week most of our carriage went down with Spanish flu. As a junior passenger, I was then taken in hand by the train's senior sister, who with great kindness gave up her own seat to me.

To cross the border between Soviet Russia and Ukraine was a huge relief. It meant leaving behind a Bolshevik society, violent, hungry, and always dangerous, for a world which in contrast, despite the presence of the German army, must have seemed strikingly normal, and where there was at least enough to eat.

Life in that same year 1918 in Kiev is described in hauntingly evocative detail in the autobiographical novel *The White Guard* by Mikhail Bulgakov (the author of *The Master and Margarita*) who lived in the city at that time. He tells of the endless flow of refugees from the north, many with forged papers acquired to cross the frontier, begging for visas, dreaming of Paris, some of them grateful for the

* A Polish or Cossack military commander, probably from the German *Hauptmann* "captain".

reassuring presence of the German army, all united by their hatred of Bolshevism.

Kiev, where they had found refuge from Moscow or from the war zone, had "swelled, expanded, overflowed like leavened dough rising out of its baking tin". The city, the true heroine of *The White Guard*, had to endure in three years, in Bulgakov's reckoning, no fewer than 14 changes of government, some of them violent. Its true symbol, frequently referred to in the novel, is the huge statue of St Vladimir, the baptiser of Rus', standing on a hill overlooking the Dniepr, upbearing an iron cross which, at night, lit up electrically, seemed to be floating in mid-air. Bulgakov's love of his native city, "the mother of the cities of Rus", to quote the Russian chronicler, gives at times an epic character to his account.

The novel opens with the words: "Great and terrible was the year of Our Lord 1918, of the Revolution the second. Its summer abundant with warmth and sun, its winter with snow, highest in its heaven stood two stars: the shepherd's star, eventide Venus; and Mars – quivering, red." *

None of the changes in Kiev's fortunes could be foreseen by those who, like my family, passed through the city in the autumn of 1918. The closest in time, following the victory of the Allies and the Armistice of 11 November, were the departure of the Germans (and Skoropadsky with them) and, on 14 December, the seizure of Kiev by the army of the Ukrainian Social Democrat leader Simon Petlyura. His reign lasted 47 days, and was followed by a rapid succession of mutually hostile regimes – the Bolshevik Red Army, Petlyura again (for one day), General Denikin's White Army, and the Red Army once more. No wonder that the year 1919 was described by Bulgakov as "yet more terrible" than the year that preceded it.

All in all, we were fortunate to pass through Kiev during the relative quiet between Skoropadsky's appointment in April 1918 and the first rumblings in November of Petlyura's approaching forces. After a week

---

* *The White Guard*, translated from the Russian by Michael Glenny, The Harvill Press, 1996.

in the city, we left for Odessa and then sailed to Yalta, where we arrived on 21 October.

In the autumn of 1918, for anti-Communist Russians seeking to escape the Bolsheviks, migration to the Crimea made good sense. In the civil war which, some months ago, had flared up in the neighbouring Kuban region the White armies of General Denikin seemed to be winning. Allied interventionist troops, mainly British and French, were supporting them. A growing number of refugees, some of them belonging to the Tsarist aristocracy, had succeeded in reaching the Crimea.

One of them was the Dowager Empress Maria Feodorovna, widow of Alexander III and mother of the late Nicholas II. There, in relative security, they could afford to wait for the day when, they hoped, Denikin's "Volunteer Army" would re-enter Moscow. And in the event, still unlikely in 1918–19, that the Bolsheviks would win in the end, before them lay the Black Sea and the chance of evacuation by the ships of the Allies.

The political situation in the Crimea when we arrived was somewhat confused. As in Kiev with Skoropadsky, the Germans had appointed as military governor the obscure and unpopular Muslim general Sul'kevich. He and his masters, however, had less than a month left to exercise power. Soon after the signing of the armistice by mid-November, the Germans evacuated the Crimea, except for Sevastopol. Almost immediately they were replaced by detachments of Denikin's army. The remainder of our stay in the Crimea was marked by an administrative duality between Denikin's military commanders and the local civilian district councils presided over by a distant relative, Vladimir Obolensky. The two were frequently at loggerheads.

Perhaps the most colourful event in our six months' stay was the arrival in early December 1918 of the Allied fleet sent to accept the German surrender of the naval base of Sevastopol. It is described sardonically by Vladimir Obolensky.

The news of the fleet's imminent arrival from Constantinople came as a surprise to the Russians, who had been largely cut off from news by the Bolsheviks in South Russia and by German censorship. On a clear, sunny morning, sixteen warships were sighted, approaching Sevastopol. Ahead steamed a battleship of the Royal Navy, carrying Admiral Colesorp. It was followed by two French battleships and by an Italian cruiser, gleaming white in the sun.

The Russian representatives, some from Denikin's army, others from the civil authorities in Simferopol, requested permission to board the British flagship to pay their respects to the admiral. They seemed, at this stage, persuaded that the sole purpose of the Allied fleet's arrival was to save Russia from the Germans and the Bolsheviks.

In expectation of their meeting with the admiral, some of their leading representatives had, the day before, begun writing and learning by heart grandiloquent speeches of welcome. The inadequacies of their English meant that the speeches had to be delivered in French. In their fertile imagination, the speeches would be accompanied by national anthems, music, and endless toasts. A banquet would be prepared in Sevastopol for the admiral and the officers.

Things turned out rather differently. The Russians were courteously received on board the flagship but, to their bewilderment and eventual exasperation, made to wait several hours while the admiral was cloistered with the German commandant, come to surrender the keys of the fortress. The audience was postponed till the afternoon. It fell to Obolensky to act as the Russian spokesman during the meeting with the admiral. The latter's knowledge of French proved as inadequate as the Russians' English. Obolensky was reduced to mumbling at full speed his prepared French speech to a manifestly puzzled admiral who was unsure who was in charge of the Crimea, the Bolsheviks or the Whites. Seldom, wrote Obolensky in his memoirs, was he made to feel so foolish.

The admiral, meanwhile, had cabled home for instructions. These arrived in a few days' time. As a result a group of Allied naval officers (of middle rank) were allowed to travel to Simferopol to a banquet given them by the Russians. The famed Russian hospitality was put into play, and much vodka was consumed. The hero of the day proved to be V. D. Nabokov (the writer's father). In describing at dinner his experiences both on the western and the eastern front, he was able to pass effortlessly from French into English and back, noisily saluted each time by shouts of "Bravo! Bravo!" by the French and of "Hip, hip, hurray!" from the British.

Obolensky's judgement on this first meeting of the Russians with their allies in the Crimea was less ebullient. "On us," he wrote, "it produced a sobering impression."

To return to family matters. The day after our arrival in Yalta, I was moved into the Vorontsov Palace in Alupka. I was there without my parents. My father had remained behind in Odessa, doubtless preparing to join the White Army of General Yudenich, which he did a year or so later. As for my mother she was banned from the palace by its redoubtable chatelaine my great-grandmother Elizabeth Vorontsov-Dashkov who, I gather, disapproved of her marriage.

After a week, during which I was looked after by a non-excluded aunt, I joined my mother in a local pension.

I know next to nothing about our subsequent life in the Crimea. My mother, whose brief memoirs are here my sole source of information, breaks her silence only once, when she comes to the fateful 9 April 1919.

The day before we were told to prepare for a hasty evacuation. An emergency situation had arisen from the unexpectedly rapid southward advance of the Bolshevik armies. After capturing Kiev and (after its evacuation by the French occupying forces) Odessa, on 7 April, having invaded the Crimea, they were within two days of entering Simferopol.

Urgent measures called for the evacuation of the civilians who, after their more than willing collaboration with the now fleeing Denikin troops, could expect little mercy from the Reds.

Plans for the evacuation were drawn up jointly by the French General Franchet d'Esperey (Commander-in-Chief of the French Forces de l'Orient) and the Royal Navy. One of its key operations was entrusted to HMS Marlborough, sent by the Admiralty to the Crimea to pick up the

Dowager Empress, the sister of Queen Alexandra of England, and to bring her to the safety of Malta. Others given refuge on board the British battleship were the Grand Duke Nicholas (one time commander of the Russian armies in the war), various other members of the Romanov family, and my great-grandmother. We were to follow in a humbler craft.

On the morning of the 9th we were told to assemble in Yalta for embarkation. Three British destroyers lay alongside. We were late arriving (due to the fact that, as we were waiting by the pier earlier in the day, I was drenched by a strong wave, and had to be taken back to the hotel to be dressed in dry clothes and then fed) and were supposed to board the third destroyer, which we reached by walking across the first two. According to my mother I proved a huge success with the naval ratings who for hours carried this one-year-old baby all over the ship; the feelings were evidently reciprocated, for I showed no wish to return from their arms to those of my mother. Meanwhile the embarkation plans were altered and in the evening a large British transport ship, the *Princess Ena*, took us on board.

Its size allowed all elderly persons and children (including myself) to be given separate cabins. We sailed from Yalta the same night, in fairly heavy seas, and at dawn arrived in Sevastopol, where my father joined us. On the same evening – 10 April – we left Russia, and set course for Constantinople.

The dates make it on the whole unlikely, though not impossible, that we witnessed the scene described by Vice-Admiral Sir Francis Pridham, then Gunnery Officer of HMS *Marlborough*, which took place at Yalta shortly before evacuation:

> A British sloop embarked about 400 of the Imperial Guard, mostly officers, who had collected at Yalta, for transport to Sevastopol. On sailing, the sloop steamed slowly round the *Marlborough* to allow those on board to salute the Empress Marie and obtain a last sight of her. Gathered on our quarter-deck were a number of our distinguished passengers, including the

Empress and the Grand Duke Nicholas. The Empress, a little lone figure, stood sadly apart from the others near the ensign staff, flying, of course, the White Ensign, while the voices of the Imperial Guard singing the Russian Imperial Anthem drifted across the water to her in last salute. None other than that beautiful old tune, rendered in such a manner, could have so poignantly reflected the sadness of that moment. The memory of those deep Russian voices, unaccompanied, but in perfect harmony, which few but Russians can achieve, has surely never faded from the minds of those who were privileged to witness this touching scene. Until long after the sloop had passed there was silence. No one approached the Empress, while she remained standing, gazing sadly after those who, leaving her to pass into exile, were bound for what seemed likely to be a forlorn mission.

The Bolshevik invasion of April 1919 was not, however, the end of the civil war in the Crimea. A year later the Whites were in control of the peninsula again, under the command of General Peter Wrangel, elected in April 1920, Denikin's successor as Commander-in-Chief of the armed forces of southern Russia. He was by far the ablest of the anti-Bolshevik military leaders.

Unlike Denikin, he believed neither in rapid forward advances, nor in the furtherance of ethnic Russification. His policy was to firmly establish his government and regime in one region of Russia, in the hope of attracting more widespread support for the campaign against Bolshevism; and, although a convinced monarchist, he was wise enough to realise that, unless he recognised the rights of the constituent national groups within the Empire, he stood no chance of winning the war.

His strategic ability and personal prestige were at first remarkably successful. By June 1920 his forces had broken out of the Crimea, and occupied part of the grain-producing plain of "Northern Tauria". But by early November the tables had been turned, and the Soviet armies, led by Trotsky and Budenny, having forced the Perekop isthmus, began their deployment into the Crimea. This "last stand" of the White armies in the civil war ended on 14 November 1920 in Sevastopol, with the evacuation, partly by the French Navy, of the entire National Army.

By contrast with the chaos and panic that had accompanied the evacuation of Denikin's armies from Novorossisk earlier that year, Wrangel's operation was a model of discipline and careful planning. The commander-in-chief was the last man to leave the quay at Sevastopol. Readers of the earlier section of these memories will recall that one of the aides-de-camp who accompanied him was André Tolstoy, my future stepfather.

Nice
(1923–29)

My earliest memories, still very fragmentary, are of my family's wanderings during the first years after our escape from Russia. The first three years remain a total blank. The *Princess Ena*, after crossing the Black Sea, anchored off Halki (Heybeli), one of the Princes' Islands. The island then housed a Greek Orthodox seminary which, some 30 years later, I was to visit in the company of the Ecumenical Patriarch Athenagoras.

Together with other refugees from the Crimea, we were then moved to neighbouring Constantinople, where we boarded the British merchant vessel SS *Bermuda*, and sailed for Malta.

We arrived there on 24 April 1919, a few days after HMS *Marlborough*, and stayed for about six weeks, after which we embarked on the second stage of our journey. It took us, through Rome and Paris, to England, where we settled for a few months in the small town of Southborough in Kent.

The reason for the choice of England was my father's intention of joining the White Army of General Yudenich in north-west Russia, which was being armed and equipped (with rapidly diminishing enthusiasm) by the British.

Yudenich's planned advance on Petrograd (St Petersburg) led to one of the crucial battles of the Russian Civil War. By 20 October 1919, his units had reached the outskirts of the city, only to be driven back into Estonia by the Red Army, commanded by Trotsky.

These family peregrinations ended in Stockholm, where my mother, with me in tow, went to be closer to my father, in case he needed her.

And here her diary, on which the account of our movements of 1918–19 is largely based, comes to an abrupt end.

My memories take shape a little later. The year is 1921, and the place Cannes, on the French Riviera. My mother's marriage had ended in divorce, and on 15 February 1922 she married, in the Russian church in Cannes, Count André Tolstoy, a distant relative of the writer.

He had recently arrived from the Crimea, where he served in 1920 as aide-de-camp to General Wrangel, the Commander-in-Chief of the armies of southern Russia. My stepfather – "Andrik" to his friends, "Papasha" to his children and me – always treated me as a son, and I came to love him dearly. It is him that I first remember, probably soon after he appeared in my mother's life, offering me with a gentle smile an empty matchbox with a Gallic cockerel depicted on the cover – a tall, elegant, and handsome figure.

Fragmented recollections jostle each other for another year or so. They follow the family's rather restless wanderings in western Europe and the Balkans – in Germany where we lived in Baden-Baden and holidayed in the Black Forest and, one summer, in Dubrovnik, to visit my stepfather's parents and of which I remember only the cockroaches.

In the meantime, two new persons had joined the family. The first was my half-brother Ivan, born in Germany, five years my junior, and now, largely retired, a distinguished geophysicist. He was far more adventurous and fearless than I. We would often be found in Nice swimming in the bathing establishment of La Grande Bleue, or roller-skating on the Promenade des Anglais.

The other addition was Nanny. Short of stature, freckled and inclined to be over-critical and fussy, Miss Clegg was engaged by my mother through an agency in England. During the long years she stayed with us, her age always seemed strangely indeterminate. Ivan and I made frequent and indiscreet attempts to satisfy our curiosity by searching for her passport. To our repeated and intemperate question "Nanny, how old are you?" she would simulate anger and rebuke us for rudeness. Yet basically she was a kindly soul, and was deeply devoted to the family.

My mother's first impression was that Miss Clegg lacked positive opinions of her own. How wrong she was! Resolutely Victorian in her views, especially on matters of education, Nanny was convinced of the innate superiority of English ways.

"We in England don't do such things," she would forcibly remark whenever my brother or I did something of which she disapproved. Hence, living as I did in an actively anglophile environment, I became convinced that, however much I tried, the English way of life would forever remain an unattainable ideal.

It is from our move to Nice in 1923 that my coherent and continuing memories begin. By migrating there we joined a complex society whose origins go back to the mid-nineteenth century, and in which at least three separate strands can be distinguished.

Best known, at least to the outside world, were the wealthy residents and distinguished visitors who had come to enjoy the sun-baked climate, the mild winters, and the enchanting scenery of the Côte d'Azur. Some of them had probably arrived by "*le train des grands-ducs*", as the luxury train linking St Petersburg with Nice was colloquially known before 1914. Others came by sea. There is a story about one of them which I have always liked: it is of a Russian admiral who, having anchored his warship outside Monte Carlo, gambled and lost its entire reserves at the casino. Undeterred, he returned to his ship, trained his guns on the building and threatened to fire on them unless his debt was remitted . . . I was disappointed to learn from a friend who was writing the casino's history that the story is apocryphal.

Another story, true this time, is of two lengthy visits paid to Nice during the winters of 1856–57 and 1859–60 by the Dowager Empress Alexandra, the widow of the Emperor Nicholas I. Winters were then considered the beneficial season for visits to the French Riviera; yet things were already beginning to change. Thus the Empress's sister-in-law, the Grand Duchess Helen, boasted of inaugurating summer bathing in Nice. During the first visit the Empress Alexandra arranged for the building, by public subscription, of the first Russian church in the city, a rather sombre and still extant edifice in the rue de Longchamp.

The Empress's second visit coincided with an event of international importance: the cession to France by the King of Sardinia of Nice and the Duchy of Savoy. This decision was extremely unpopular among the Russians in Nice, who must have reckoned that Napoleon III would prove a harder nut to crack than Cavour, King Victor Emmanuel's Prime Minister.

Politics must also have played some part in the Dowager Empress's two visits. Russia's defeat in the Crimean War (1856) led to the country being forbidden to maintain naval forces in the Black Sea. In an effort to counteract this vexatious clause, the Russian government sought to establish a naval presence in the Mediterranean.

Its choice of a station fell on the deep-sea port of Villefranche, a mile or so east of Nice. It was in this bay that the Empress arrived in October 1856 on board a Sardinian frigate. By 1858 the Russians were openly using its naval facilities. When in 1860 Nice and Villefranche became French, the government of Napoleon III raised no objections. Not so the British, whose press, echoing Palmerston's indignation, voiced the strongest suspicions of these manifest attempts by Russia to evade its contractual obligations by using the Bay of Villefranche. The Globe was particularly eloquent: it claimed that this "capacious and well-sheltered harbour" was "in the most favourite position for becoming a small Sevastopol in the heart of the Mediterranean", and that the people of Nice were "delighted at the chance of being a permanent Russian Brighton" (10 September 1857).

This attempt by the Russians to find a naval point d'appui in the central Mediterranean was short-lived. By 1870, Russia had freed itself from the restraints on her movements in the Black Sea imposed by the Treaty of Paris, so her naval strategy no longer required a Mediterranean base.

In the nineteenth century, Nice played another role in European history, by providing a refuge for political exiles. The most distinguished was Alexander Herzen, often described as the father of

Russian radicalism. His fervent admirer, Isaiah Berlin, has applauded his view "that the goal of life is life itself, that to sacrifice the present to some vague and unpredictable future is a form of delusion which leads to the destruction of all that alone is valuable in men and societies, to the gratuitous sacrifice . . . of live human beings upon the altar of idealised abstractions". Herzen's presence in Nice is recorded several times between 1847 and 1867. When in England, he founded the earliest Russian free press abroad. He died in Paris in 1870, and was buried in Nice, next to his wife.

Another, and more numerous, group of political *émigrés* began to arrive in Nice after 1917: refugees from Communist Russia, mostly holders of "Nansen passports" and entry visas to France. Some, like ourselves, had come from the Crimea, others from General Wrangel's camps in Gallipoli. Most of them were penniless and obscure. A few belonged to distinguished families or had held prominent positions in imperial Russia. They included Count D. I. Tolstoy, the last pre-revolutionary director of the Hermitage Museum; Alexander Naumov, former Minister of Agriculture; Serge Sazonov, Foreign Minister; and the more recluse figure of Princess Catherine Yurevsky, the morganatic wife of the Emperor Alexander II (she died in 1922, and is buried in Nice).

A third category of Niçois were Russians who had come to the Riviera because they were gravely ill. The archives of the Russian consulate in Nice mention the presence of numerous compatriots in search of a cure for the ever-rampant tuberculosis. Not a few are buried in the cemetery of Caucade, high above the town, acquired in 1867 from the English colony. It now contains over 3,000 Russian graves.

The most distinguished of the imperial visitors to Nice arrived in November 1864. He was the Grand Duke Nicholas, the eldest son of the reigning Emperor, Alexander II, and thus the heir to the Russian throne. For the past four years he had suffered from tuberculosis, and died of it in Nice on 24 April 1865, aged 21. His immediate family were assembled round his deathbed: his father the Emperor, who had arrived two days earlier; his brother, the future Alexander III; and his fiancée Princess Dagmar, daughter of King Christian IX of Denmark, who had come with her mother from Copenhagen, and who later married his brother, becoming known in Russia as the Empress Maria Feodorovna. The funeral service was held in the small Russian church in the rue de Longchamp, after which the body was taken to Villefranche, and then in a warship to St Petersburg.

On the site of the Grand Duke Nicholas's death, the Villa Bermond, a commemorative chapel was built. The park attached to the Villa later became the emplacement for the building of the handsome Russian cathedral, still one of the best-known and prominent buildings in Nice. The first stone was laid in April 1903, and the cathedral was consecrated on 18 December 1912.

In my memories of childhood and adolescence, the Russian cathedral plays an important role. It was there that my earliest religious feelings and views found focus and expression. It was about half an hour's walk from home; and, as I made my way there alone on Sunday mornings (as one of the altar boys I had to be there before most of the others) I still remember the feeling of happiness that overcame me on hearing the tolling of the cathedral bell. The Holy Week services were particularly impressive. Nanny's Anglican instincts rebelled at their number and length.

"We in England," she declared, when my mother and I returned one evening from a Good Friday service lasting some three hours, "go to church so as to become better; you Russians do so to see for how long you can stand."

Russian churches, as everyone knows, have no pews.

Not far from the Orthodox cathedral was the Russian school. Both recalled, in their location, the late Grand Duke Nicholas: Boulevard Tzaréwitch was the address of the cathedral, and Boulevard Tzaréwitch prolongé that of the school, further up the road. The history of this school is an impressive example of the initiative and devotion shown by educated and well-to-do Russians, in the early years of the emigration, in providing their younger compatriots with a means of safeguarding their language, religion, and culture and, as the more hopeful intended, of preparing them for the return one day to their homeland.

Some were wealthy enough to provide solid financial support for this enterprise. They included Ryabushinsky, a banker who had wisely transferred important assets to France before the Revolution; the Grand Duke Andrew, who became the patron of the school; Paul Demidov, and perhaps inevitably Sir Basil Zakharoff.

The headmaster was the highly enlightened Arkady Yakhontov, the former general secretary of the Russian council of ministers, who founded the school, named Alexandrino, in October 1925. The fifty or so pupils, some of them boarders, were Russian by origin and Orthodox by religion. The teaching was in Russian, except for instruction in the French language, which followed the methods used in the national *lycées*.

Several of the teachers were highly gifted. Two of them, both *émigrés*, proved lastingly influential: Nataliya Tomilova and Father Alexander Elchaninov.

I studied at this school for four years, between the ages of seven and eleven. Father Elchaninov, whose personal notes were later published by his widow under the title *The Diary of a Russian Priest*, possessed rare gifts as a teacher and spiritual director. To Madame Tomilova I owe a solid grounding in the Russian literary language. My debt to both these outstanding teachers is very great.

Sadly, the school failed to survive the manifold burdens of *émigré* life, and the financial crisis of 1929. In 1934 it had to close. Arkady Yakhontov and his family moved to Cannes, where he died of a heart attack in 1938. Russian culture in France owes him and his wife Adelaida a considerable debt.

We lived in Nice from 1923 to 1929. These were, I think, the happiest years of my life. My stepfather had a paid job as co-director of a small local bank. Finances went somewhat downhill when his Russian colleague absconded with the funds. Yet there was still a little money left, with which we rented a small house in the district of Les Baumettes, overlooking the sea. But the financial crisis had started to bite, and employment was increasingly hard to find. The move to Paris, where jobs were more easily available, seemed the only solution.

Lynchmere
(1929–31)

Our decision to leave Nice and move to Paris was prompted mainly by economic considerations. The 1929 crash had a disastrous effect on the labour market in France, and hit with particular severity those foreigners like ourselves who were required by law to obtain a work permit.

Large cities such as Paris offered a greater chance of gainful employment. Hence a minor exodus of Russians from Nice began in the late 1920s. In the summer of 1929 we moved to Versailles, where my stepfather found a job with an insurance company.

For a year or so we lived close to the immense park of the palace (the château) built for Louis XIV. These formal gardens, designed and embellished by Le Nôtre, included the Trianon pavilions, later graced by Marie Antoinette, and the two huge fountains, named after Apollo and Neptune. The view from the front of the palace, in a sweeping perspective extending past the Grand Canal into the far distance, was one we often admired.

Two important family events marked our year in Versailles. The first was the birth of my second half-brother Paul. A delicate child, he narrowly escaped death in an attack of double pneumonia. He was also unusually precocious, displaying by the age of ten an alarming interest in embryology and spending hours on Sundays endeavouring to teach Latin to our Aunt Seta, who adored him. He is now professor of anthropology at the French university of Montreal.

The other event was the totally unexpected appearance in our lives of Harry Upfield Gilbert. This remarkable man had, in 1904 in Russia, been engaged by my stepfather's father, Count Dimitri Tolstoy, to teach English to his two sons. A graduate of Merton College, Oxford, he came up as a Classical Scholar in 1891. His undergraduate career was a mixed one: he obtained a Second Class in Honour Moderations and, no doubt to the disappointment of his College authorities, only a Third in Greats. At Merton, it is curious to note, he overlapped with that notorious impostor Edmund Backhouse.

On the Tolstoy estate in Ukraine, Gilbert was an immediate hit. He took the boys camping and on long walks, teaching them English and Latin, nurturing their anglophilia. With their parents, however, his relations, cordial at first, soured a year or so after his arrival. The reasons were purely linguistic. Countess Tolstoy, whose English was poor, conversed with Gilbert in French, of which his knowledge, at that time, was limited.

At dinner one evening she said, probably intending this as a compliment: "Monsieur Gilbert, les garçons ont acquis des manières extrêmement anglaises."

Gilbert, no doubt misconstruing "extrêmement" to mean "excessively", and taking this to be an unjustified slur on English manners, retorted: "Et vous, avec vos sales manières russes!"

What happened then is not altogether clear. The fact is that, although the linguistic misunderstanding was soon clarified and settled, Gilbert's rudeness was not, and he had to go. The Count, a kindly man, gave him most of a year's pay and a ticket to Paris. He then took him to Kiev and put him on the train.

Gilbert's subsequent life was spent in England. Wounded at Ypres and partially lame, he was invalided out of the army and settled in Eastbourne, where he started a small preparatory school which he called Lynchmere. He had, in the meantime, lost track of the Tolstoy family. Worrying perhaps about his monumental gaffe and wishing to make amends, he eventually traced them to France. And so, one day in the late summer of 1929, in the company of two Lynchmere boys, he arrived in Versailles and found us, living on the edge of poverty.

The amends he offered (without, of course, saying so) for his indiscretion in Russia were generous in the extreme. He offered to take me as a pupil, free of charge, for at least a year, possibly two. In a few years, he added, he could take Ivan as well.

I accepted with enthusiasm. Nanny's anglophilia had clearly left its mark. Besides I knew that "games" (le sport, as the French called them) were very important in English schools, and I was becoming seriously interested in football and tennis, the latter on the way to becoming a teenage passion. So in early October, escorted by my stepfather, I crossed the Channel on the way to Eastbourne. I was then eleven.

In Newhaven, Gilbert was waiting for us in his open Morris car. The drive to Eastbourne was decidedly chilly, a foretaste of the almost constant sensation of cold which I was to experience during the winter months in the unheated gas-lit halls, staircases, and dormitories of the school.

In the afternoon, Papasha left for home. Within a few minutes I was seized by a powerful affliction which was to plague me during the first weeks of every term at Lynchmere. It was home-sickness. It would strike with lightning speed on waking in the mornings (as I recorded daily in my diary, but never dared to admit to anyone at Lynchmere). I had never before left home for any length of time, and the knowledge that months would pass before I could hope to see my family was at times unbearable.

My only recourse was to write despairing letters home (in answer to which my mother gently urged the exercise of will-power) and to open the school atlas on the page marked "France" to gaze with longing on the point marked "Paris". With time, the affliction diminished in intensity, as I became more involved in the school's activities, and the approach of holidays at home became more tangible. But it never entirely left me.

All told I was not altogether unhappy at Lynchmere. I made several good friends among the school's thirty or so boys. I greatly enjoyed the team games and the soccer and cricket matches we played against other Eastbourne schools. There were other agreeable memories: walking with a chosen school-mate on Sundays to Beachy Head (this was known as "pairing"), jogging when muscles, limbs, lungs, and heart all seemed to be working in unison, or looking out in broad sunshine onto the school lawn on endless summer afternoons – these still remain in my old age happy and heart-warming recollections.

Gilbert was an excellent teacher, provided your memory was good and you responded to his questions with alacrity. Latin prose composition was the subject in which he excelled. Years later when, as a pupil in a French lycée, I outclassed my school-mates in Latin composition, and in an official interlycée competition was placed fourth in France, I liked to think that I had learned from Gilbert a little of that skill in imitating the language of classical writers in a style which, in the words of A. E. Housman, was "written in England . . . better in the nineteenth century than anywhere in Europe since classical antiquity itself".

Memory and speed were qualities highly prized in Gilbert's oral interrogation. He would line us up facing him in what he regarded as the order of merit. A searching question of Latin grammar would be passed down the line; and the first to get it right would then advance to the top of the class. We were also encouraged to recite long poeticised lists of exceptions to rules of Latin gender taken from Kennedy's grammar. I can still regurgitate them at will.

School discipline, though fairly strict, was not over-severe. I discovered later that Gilbert, a firm believer in and an expert practitioner of, corporal punishment, had been made to promise the parents that neither Ivan nor I would be subject to it. This promise he loyally kept.

My worst problem was the cold. I had never heard of chilblains before coming to Lynchmere. The dormitories were unheated, and we were allowed only one blanket, except when the thermometer dropped below freezing. One night, in some discomfort, I spread a dressing-gown over my blanket, only to see Gilbert stalk in after lights-out, rip the offending object off the bed, and address me as "You sweaty hog".

A more frequent indictment was being "feeble-minded". It covered a large and ill-defined number of failings and misdemeanours, and few of us ever escaped it.

We endured further discomfort at an early morning activity known as "plunge". Before breakfast each of us had to dive into a 15-metre swimming pool and do two lengths. Sometimes, after a very cold night, there would be ice in the corners of the pool. A row of shivering, naked boys stood against a damp stone wall, waiting in deep misery for their turn to jump. Any visible lack of enthusiasm was rewarded by a kick on the backside from the headmaster and the spluttering victim had to swim or sink. A long pole was propped up in a corner just in case. However, I don't remember it ever being used.

Occasionally a recent arrival, unfamiliar with the harsh rules of "plunge", would try to hoist himself out before completing the statutory two lengths. He would have his fingers smartly stamped on by the ever-watchful Gilbert (known among the boys as "The Man"), with a commanding roar: "Get back, you rotter!"

More than once I blessed my Mediterranean childhood, which at least had taught me to swim.

One of the masters presided over breakfast. Our staple food was porridge and bread and butter (more likely margarine), washed down with tea. The master was given toast; he would cut off the hard edges and distribute them to the boys sitting near him. I remember being rather puzzled by the indignation aroused by this generosity, which we accepted gratefully enough, when I spoke of it at home.

An experience new to me was a cross-country run known as "harriers", in which we followed the local hunt across the Pevensey marshes. In my ignorance of hunting, it seemed to me to amount to a bizarre sequence of goose-chases: the hounds pursuing the hare, the huntsmen the hounds, while the boys, escorted by the junior masters, ran after the huntsmen. Gilbert, being lame, either took short cuts or occasionally pole-vaulted over the dykes. We ended up, I need hardly say, feeling cold and wet.

Gilbert's eccentricities, occasionally outrageous, masked, I believe, a warm heart and a not ungenerous character. As most of the other Lynchmere boys, I suspect, I grew genuinely fond of him. It was sad to learn of his death in the summer of 1939 of a heart attack while bicycling in Normandy with two of his boys.

Paris
(1931–37)

My return to France in 1931, at the age of 13, was a move from an English boarding school to a French lycée. The change was considerable. It meant living at home and accepting a widely different educational philosophy and programme of studies.

Unlike the empirical approach of Gilbert and his team of masters, and the English emphasis on "games", with their physical and social value, our French teachers laid the main stress on the accumulation of knowledge and, understandably enough, on the literary and intellectual achievements of their own national culture.

We worked far harder than at Lynchmere, with "prep" often running on till late in the evening, and only the briefest acquaintance with "gym" at the most once a week. Our progress in each subject was tested once a term in a written exam known as "composition", a competitive and much feared ordeal, not devoid of drama. Half-way through a class the door would suddenly open, and the two principal officials of the school – the Proviseur (headmaster) and the Censeur (responsible for discipline) – would march in and proceed to read out to some 20 or 30 boys the classified results. Works of literature were often learned by heart, which suited me as I had inthose days an exceptional memory.

On my return from Lynchmere, I studied successively at two lycées on the western outskirts of Paris: at the Lycée Hoche in Versailles (in 1931–2) and the Lycée Pasteur in Neuilly-sur-Seine. Two teachers, both at Pasteur, proved influential. One was the well-known Catholic writer Daniel-Rops, whose real name was Petiot. A gifted and imaginative teacher, he certainly stimulated my interest in history. The other, Perret, who taught philosophy in my terminal year, was no doubt responsible in some measure for my choice of that subject, then called Moral Science, in my first year at Cambridge.

Each of the last two years of secondary education ended with a rigorous exam known as the *baccalauréat*. Success in both entitled you to enrol, without further test, in a university.

As I grew older I became increasingly aware of the *émigré* community of which my family and relatives were a part. It was a large and socially complex society, far more numerous and less homogeneous than the Russian community in Nice. Out of a million or so refugees who fled the Bolsheviks in 1918–21, some 400,000 are believed to have settled in France. Most of them had escaped across the Black Sea. The majority were the defeated remnants of the White armies who, under Generals Denikin and Wrangel, had fought the Bolsheviks in South Russia, Ukraine, and the Crimea.

A sizeable minority belonged to the educated classes. They had the inestimable advantage of knowing French, and sometimes other foreign languages, and could mitigate their painful awareness of being exiles by the sense of belonging culturally to Europe. Their influence was further reinforced by Lenin's decision in 1922 to expel from Russia over 150 distinguished intellectuals together with their families.

From 1925 to 1940 the most important centre of the Russian emigration was Paris. It was there that the political, literary, and artistic activity, as well as the religious life of the *émigrés* was in the main concentrated. Their leaders were convinced, often rightly, that in the face of the deadening and in many respects iconoclastic Soviet tyranny, it had fallen to them to act as the standard-bearers of Russian culture.

The fact that this culture had flourished so mightily in the decades preceding the Revolution added force to this conviction. Not a few of these *émigré* masters spent many years in Paris, and were culturally and spiritually active there. Their names rank high in the annals of

Russian and world twentieth-century achievement. They include in the political field Kerensky, Maklakov, Miliukov, and Struve; in religion and philosophy Berdyaev, Bulgakov, Metropolitan Evlogy, Florovsky, and Vladimir Lossky; in literature Bunin, Khodasevich, Merezhkovsky, and Tsvetaeva; in art Benois, Bakst, Chagall, Kandinsky, and Soutine; in music and ballet Chaliapin, Diaghilev and Stravinsky; in scholarship André Grabar; and in chess Alekhin.

Most of the Paris *émigrés*, it is true, were too busy struggling to survive with their families to be able to share, even passively, in those cultural activities. Life for them became even harder after the Great Crash, with its adverse effect on economic prosperity. Work permits became even more difficult to obtain, especially for those stateless persons whose sole credential was the "Nansen passport", issued by the League of Nations and so called after Fridtjof Nansen, the Norwegian polar explorer who was appointed High Commissioner for Refugees in 1921. It was merely a legal means enabling them to cross state borders, provided they obtained the necessary foreign visas.

The relations between the Russian *émigrés* and the French authorities were fitful. In October 1924, to the despair of the Russian community, the Soviet government was officially recognised by France. Henceforth, in the eyes of the *émigrés*, the Soviets began to present a tangible threat.

In January 1930 General Kutepov, a hero of the civil war, a companion-in-arms of Wrangel and then head of a veterans' organization, the Russian All-Military Union (ROVS), was kidnapped in broad daylight in a busy Paris street. Recently uncovered Soviet archives confirm the widely held suspicions that the assailants were agents of the GPU, the precursor of the KGB. Kutepov was drugged and taken to Marseilles, where he was embarked on a Soviet ship bound for Novorossiisk. He seems to have died of a heart attack during the voyage. The event received wide publicity in the French press and, needless to say, in Russian *émigré* newspapers. Seven years later, an almost exact replica of this outrage was perpetrated in Paris: General Miller, Kutepov's successor as head of ROVS, was similarly kidnapped by Soviet agents and, in all probability, embarked on a Russian vessel in Le Havre.

In May 1932, two years after the Kutepov affair, the President of the French Republic, Paul Doumer, was assassinated in Paris by a Russian émigré, Paul Gorgulov. Though he was certifiably mad, the assassin was guillotined. A wave of anti-Russian xenophobia swept France; its favourite slogan was "*La France aux Français*". Doumer's assassination, it has justly been said, heralded "the worst months in the history of the Russian emigration".

The more sophisticated were still capable of black humour: one émigré, it is said, was greeted next morning by his French employer with the words: "*Il a crevé: faites vos valises!*" ("He's snuffed it: pack your bags!").

The next year, 1933, fate smiled at last on the Russian exiles. On 10 November it was announced that one of their number, Ivan Bunin, who lived in the South of France, had been awarded the Nobel Prize for Literature. In this, their proudest moment, the exiles were able to lay aside for a while their political and other disputes and to recognise that, whatever the claims of their Soviet adversaries, the true values of Russian culture rested with them.

The variety and complexity of the émigrés' daily existence can be illustrated by three examples, all taken from the lives of members of my family. These are my father, my stepfather, and my uncle.

My stepfather was the most stolid of the three. In 1915 he enlisted in the highly exclusive Chevalier Guards regiment, fought the Germans, and after 1917 spent another three years on active service in the civil war, ending as a captain on the staff of General Wrangel. The revolution and exile ended his hopes of a scholarly career in natural science.

In France, where most of his energies went into supporting his family, he had little time for relaxation. He was fortunate in finding a steady job in a film factory on the outskirts of Paris, eventually becoming assistant to the director. His knowledge of languages certainly helped. His holidays were often spent hiking or mountain-climbing, for which he had something of a passion.

Sometimes he attended regimental dinners, and lavish parties in the home of a long-standing Polish friend, Dolly Radziwill, who was married to the Norwegian architect Mogens Tvede. They lived in some splendour near the Invalides, in conditions he and my mother had almost forgotten and I had never known. There were several servants, a first-class chef, a chauffeur, as well as a Rubens and a Gobelin in the drawing room. Occasionally there were lunches to which Ivan and I were invited. We greatly enjoyed these gastronomic events, pretending, during meals, not to notice the frowns of the parents, who evidently feared that our undisguised gluttony would be seen by our hosts as a sign of near starvation at home. On returning from one of these Lucullan occasions I was once sternly reprimanded for accepting to be served three times with a particularly delicious soufflé.

One day, hearing that mother was unwell, Dolly sent her private doctor to help. He arrived with some formality, in a frock coat and pin-striped trousers, wondering no doubt as he surveyed our modest *intérieur*, at the ill-fortune that had struck our expatriate, though titled, family. At the end of his visit, as he sat writing out a prescription, the table on which he wrote suddenly collapsed with an ear-splitting crack. Memories of this event never lost the power to send the family into hoots of merriment.

My father's life as an *émigré* was more colourful. In the 1920s and 1930s he held a large variety of jobs, whose details he would recount with unfailing glee: purser on the transatlantic liner *Isle de France*; riding instructor in an American school of equitation; dealer in rabbit skins in Normandy; guide to the night-life of Paris for wealthy Americans; secretary to a "crazy Scot" who wanted to buy up the rivers of Corsica for salmon fishing; and night watchman who, under the authority of the police, patrolled the district of the Paris Opéra.

Many of these watchmen were, like he, impoverished though honest Russians. Each, he explained, was issued with a revolver, with the strict warning that, if he used it except in self-defence, he risked hard labour. Great was his chagrin when one night, about to apprehend from behind a lamp-post a suspicious-looking figure emerging from a bank, he discovered it was the bank manager. Gone was the chance of the expected tip!

Another adventure befell my father in the South of France. As he was cycling down a path leading to the coastal road, he inadvertently collided with a medium-sized car. Projected high above the road, he turned a complete somersault, and landed on his feet. To the astonished driver he announced: "I served in the Russian cavalry – and they taught us how to fall."

My father ended his life on the French Riviera, tending on behalf of two eccentric ladies something they called an estate, in fact little more than a kitchen-garden. He was particularly proud of his black tulips, loving above all the earth and all that grows on it.

His younger brother, Peter, had an almost equally adventurous career in emigration. He too had been a night watchman, not on the streets but in two hotels – the Napoléon Bonaparte in the centre of Paris, and the other in St Tropez. My uncle rose to the more prestigious activity of taxi-driver, a career proverbially embraced by Russian aristocratic émigrés. It was valued for the independence it conferred, making it attractive to war veterans. Peter himself reckoned that on the eve of the Second World War, of the 17,000 taxi-drivers in Paris, 7,000 were Russians. The latter were grouped in two rival factions, divided by their opposing political views, and battling with each other on the pages of their respective fly-sheets: Za rulyom = "Behind the steering-wheel" (conservative) and Russky shofyor = "The Russian driver" ('democratic').

In 1955, in the short-lived and mistaken hope that freedom was on the rise in the Soviet Union, and probably from genuine homesickness as well, my uncle returned to Russia. Being a composer and the author of several studies on Russian music, he got to know Shostakovich, who had him appointed a member of the Union of Soviet Composers. His meagre salary was eventually succeeded by a retirement pension. Judging this to be inadequate, he is said to have written to Nikita Khrushchev complaining that "even a prince can't live on so low a pension". The Soviet leader, who shared some of my uncle's sense of humour, promptly had his pension raised.

Peter died in Moscow in December 1969. His memoirs, though brief, are surprisingly free of the irrelevant propaganda normally required by Soviet censorship. One of his Moscow friends, who later emigrated, wrote his obituary in a Russian Paris newspaper. He felt that Peter was a deeply disappointed man, though afraid to acknowledge it.

My own active participation in the world of Russian Paris was limited mainly by the time-consuming school studies, but some outdoor activity was possible. Having grown up, partly under the influence of my mother, as a practising member of the Orthodox church, I would travel on most Sundays from our home in Neuilly to the centre of Paris, where I served as an altar boy in a small church belonging to the Russian branch of the YMCA. One of its priests, Father George Florovsky, was already then a world-famous patristic scholar. These religious influences, in what I hope is a maturer and perhaps more critical form, are with me still.

Another form of companionship which I greatly enjoyed were the summer camps organised annually on the French Riviera by the Russian Student Christian Movement. My friends and I would cycle by the shore between Toulon and the Italian border, and in the evenings, sitting round a campfire, sing traditional Russian songs whose words, if not always the tunes, I long remembered.

Another kind of outdoor activity for which I developed a real passion was tennis. There were times when I would have liked to devote my life to this rhythmic and elegant sport; fortunately I was not good enough for that. In Courbevoie, a suburb of Paris, there was a Russian tennis club. My family could not afford the full membership fee: so, as a special favour, I was allowed to use its courts at a much reduced rate, and on one condition: I was to play regularly with the club secretary (repressing a strong irritation, as he was not good at all at the game, being capable of little more than gentle lobbing).

Some entertaining went on at home, especially on Sunday after-noons, when various relatives converged at our little house in Neuilly (we lived near the Bois de Boulogne), where, under the stimulus of my grandmother, family news and politics were discussed at length. Occasionally some grander figure would be invited to dinner.

One such was Berdyaev. He would discourse learnedly on the latest intellectual and spiritual groupings in Europe – such as Eurasianism and the Ecumenical Movement – while my brothers and I stared incredulously at the nervous tic which every so often made him open wide his mouth and stick out his tongue. He detested all forms of anti-Semitism. I once attended a lecture by him on the relationship of Judaism and Christianity, which was interrupted by two loutish young men who shouted pro-Fascist slogans. White with rage, Berdyaev silenced them by threatening to close the meeting.

One of my last memories of the pre-war world of Russian France was a ceremony that took place in Paris on 10 February 1937, marking the hundredth anniversary of Pushkin's death. Usually celebrated on the anniversary of Pushkin's birth, 6 June 1799, it has been observed annually in Paris and other *émigré* centres since 1925. On 6 June 1926 a large group of distinguished Russians gathered at the Sorbonne to pay homage to Pushkin (the one name, it was hoped, that could unite them all). It included Merezhkovsky, Miliukov, and Vasily Maklakov, the ambassador of the 1917 Provisional Government.

Maklakov, now the dean of the Russian *émigré* community, speaking to a packed audience, stressed the *émigrés*' duty to preserve and protect their cultural tradition, particularly their literary culture, under threat in their native land. Echoing these sentiments, Dimitri Merezhkovsky was later to write: "For those of us who have lost our country, Russian literature is our final homeland, all that Russia was and will be."

Cambridge
(1937–48)

It is not easy to identify and classify in order of importance the reasons that impelled me – when my days at the lycée were drawing to a close – to re-cross the Channel and seek admission to an English university.

There were certainly more than one: deep-seated anglophilia at home; the years spent at Lynchmere; and, more difficult perhaps to explain, a certain failure to adapt to French life, coupled with a degree of inertness in accepting the ghetto-like existence of so many Russian communities in France. All these were no doubt contributory factors. The decisive occasion, however, was a tea party in Paris.

The tea party, which I suspect was instigated by my mother and stepfather, was given by my great-uncle and godfather, Alexander Polovtsov. There I met a Cambridge graduate, Gray Skipwith, who had recently studied at Trinity College. He told me that, after a competitive examination, his College awarded scholarships to suitably qualified candidates. He promised to write to Trinity about me, thus initiating a number of useful moves: a letter of enquiry from my stepfather to Trinity; the College's reply, explaining the mechanism of the scholarship examination and informing me that, if I wished, I could offer French and Russian as my main subjects. Realising that this would give me an initial advantage, and that financial aid would be necessary if I had any hope of going to Cambridge, I decided to sit for a scholarship in December 1936.

Certain preparations now became necessary. While I was reasonably confident of my ability to cope with texts in French and Russian, I knew that the scholarship exam also had papers in Latin, an English essay and, worst of all, "general knowledge questions". The latter, I suspected, required an acquaintance with English culture which, having left England at the age of 13, I did not sufficiently possess. This could easily prove a stumbling-block. The sensible thing was to spend at least a month or so in England before the examination, under the guidance of an experienced tutor.

One was found through family contacts, and in November I was sent to stay with the Reverend Derwas Chitty, Anglican vicar of Upton Rector, near Didcot in Berkshire, who later became known as the author of *The Desert a City*. The other problem was my duties to the *lycée*. I had another school year before completing my secondary education. The authorities of the Lycée Pasteur gave me leave of absence for the whole of the autumn term, knowing full well that I would use it with the intention of moving to England – an act of academic altruism worth a grateful mention.

Derwas Chitty proved an admirable tutor. A delightful man, still young and full of vigour and enthusiasm, he had been a naval chaplain in Greece, where he became a devotee of the Greek Orthodox Church. His parishioners, who were devoted to him, were treated from time to time to the sight of some bearded and black-robed Orthodox prelate alighting from the London train on his way to the rectory. The latter was largely unheated and, on winter nights, bitterly cold. One of the window panes on the staircase, I noticed, was missing. His housekeeper, when I asked her why, replied with a smile, as though it happened all the time: "The rector put his fist through it the other day."

Derwas set me Latin unseens and prose compositions, and English essays to write. I remember the title of one of them: "Which was right: Galileo or the Inquisition?" After dinner we would retire to his study, lined with Greek and Syriac sources. He often read poetry aloud, usually Romantic in content. Flecker and Housman, to whom he introduced me, were among his favourites. I can still hear his voice, reciting, as he often did, Francis Thompson's *The Hound of Heaven*.

In mid-December, coached by Derwas and, I hoped, groomed a little in English (in his case, Welsh) ways, I took the train to Cambridge. It was very cold and foggy, and I still remember the feeling of melancholy that overtook me at the sight of the city's single railway platform poking out of the gloom.

For a week we wrote two three-hour papers a day. On my return to London, where I stayed with family friends, I listened on the radio with some bewilderment to the King's abdication speech. I was told that, if successful, I would receive a telegram from Trinity.

On the afternoon of the fateful day I went with my mother for a long walk in the nearby Bois de Boulogne. On our return I saw, lying on the floor, a telegram. It was from J. R. M. Butler, the Senior Tutor of Trinity, and read: "A hundred pounds scholarship – congratulations!"

This was certainly the most important telegram I ever received.

I remember sparing a moment of gratitude for Gray Skipwith, without whom none of this might have happened. He was killed in the RAF during the war, flying over Germany.

I returned to the lycée for the remaining two terms. Meanwhile a number of practical problems had arisen, some of them urgent. Two were questions asked by Trinity: what subject did I propose to "read" at the university? And did I need furnished or unfurnished rooms in College? A third problem stemmed from my nationality. As a stateless person with a "Nansen passport", I needed a visa from the British consulate in Paris. Finally, the most demanding question of all: the £100 scholarship I had been awarded, the maximum amount, was insufficient to live on. The minimum required, in those days, was said to be £220. Trinity might come to the rescue.

My poor stepfather wrote to the College, regretting that he could give me annually no more than £5, a sum whose smallness he ascribed to the recent devaluation of the franc! In the event, the College's generosity proved boundless: for the next five years, until my election to a College Fellowship, I was entirely supported by Trinity.

My choice of a subject was influenced by the excitement and joy I had felt at being taught philosophy during my last year in Paris by a gifted teacher. Although it then masqueraded under the title of

"Moral Science", I resolved to study this subject at Cambridge. Little did I realise the trouble I was stirring up for myself.

As to furniture, possessing none of my own and unable at that time to buy any, I had naturally asked for furnished rooms in College. Someone, however, probably in the College office, had blundered; and when I arrived on a Sunday evening in October 1937 and, full of excited anticipation, entered my set of rooms, I found them completely bare save for a case of books I had sent from Paris.

Almost in tears, I appealed for help to my tutor, Mr Butler. He was kind and sympathetic, arranged for me to be put up for the night elsewhere in College, and there and then handed me a cheque for £20 to enable me to buy some furniture next morning: another novel experience!

In a day or so I called on my director of studies, John Wisdom of Trinity, later to become Professor of Philosophy. I have little recollection of our meeting, but I must have told him something about my philosophy course in France. I strongly suspect that he found the course, and probably me, inadequate for the task of reading Moral Science. Apparently there was in the late 1930s little of any intellectual contact between British and French philosophers, more of a cultural blockage. I do not remember having so much as heard in France of logical positivism or linguistic philosophy, which seemed to reign supreme at Cambridge.

Why Mr Wisdom failed to explain even briefly what the local school of philosophy was all about I never understood. As far as I can remember, all he did was to send me to the Cambridge University Library with a list of books to read. One of them, I remember, was Susan Stebbing on logic. I don't believe I ever got beyond page four.

The sequel to this unpromising beginning was later told as a funny story by my then tutor Patrick Duff. It went roughly as follows:

I went to see him in some despair.

"Sir, I can bear it no longer. This morning I went to a lecture by Mr Wisdom. All he did was to pace up and down with an agonised expression (in imitation, I later suspected, of Wittgenstein, who had a naturally agonised expression), discussing one single proposition: 'What do I mean when I say there is a blackboard there?'"

Many years later I repeated these words, when telling this story, in a somewhat frivolous tone, to the eminent Oxford philosopher Freddie (Sir Alfred) Ayer.

Looking at me severely, he said: "But I have kept audiences riveted to my words for an hour, saying precisely that."

I was evidently unlucky when relaying the *ipsissima verba* of philosophers to their colleagues.

One day I encountered Wittgenstein – whom I knew as a Fellow of Trinity – in a Cambridge street. After chatting amiably he said to me: "Do you know what my next work will be? – 'On the Humour of the Marx Brothers' . . . "

Professor C. D. Broad, who was present in the Trinity Combination Room when I narrated this encounter, looked at me *very* severely, and said: "I am sure Professor Wittgenstein meant that in jest." I am equally sure Broad was wrong.

As a result of all this, I was allowed to switch from Moral Science to Modern Languages (Russian and French). I have often thought that, had I persisted with the study of Moral Science, I might have ended like Hilaire Belloc's anti-hero Godolphin Horne, who concluded his disappointing career by "blacking the boots at the Savoy".

I was assigned two new directors of study. One was Elizabeth Hill, the recently appointed Anglo-Russian lecturer in Slavonic Studies. She was on the lookout for pupils who knew, or could learn, Russian; these were somewhat scarce at the time. She must have thought I fitted the bill rather well.

My teacher in French was the Reverend Dr H. Stewart, of Trinity, a well-known authority on Pascal, and responsible, it was said, for persuading the College to subscribe to the *Daily Worker*. He soon realised that what I needed was not teaching in French, but more knowledge of English literature. On his suggestion I read a number of English classics, including, I remember, *Vanity Fair*.

Before long I found myself having an absorbing social life. Being invited to numerous parties by undergraduates and dons was a novel and exciting experience. The feeling that I was liked and appreciated added to the many attractions of Cambridge. Had I then been familiar with Vladimir Nabokov's autobiography *Speak, Memory* I would probably have wondered how the author, a Russian undergraduate at Trinity in the early 1920s, could so signally have failed to enjoy himself.

Once a week Elizabeth Hill invited Russian-speaking undergraduates, and those who were learning the language, to evenings in her flat where we sang Russian songs. During a whole term some of us rehearsed for a production in Russian of Gogol's *Government Inspector* (*Revizor*) at the ADC Theatre, in which I played the part of Khlestakov, the bogus inspector-general. Even foreign travel, until the war, was there to be enjoyed. In 1938 I was given a grant to attend a summer school at Tatranská Lomnica in Slovakia, organized by the League of Nations Union. It rained for most of the week, so we sang: "Czechs and Slovaks everywhere . . . Stormy weather . . . "

On my way home I stopped for a few days in Prague, an overwhelmingly beautiful city. In the summer of 1939, I was given a vacation job by the National Union of Students. I had to act as a guide to a group of British and Commonwealth students going on a tour of north Italy (Milan, Florence, Venice, Stresa, Lake Como). The fact that I had never been to the country and spoke virtually no Italian did not appear to matter. The students – six men, six girls – paired off conveniently, leaving me free to do some sightseeing on my own.

One hot day I had to go to the office of the Brera Gallery in Milan to collect some tickets. As I entered, an official started yelling at me ferociously and pointing to the wall behind me. I was apparently standing, with my hat on, beneath a photograph of Mussolini!

We got to Stresa the day after the signature of the German-Soviet pact. With war now inevitable, I received a telegram from the NUS headquarters in London, demanding our immediate return. We got back at the end of August. On 3 September we were at war with Germany.

The first year of the war coincided with my third and final year as an undergraduate (1939–40). In those early months the war seems to have had little impact on Cambridge. For all the absence of dons and senior undergraduates who had been called up, university life continued much as before. Trinity undergraduates could still have lavish meals sent up to their rooms, including the College's famous *crème brûlée*.

In the summer of 1940, when I passed my final exam and became what would today be called a graduate student, the question arose as to what I should do next. The natural thing was to enlist in the armed forces. So, in expectation of this, and with the encouragement of my College, I joined the local branch of the Officers' Training Corps (OTC). After several weeks of fairly intense military training we, its cadets, if successful in the passing-out examination, would qualify for an officer's commission.

In my case, however, it was not so simple. To become an officer you normally had to be a British subject. A stateless person like myself – unless he was held to be an "enemy alien" (German, Austrian, or Italian), in which case he was usually sent to an internment camp under Clause 18B – had the choice of serving in the Pioneer Corps, reputedly mostly staffed by Czech refugees. Perhaps the authorities of the Cambridge OTC wished to find out how I would get on as an officer cadet. If so, they were unlikely to be impressed. I proved quite hopeless in dismantling and reassembling the Bren gun, and less than sharp in drilling a platoon of recruits.

After observing me from his hut, an officer came out and pronounced: "Obolensky, you don't sound convincing!"

I did rather better in the last few days of the camp exercises. We were taken on a "route march" over the neighbouring hills, which lasted all night. As we marched back in deep misery and pouring rain, I began, as a way of boosting my morale, to sing some of the soldiers' songs I had picked up at the camp. My marching companions joined in the singing, to the evident satisfaction of our sergeant major, who complimented me on what he was pleased to call my "leadership qualities".

In the event, however, the military authorities, perhaps to avoid any embarrassment due to my lack of national status, declined to allow me to take the passing-out examination. So I returned to Trinity and life as a graduate student.

I began my historical research, under the largely nominal supervision of Elizabeth Hill. Though no historian herself, she gave me a subject that did much to nurture my interests in this field. This was the history of a dualist sect of indirectly Manichaean origin known as the Bogomils, which acted as a strong and dangerous competitor to Orthodox Christianity in the medieval world of the Balkans.

In the 1940s, during and immediately after the war, I acquired three new friends, all considerably older than I, who came to matter a great deal to me. The first was Greek, the second Czech, and the third French.

Marco Pallis, the son of a distinguished Greek poet, was a writer and composer. He became a Buddhist as a result of two journeys he undertook in 1933 and 1936 to the Himalayan lands on the borders of Tibet. The second in particular, to Sikkim and Ladak, the two "antechambers of Tibet", had as its principal aim the study of Tibetan civilisation. Though Marco and his companions failed to gain permission to visit Tibet, he became an acknowledged expert on the country's traditions and culture. This is apparent in his substantial book *Peaks and Lamas* (1949), in which a description of Himalayan mountain-climbing gives way to a full-scale account of Tibetan Buddhism, entitled "The Round of Existence".

This account, and several of Marco's later studies, were enriched by his attempt to authenticate them in the light of the numerous works by René Guénon, a Muslim writer of French origin, in whom, at least at the time of writing, he seems to have had unlimited confidence. These are mainly concerned with Oriental doctrines, above all with Hinduism, and illustrate Guénon's belief in a primordial metaphysical tradition, from which all other genuine traditions and religions are derived, and in a basic distinction, within each tradition, between its "esoteric" and "exoteric" aspects.

Under Marco's influence, exerted through his writings and in lengthy conversations in Cambridge and at his Liverpool home, I read, spellbound, volume after volume of Guénon's works, excited by the discovery of the intellectual element that can underlie religious belief and experience. Gradually, however, I cooled to Guénon, disconcerted and eventually repelled by what seemed to me his prejudiced and at times arrogant critique of Christianity. This, I fear, may have affected my relationship with Marco, of whom with time I saw less, but whom I remember with affection and gratitude. He, like Guénon, has influenced many; and there is now in London a Marco Pallis Foundation.

My other friend from those days was Father Francis Dvornik, a Czech from Moravia, formerly professor of church history at the Charles University in Prague and a distinguished Byzantinist. When the Germans invaded Czechoslovakia in 1939, he was in London, working in the Library of the British Museum, and decided not to return home. England became his home for the next seven years.

Dvornik became famous for his works on three ninth-century Byzantine figures, the missionaries Cyril and Methodius and the Patriarch Photius. In his original central European environment – the meeting place since the early Middle Ages of cultural influences from East and West – he acquired the outlook of a true European; and his first-hand acquaintance with the traditions of his own Roman Church helped him to interpret with sympathy as well as learning the thought-world of Eastern Christendom to the Christians of the West.

During my frequent visits to Paris in 1945 and 1946, I met a friend of my family, who eventually became my own: Pierre Pascal. In 1916, as a lieutenant in the French army, he was appointed a member of its mission to Russia, whose aim was to provide the Russians with military support and technical knowledge. He grew to love the country and its people, and for a few years after 1917 became a genuine admirer of the achievements of the Revolution.

When the French military mission returned home in October 1918, Pierre refused to follow, remained in Russia, and was eventually condemned as a deserter by the French authorities. He held several minor posts in the Soviet ministry of Foreign Affairs, but by 1921, disappointed by Lenin's New Economic Policy, which he condemned as an unprincipled concession to market forces and a betrayal of socialism, as well as by his persecution of religion, he had ceased to regard himself as a communist. He was eventually able to return to France, was pardoned for his desertion, totally rejecting his ideological and political errors and remaining, as he had never ceased to be, a practising member of the Catholic Church. A notable scholar, he became Professor of Russian first at the Ecole des Langues Orientales, and later at the Sorbonne.

I came to know Pierre and his wife Jennie very well, sometimes staying with them in their flat in Neuilly. After his retirement and her death, he suffered a severe stroke. My last memory of him was in hospital, where I paid him a visit. He was brought some food, which I fed him with a spoon. He could no longer speak, and I don't know whether he even recognised me. To my family and myself, Pierre and Jennie seemed a wonderful exception to the aloofness which, together with many other Russian refugees, we ascribed, rightly or wrongly, to the French.

In the spring and summer of 1940, the war entered a new and more active phase. With the end of the "phoney war" came the German invasion of France, Dunkirk, the fall of Paris, and the Battle of Britain. I was virtually cut off from my family.

What remained of our contact during the next five years was tenuous: Red Cross messages, open to scrutiny and restricted in length, and an occasional clandestine letter, written from Paris by my mother to her sister in Italy, who sent it on to Lisbon, where she knew the British Council representative.

On 22 June 1941, news reached us of the German invasion of Russia. My feelings were mixed. I felt unable, or unwilling, to hope for either a Soviet or a Nazi victory. Stalin, I was convinced, was as bad as Hitler; and I could not identify, at least without strong reservations, with the enthusiasm (understandably widespread in Britain) for the resistance of the Russian troops to the invader. This made me careful in what

I said about the war on the eastern front, except to close friends. One of them was Marco, who shared my views, except for the pacifism he professed as a Buddhist.

So for the present I felt free to concentrate on my research. My thesis on the Bogomils was making headway: most of it was written in the 18 months between the spring of 1941 and the late summer of 1942, partly in the hospitable Sussex house of Sylvia Fennell, the mother of my Cambridge friend John Fennell. By the autumn I was to present it for a "Prize Fellowship" at Trinity.

On the day of the election, to lessen the tension I spent the day in London, returning as late as I could. Above all I wished to get unseen to the notice board outside the dining hall where, I knew, the names of the successful candidates (two that year) would be displayed.

But as I entered the Great Court about six o'clock, I saw to my alarm one of the senior Fellows, the Russian mathematician Besikovich, who undoubtedly knew the results, walking ahead of me.

He suddenly looked round, saw me, turned and slowly started to walk towards me. I expected condolences, but he said in Russian: "Congratulations!"

Gaping, I said: "With what?"

When he said that I had that afternoon been elected to a Trinity Fellowship, I turned, without saying a word, and ran up the steps to the hall. There, unbelievably, I saw, displayed, my name.

Thus my whole life was changed. I was no longer in statu pupillari but a Fellow, entitled to meals at the High Table, elegant rooms in College, and – rather quaintly – to walk across the lawns of the College courts.

I suppose I must have realised that I had achieved, as far as it was possible in wartime, total security.

Now that I had ceased to be a student, I felt able to make a slightly more substantial contribution to the "war effort". My first job was to teach Russian at a military course at Cambridge, designed to train liaison officers.

Under the command of Gerald Wellesley, the future Duke of

Wellington, the course was remarkable for the obscurity of its teachers and the eminence of its pupils.

One of the latter was Fitzroy MacLean, then a second lieutenant, a newly elected Member of Parliament and until recently a diplomat attached to the Moscow embassy. He had, it was said, greatly wanted to enlist in the army, but had discovered that the only way he could legally resign from the Foreign Office in wartime was to become an MP.

Churchill, who heard of this, is said to have referred tartly to "that young man who wants to use the Mother of Parliaments as a public convenience".

A fluent Russian speaker, he did not stay on the course for very long. He was soon transferred to Cairo from where, with the rank of brigadier, he was dropped by parachute to Yugoslavia, to act as liaison officer with Tito.

My second job was perhaps less predictable. I became for some two years a Temporary Assistant Keeper in the Department of Printed Books in the British Museum.

The reason for this was the Museum's need to have on its staff someone with a knowledge of Slavonic languages, its own experts on this subject being away on more active war duties. My day was divided in two: in the mornings I was taught the technique of cataloguing; in the afternoons I was let loose on the readers, whose queries I was supposed to answer. To my great benefit, the reverse was usually the case: for among the readers were several distinguished Byzantinists, including Father Dvornik, who promptly answered my own queries.

The experience proved valuable: in those two years I acquired a knowledge of the proverbial intricacies of the catalogue of the British Museum (now the British Library), an undying affection for the Round Reading Room (then largely unused because it had been bombed), and further experience of the London "blitz", which I had already tasted during the winter of 1940–41; this time the unwelcome visitors were the "doodlebugs" or "flying bombs".

In the autumn of 1945, to my great joy, I obtained a French visa to visit my family in Paris. We had not met for over five years.

On 1 October 1947, I married Elisabeth Lopukhin, a Russian whose parents had emigrated to Paris via Manchuria and the United States. We had met in London, where she was working as a translator at some international conference. My father and grandmother attended the wedding in Clamart, a suburb of Paris. Our marriage survived for 42 years: we divorced in 1989.

On 12 June 1948 I became a British subject. The final event in those years full of change was our departure from Cambridge. Oxford University had created a Readership in Russian and Balkan Medieval History, and offered it to me. With its explicit reference to history it was clearly closer to my interests than the rather insubstantial "Slavonic Studies" which, as a lecturer, I had taught at Cambridge. It was also, in academic terms, a promotion.

I was sad to leave Trinity, which for the past eleven years had given me so warm and secure a home. I was grievously to miss some of my senior colleagues. Among them Denys Winstanley, the Vice-Master, and Donald Robertson, Regius Professor of Greek, were outstanding for their kindness.

Oxford
(1948–85)

The two largest Colleges in our oldest universities, both founded by Henry VIII, have a personal, and in some degree social, link with each other. So it was natural that, on leaving Trinity, I should be offered a College home in Christ Church. When compared to Trinity, it has several original features: it is both a College and a Cathedral; its head is the Dean of the Cathedral; and its Fellows are known as Students.

On my arrival in Oxford in the autumn of 1948, I called on one of the two Students in charge of College administration: Hugh Trevor-Roper (now Lord Dacre of Glanton). His temporary College duties imposed on him the title of Junior Censor. He welcomed me to Christ Church, and with great kindness invited me to stay in one of his College rooms whenever I had to lecture, until I found permanent accommodation.

He mentioned a striking coincidence: one of the Students and history teachers currently at Christ Church, Charles Stuart, had been with me at Lynchmere. We met again in more august surroundings, and became friends until his death.

In the event, the University soon found us a flat. The College, meanwhile, gave me the warmest of welcomes. In 1950 I was elected to a Studentship of Christ Church, thus becoming a member of the College's Governing Body. For the next 35 years Christ Church was, as much as Trinity had been, a true academic home. Yet for some time to come, I continued to feel nostalgia for Trinity and, using my rights as a Past Fellow, often stayed for weekends there.

I spent the 1952–3 academic year at Dumbarton Oaks in the United

States. It was enlivened by visits to my family, who in the meantime had left Paris for New York. It ended in an agreeable and unexpected diversion.

Having just learned to drive in New York, and acquired a second-hand car, I decided, as soon as the University year was over, to drive with my wife across the United States, from coast to coast.

Driving west along the Pennsylvania Turnpike, we crossed Ohio and Indiana and, by-passing Chicago, we reached the Pacific coast at Seattle. Turning south, through Oregon, we reached San Francisco, where we stayed for a week with friends. From there to Los Angeles, then eastward through Arizona to the Grand Canyon, and back through the Californian desert to San Francisco. There, having driven all the way, I sold the car, and we returned to New York by Greyhound Bus.

The memories of this 6,000-mile-long odyssey are too numerous to recount. What still stand out with clarity are Yellowstone Park with its mountain scenery, geysers, bears, and moose; Yosemite Park and its waterfalls; the big earthquake in Los Angeles at five o'clock in the morning (its epicentre was in Tehachapi); the enormous heat of the night drive through the Colorado Desert, with ice-packs attached to the bonnet of the car, and the joy of finding iced water in the motel at night; and finally the endless weariness and monotony of the bus drive home.

I returned to Dumbarton Oaks on numerous occasions, sometimes for several months. The last time, in November 1990, was to celebrate in Washington the fiftieth anniversary of the donation to Harvard University by its owners, Robert Woods and Mildred Bliss, their collection of works of Byzantine art, as well as the library needed for their study, and the house containing it and the extensive gardens. Thus, in a great American example of private munificence, was founded one of the world's major institutions devoted to Byzantine studies.

I was fortunate in acquiring several close friends. One was Alexander Schmemann. Like me a child of Russian émigrés and brought up in Paris, he became a church historian and a Byzantinist. In the early 1950s, an ordained priest, he migrated with his family to New

York, where he became dean of St Vladimir's Orthodox Seminary. Despite his heavy pastoral and administrative duties, he maintained his scholarly work, and became a much respected authority on liturgical history and life. In December 1983 he died of cancer, after writing me a farewell letter which I treasure. I never ceased to enjoy his knowledge and love of Russian poetry, and his sense of humour.

Here again, another friend from those days was my second cousin Ivan Meyendorff. He too was brought up as an *émigré* child in Paris, and became a theologian and church historian, specialising in the teachings of hesychasm (from the Greek *hesychia*, best translated, perhaps, in this context, as "inner stillness") and fourteenth-century Byzantine culture. He was the third in a line of teachers and theologians to migrate to New York from the Orthodox seminary of St Serge in Paris.

The first, in 1948, was George Florovsky. He was followed, at his urgent invitation, by Alexander Schmemann, who in turn paved the way for his friend John Meyendorff. All three in turn became deans of St Vladimir's Orthodox Seminary, thereby cementing an academic and cultural link between Paris and New York that proved greatly beneficial to Christianity in the New World.

A third friend was Ihor Sevcenko, a Byzantinist of Ukrainian origin and a professor at Harvard. He was much in evidence in those early years at Dumbarton Oaks, impressing pupils and colleagues by his extensive knowledge of the classical world, gift for languages, and vivid historical imagination. Shortly before his retirement he was elected president of the world association of Byzantinists. His friendship brought me intellectual stimulation and personal happiness.

In the summer of 1954 I was a passenger on the French transatlantic *Isle de France*, on my way to visit my family in New York. Another passenger was a French priest known as the Abbé Pierre. Although I did not know it at the time, he was famous as the founder of a Paris community whose aim was to house the homeless. One of its strikingly original features was the attempt to enlist the homeless and dispossessed in a common work of rehabilitation and faith. Gradually, under the guidance of the Abbé Pierre, a community was moulded whose twin aims were spiritual awareness and the readiness to help the destitute. To this community he gave the name "Emmaus".

The name was both eloquent and symbolic: a village not far from Jerusalem, mentioned in the Gospel of St Luke. Two of Jesus's disciples were walking towards it, crestfallen after their master's crucifixion and death. They were joined on the way by the risen Christ, whom they failed to recognise. At supper their unknown companion took bread, broke it, blessed it, and gave it to them, as he had done at the Last Supper. And, says St Luke, "their eyes were opened, and they knew him; and he vanished out of their sight".

The Abbé's fame, in France and abroad, had begun in January of that same year, 1954. During an exceptionally cold winter, a baby, sheltering with his parents in a broken-down bus on the streets of Paris, died of cold. The Abbé Pierre, who had been a deputy in the French National Assembly, wrote to the Minister of Reconstruction, telling him of this and mentioning the date of the child's funeral. And he added: "Think of him. It would be good if you could come and be with us at that time."

The minister came to the funeral and walked with the procession. A few days later the Abbé, in a radio broadcast, told his listeners of yet another death from cold in Paris. Almost immediately the Government made available several thousand dwellings to the homeless in Paris.

The Abbé's eloquence and ability to touch human hearts, sometimes in a deliberately dramatic way, had their effect: from all over France, money in aid of the homeless in the cities poured in.

He spoke of these events to the passengers, explaining the aims of "Emmaus" and their moral and spiritual significance. Many of us were clearly moved by his words. I met him later in New York and asked whether I could, for a few weeks, work for "Emmaus" in Paris. He gave me an address.

By early September, back in Europe, I joined three of the "Emmaus" communities. Each provided a vivid picture of their activities:

(1) We collected, no doubt with the agreement of their owners, furniture from Paris flats, which was then sold for the benefit of "Emmaus". Some of these objects were quite large, such as cupboards and pianos. This was known as "*la chine*".

(2) We helped to build in an eastern suburb of Paris houses for the homeless, prefabricated in fibro-cement.

(3) I was sent to a small community east of Paris, specialising in the recovery from sewage farms of waste products, usually from dustbins. This was regarded as the most demanding activity. Some 20 of us stood in a circle, working with rakes on piles of refuse, immersed in a cloud of flies. This was called "*la biffe sur le tas*". The members of this community, fed much better than the others, were regarded as "the aristocracy of Emmaus". We recovered paper, rags, scrap iron, old shoes, tins of food, which were then washed, cleaned, and sorted, becoming, as one writer put it, "raw material in money and bread for the life of Emmaus". The Abbé Pierre called this "the resurrection of things".

As this dustbin raking required a modicum of training and experience, I was placed under the guidance of a mentor, an amiable rag-picker called Gabriel. I still possess a cigarette lighter, no doubt extracted from a dustbin, which he gave me as a parting gift.

Meanwhile, professional life became more interesting and diverse after my promotion to a chair at Oxford. I was appointed a member of a sub-committee of the university Grants Committee (UGC) concerned with Asian, African, and East European Studies. The UGC, which alas no longer exists, was an admirable body, consisting mainly of academics, which every five years dispensed government money to universities, acting as an intermediary between them and the government. Our brief was to advise the UGC on how to apportion the funds, which amounted, in the value of the time, to about £300,000, now made available to universities. They were intended to cover the expenses of up to 125 new lectureships, 100 post-graduate awards in non-language departments, six to eight centres of "area studies", as well as travel and library grants in the above-mentioned three areas.

Oxford did well out of these transactions: the University received funds for the endowment of a centre of Middle Eastern studies and of ten new lectureships in East European studies. Middle Eastern and East European Studies at Oxford were utterly transformed and immensely expanded thereby.

In June 1965 an important event took place in Anglo-Russian cultural relations. At the invitation of the British Council, the foremost Russian poet, Anna Akhmatova, travelled to England and, in a ceremony on 5 June, was awarded by Oxford University the degree of honorary Doctor of Letters.

For years she had been persecuted by Soviet officials, who disliked her poetry of intimate human emotions and distrusted its widespread popularity, particularly among the young. But in the more relaxed atmosphere after Stalin's death she was openly held in honour and reverence by all true writers and lovers of literature in Russia, a reverence enhanced by the dignity with which she bore her personal trials. The recognition she received in Oxford was an experience as moving to her as it was to her friends and Russian admirers, some of whom had come far to pay tribute to, as a fellow poet once called her, "Anna Chrysostom of All Russia".

The most distinguished of these friends, of Russian origin, was Isaiah Berlin, philosopher and historian of ideas, who later became the first President of Wolfson College, Oxford. The two met in the autumn of 1945, when he served at the British embassy in Moscow, and visited her in Leningrad, in her modest home in the former Sheremetev Palace. The friendship came to mean a great deal to both of them. Their first meeting was described by Isaiah as "one of the most – perhaps the most – memorable experiences of my life".

For her part, during the next twenty years Anna Akhmatova wrote numerous poems about their relationship. In her lengthy masterpiece, *Poem without a Hero*, which is partly dedicated to Isaiah, he appears as the mysterious "Guest from the Future".

Much of my work has been concerned with Byzantium's relations with the peoples of Eastern Europe. I have studied these relations – political, diplomatic, economic, cultural, and ecclesiastical – both in the light of the Byzantine Empire's foreign policy, and from the point of view of the East European peoples – Greeks, Bulgarians, Serbs, Roumanians, Ukrainians, Russians, and Albanians – who, whether on their own initiative or in response to impulses emanating from Byzantium, were drawn into its orbit. To the community formed by the contact, the "dialogue", between the Empire and its East European satellites, I gave the name "the Byzantine Commonwealth".

I inevitably became interested in the geographical aspect of this community's history. This has meant studying the historical geography of two distinct, though interrelated, areas: the Balkan peninsula, bounded in the north by the Danube; and the land lying to the north of the Black Sea, called Rhosia by the Greeks and Rus' by its medieval Slav inhabitants, one of whose names today is Russia.

The quiet life of the Oxford don was therefore punctuated by travels in Eastern Europe. The Communist authorities put strict limits on what I could see, whom I could meet and what they could say during my visits to the Balkans. This put into even sharper relief the times I spent in Greece, which eventually became quasi-annual events, often lasting for weeks, sometimes months.

I went several times to Mount Athos, at a peninsula jutting out into the Aegean from Halkidiki, capped by a summit of 2,030 metres. For over a thousand years, Athos, the "Holy Mountain" as it is known locally, has been the nerve-centre of East Christian monasticism, a pan-Orthodox, multi-ethnic focal point.

There were once monasteries for Bulgarians, Georgians, Italians (Amalfitans), Moldavians, Russians, Serbs, and Wallachians as well as Greeks. There are still houses for Bulgarians, Greeks, Roumanians, Russians, and Serbs. In the late Middle Ages the international role of Athos was marked by a movement known as hesychasm, of which the revival of contemplative monasticism was the original and most characteristic feature.

By spreading from Mount Athos to the Balkans, Roumania,* Ukraine, and Russia, hesychasm did much to link together the different parts of the Byzantine cultural commonwealth; it still plays an important intermediate role between the Greek, Slav, and Roumanian traditions.

There are twenty "ruling" (self-governing) monasteries, now all coenobitic, under the spiritual authority of the Ecumenical Patriarch. When I first visited Mount Athos in the early 1950s, walking from monastery to monastery, I gained the impression that they were inhabited mostly by old men, whose communities were slowly dying. On my subsequent visits, however, that picture began to change. In the early 1970s, a powerful revival of monasticism began on Athos. From 1972 to 1996, when the last census was taken, more than a thousand new monks arrived.

In the last ten years the Athonite community more than doubled. It now numbers some 2,000 monks, a figure still rising. Most of the newcomers were young men, not a few with university degrees. They gradually took over the administration of the houses in which they settled, and where, thanks to them, the hesychast traditions and the coenobitic life began to revive.

The reasons for this resurgence have often been discussed. Two, I believe, were of major importance. Firstly, some of the new arrivals came in groups, migrating from communities in other parts of Greece where changing social conditions, such as mass tourism, were increasingly inimical to the monastic life. Secondly, the revival

---

* I must record a strong preference for the traditional spelling "Roumania" over the new-fangled, and today – alas – official, form "Romania". Steven Runciman has argued convincingly in favour of the traditional form: "The Principalities of Wallachia and Moldavia . . . remained the only part of the old Byzantine world never to be directly ruled by the Turks, or by the Italian merchant cities. By a timely submission to the Ottoman Sultan's suzerainty they preserved their autonomy. They were all that was left of Byzantium, as the name Roumania attests. The modern Roumanians like to spell it Romania, to show, they claim, that they are descended from the Romans. But the word is in fact derived from 'Roum', the name given by the Moslem world to Byzantium, the old East Roman Empire." (A Traveller's Alphabet, Thames and Hudson, 1991, p. 130.)

has been spearheaded by several charismatic figures who exerted a powerful spiritual and moral influence. An important role in this educational activity was played by two abbots – Father Aimilianos of Simonopetra and Basileios of Stavronikita (later of Iviron).

The local authorities of Athos were subject to the more distant sovereignty exercised over the Holy Mountain by the Ecumenical Patriarch, the head of the Church of Constantinople and, in that capacity, the senior prelate of the Orthodox Church. From 1948 to 1972 this was Athenagoras, the former Archbishop of the Greek Orthodox Church in the United States. Though a Greek himself, his office required him to be a Turkish citizen.

When, armed with a letter of introduction, I presented myself at the Phanax, Athenagoras's residence, I was immediately struck by his appearance. Immensely tall and dignified, with a flowing white beard, he seemed to have stepped out of a mosaic of some medieval predecessor on the patriarchal throne, while the silver two-headed eagle that hung on a chain on his ample chest evoked an avatar of the Byzantine Emperor himself. On our second meeting he clasped me in a bear-like hug.

One day he invited me to accompany him to Halki (Heybeli), one of the Princes' Islands, where a Greek monastery housed the Patriarchate's Seminary. On arrival we saw a large group of Greeks (in those days there were still many of them in Istanbul and its environs; the mass exodus came later) assembled in the harbour to greet their Patriarch. Others lined the cobbled road that climbed to the Seminary. Seated next to Athenagoras in a horse-drawn carriage, I made myself as small as possible in the face of his regal salutations.

At lunch in the monastery I was greeted by a Greek friend who had studied at Oxford and now taught at the seminary. The Patriarch was clearly amused to observe that both of us were wearing a Christ Church tie.

A man of tolerance and peace, Athenagoras was to leave a lasting mark on inter-church relations. In 1965, a year after a cordial meeting in Jerusalem with Pope Paul VI, he took part in the solemn lifting of the anathemas which, in 1054, had been pronounced between the Churches of Rome and Constantinople.

Another frequent destination was the island of Euboea (Evia). Its north-western tip, near Limni, was the home of a close friend, Philip Sherrard. Theologian, poet, and exponent of modern Greek poetry, he is widely remembered as the translator, with his friend Edmund Keeley, of the two great poets Seferis and Cavafy.

In the late 1950s, married to a Greek and already a member of the Orthodox Church, Philip chanced on an encounter that changed his life. He discovered a magnesite mine which before the war had been operated by an Anglo-Greek company, now up for sale. The place was Katounia, a few miles from Limni. He bought it for a song, including several ruined houses which had belonged to the management and which he repaired, settling with his wife on the estate.

Thanks to Philip, Katounia became for his many friends a place of happiness and beauty, with its sweet-smelling pine forest, the blue waters of the gulf of Euboea and, dominating it all, the steep limestone summit of Kandile, plunging to the water's edge.

Philip Sherrard was responsible for my meeting in Katounia the owner of another house in Greece which I was so often to visit. He was Patrick Leigh Fermor, who lived with his wife in Kardamyli, a hamlet in the Mani peninsula, high up in the Gulf of Messenia at the fort of the Taygetus, in a handsome house by the sea he had himself designed and built. Paddy is a writer of distinction who, in the words of a reviewer, "has a virtuoso skill with words, a robust aesthetic passion, an indomitable curiosity about people and places; and a rapturous historical imagination". His masterpiece, in my view, is The Violins of St Jacques. But his book on Mani, his home, was so successful that it impelled the hordes of motorised tourists who, he ruefully admits himself, now swarm over the peninsula.

At the time of writing, he is engaged on finishing a three-volume account of a journey on foot from the Hook of Holland to Constantinople which he undertook at the age of 18 and which has now reached the Iron Gates, on the middle Danube.

During the Second World War, Paddy served in Albania, Greece, and Crete. For more than two years, disguised as a Cretan shepherd, he lived in the mountains, helping to organise the Resistance, and commanding the unit which carried out the capture of the German commander of the island, General Kreipe, and his evacuation to Cairo.

One spring morning as he and the General were breakfasting in the mountains, Kreipe was so overcome by the beauty of the scenery that he started to recite Horace's ninth ode from Book I. After the first few lines, he got stuck.*

Paddy then took over and continued to the end. There was a moment's silence, then the General turned his gaze from the snow-covered mountains on to Paddy, and said: "*Ach so, Herr Major.*"

After that, Paddy averred, "our relations were never the same".

Next to the Greek world of south-eastern Europe, Russia was the country I visited most frequently in the relative security that followed Stalin's death in 1953. Some of these visits took place in the communist era, when Soviet power was still solidly entrenched. A memorable one took me to Moscow to attend an Anglo-Russian Historical Conference.

Some time in the 1950s, British and Soviet historians started the practice of holding joint scholarly meetings, alternately in London and Moscow. In 1960 it was the Russians' turn to act as hosts. The eight British historians, selected by the Institute of Historical Research in London, were Sir Charles Webster (the group's leader), George Bolsover, E. H. Carr, Philip Grierson, Sir John Habbakuk, Bruce McFarlane, Hugh Seton-Watson, and myself. The Russian party

---

* *Vides ut alta stet nive candidum*
   Soracte, nec iam sustineant onus
   silvae laborantes, geluque
   flumina constiterint acuto? Odes I. 9.
"Seest thou how Soracte stands glistening in its mantle of snow, and how the straining woods no longer uphold their burden, and the streams are frozen with the biting cold?" (Translated by C. E. Bennett, Loeb, 1968).

varied in composition, but always included Academician Guber (the chairman) and sometimes Ivan Maisky, Soviet ambassador to London in the 1930s and early 1940s. The Moscow meeting was due to be held in September 1960.

For me it had an unexpected prelude. On my way to Moscow I attended an international congress of historians in Stockholm. One of the Russian delegates was Mikhail Tikhomirov, the much respected doyen of his country's medievalists. He was also due to give a paper to our meeting in Moscow, on the sensitive subject of the conversion of Russia to Christianity. When I introduced myself to him in Stockholm, he drew me aside and, looking at me rather pointedly, expressed the hope that I would criticise his paper when it was discussed at the Moscow meeting. I took this to be a covert way of saying that, while there were things he could not say in public, I was not similarly beholden to Soviet censorship, so could I please help. I promised to do so.

For chronological reasons, Tikhomirov's paper was the first to be discussed. I had prepared a fairly long critique, dissociating myself from its habitual, if relatively mild, Marxist intonations, and stressing the religious and spiritual aspects of the subject. When I finished, all hell broke loose. Some of the author's pupils, themselves by then important scholars, attacked me severely and at length.

Finally Tikhomirov himself got up and, no doubt feeling shame-faced, added his own voice to the invectives; after which he came up to me, again drew me aside, saying that he hoped I did not mind. I assured him that I quite understood.

Later, one of my British colleagues at the conference, who had no inkling of the truth, when writing to a friend, reproached me for behaving as an apparently "devout Christian", like "a cat among birds".

But the most dramatic meeting was the final one, devoted to the discussion of the joint Soviet paper on the diplomatic background of the Second World War. Its summary, which had been distributed in advance, contained a number of severe attacks on Allied policy, listing in particular the Munich agreement, the British government's alleged intention of inciting Hitler to attack the Soviet Union, and the length of time it took to launch the Second Front.

As these charges accumulated, Sir Charles Webster looked increasingly furious. So far he had remained silent during the sessions, confining himself to issuing private instruction and advice and deploying us as a general would his troops in battle. As a historian of international relations, he had saved himself for this last, and to him crucial, session. When the Soviet authors ended their paper, Sir Charles rose to address his audience. His manner was decidedly Churchillian.

"Yes," he said, "we concluded the Munich agreement; and a regrettable thing it was, as our historians have now admitted. But you" – he added, pointing an accusing finger at the Soviet audience – "you did something even worse: you concluded a pact with Hitler; and so far not one of your historians has felt free to criticise what was done. Furthermore, you have accused us of duplicity when we negotiated with you in 1939: but you don't understand the problem that faced our government and public opinion at the time. Why, you" – again the accusing finger – "you had just had your purges, in which the greater part of your high command – from Marshal Tukhachevsky downward – had been liquidated. If these charges against your generals were true, it means that all your military secrets were then in the hands of the Germans;* and if they were false, what view could our government and public opinion entertain about you and your government?"

As Sir Charles sat down, it became apparent that this oration had now to be translated into Russian by the young, and obviously terrified, Soviet interpreters. In the circumstances, they could perhaps hardly be blamed for omitting all the references to the purges and the purged Marshal. It fell to Philip Grierson to provide an immediate and literal rendering of what Sir Charles had said.

* As far as I remember, this particular point was also made by Philip Grierson.

In this tense atmosphere you could hear a pin drop. A somewhat confused discussion followed, during which the Soviet position was reiterated with some venom by Ivan Maisky, the Soviet ambassador in London during those critical years.

Curiously enough, this acrimonious exchange seemed somehow to have cleared the air. The increased warmth of our relations with our Russian hosts, I felt, persisted until we left the Soviet Union a few days later.

The next visit, from 8 to 14 August 1991, took place when Soviet power was on the very eve of its collapse. I travelled to Moscow to attend the first International Congress of Byzantine Studies ever to be held in Russia. It took place at a high point of *glasnost* and *perestroika*; and it preceded by a few days the anti-Gorbachev *coup* which resulted in the collapse of the Soviet Union, the abolition of the Communist Party in Russia, and the replacement as Russia's leader of Mikhail Gorbachev by Boris Yeltsin.

During the Congress, a small group of us were invited to the Kremlin by the Vice-President of the USSR, Gennady Yanaev. As we sat sipping coffee, he asked a searching question: "Was there total-itarianism in Byzantium?"

The President of the International Committee of Byzantine Studies, Ihor Sevcenko, replied, equally to the point: "In intention, yes; in implementation, no: they didn't have the political means."

Apparently changing the subject, Yanaev then said: "I'm terribly busy, there's so much to do here. I've even, to my wife's displeasure, moved my bed into these offices. The trouble is, Gorbachev has departed for his summer holidays, and left me behind to do all the work."

A week later, Yanaev headed the abortive *coup* against Gorbachev. Four days later, he was in jail.

My most recent visit to Russia, from 21 June to 2 July 1997, was to join in the celebration of my election two years earlier as a foreign member of the Russian Academy of Science. Unlike most of my previous visits, this one had for me a strongly personal element.

I have often found it difficult to decide what exactly was – and is – my relationship with the Russia I left behind in 1919. A measure of ambiguity had always attended my thoughts on the matter. It surfaced again during this last visit.

Several factors conspired to complicate the issue. Among these are my lack, until 1956, of any visual memory of Russia; strong dislike of the Soviet regime and all its works; latent suspicion of all forms of nationalism; and, though this often lacked clarity and focus, belief in my own cosmopolitanism and emotional attachment to England. It is perhaps hardly surprising that, during my early visits to Russia, I would sometimes say to myself: "This is not my country."

And yet I always knew that there was another side to the picture, a positive one. The most obvious, perhaps, is family history. From an early age I knew that I descended in a straight line, on my father's side, from Rurik, the ninth-century Viking who founded the dynasty which ruled Russia until the late sixteenth-century, shortly before the Romanovs took over.

As my interest in history increased, I got to know more about my direct though remote ancestors, who included at least two saints: Vladimir, who brought Christianity to Rus' in the late tenth century, and Michael of Chernigov, martyred by the Tatars of the Golden Horde in 1246. On my mother's side too, through the Shuvalovs and the Vorontsovs, my ancestors were often close to the throne and politically influential. This I came to realise only gradually, mostly in my Cambridge and Oxford years, but the impact was, of course, a real one.

Another area of contact was music. Unfortunately, since from my early childhood I was deemed to have "no ear for music" (I always sang out of tune), I had to explore this link by my own effort, and it took a long time. But I loved to hear and, to my family's unfailing derision, to attempt to reproduce, Russian songs and especially liturgical singing which, as I grew older, began to move me deeply.

Music, of course, was linked to poetry. And for poetry I developed an attachment that, in later life, became a real need. Of all forms of speech, this is surely the one I could not easily live without. Some of this love I owe to my mother, who read poetry aloud very beautifully. Having, in those days, an exceptionally good memory, I learned to recite by heart long fragments, mainly in Russian, French, and English, but also in languages I knew less well, such as German and Modern Greek. When, in the early 1960s, I accepted to edit the *Penguin Book of Russian Verse*, little did I know what joy I was storing up for the future.

Poetry is surely the greatest achievement of human language. When all is said, Russian will surely remain the most vital and permanent of my links with the people who speak it: that language which I learned in Nice, spoke at home, and taught in Cambridge; whose "breathtaking resourcefulness" was so well described by Max Hayward; and whose familiarity, I now believe, gives the lie to my over-hasty judgement that "this is not my country".

How else than by recognising the strength and permanence of this link could I understand the emotion, mixed with tears, that seized me when I found myself alone in the garden of the Vorontsov palace in Alupka, or when I crossed for the first time one of the bridges over the Neva, bridges which, as Pushkin put it so vividly, "hang above the waters"?

I am sometimes tempted to liken this experience on crossing the bridge to the one which, in the very same years, was evoked by the Russian poet Anna Akhmatova, who in her St Petersburg home was awaiting the visit of her new friend, Isaiah Berlin:

> Guest from the Future, can it be
> that he will really come to me,
> turning left from the bridge?